RENEGADE RULE™

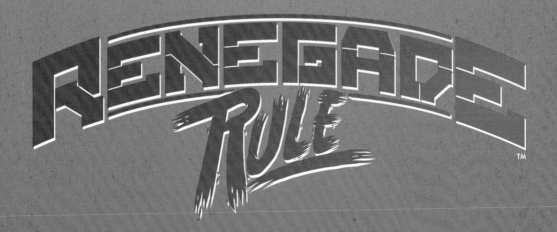

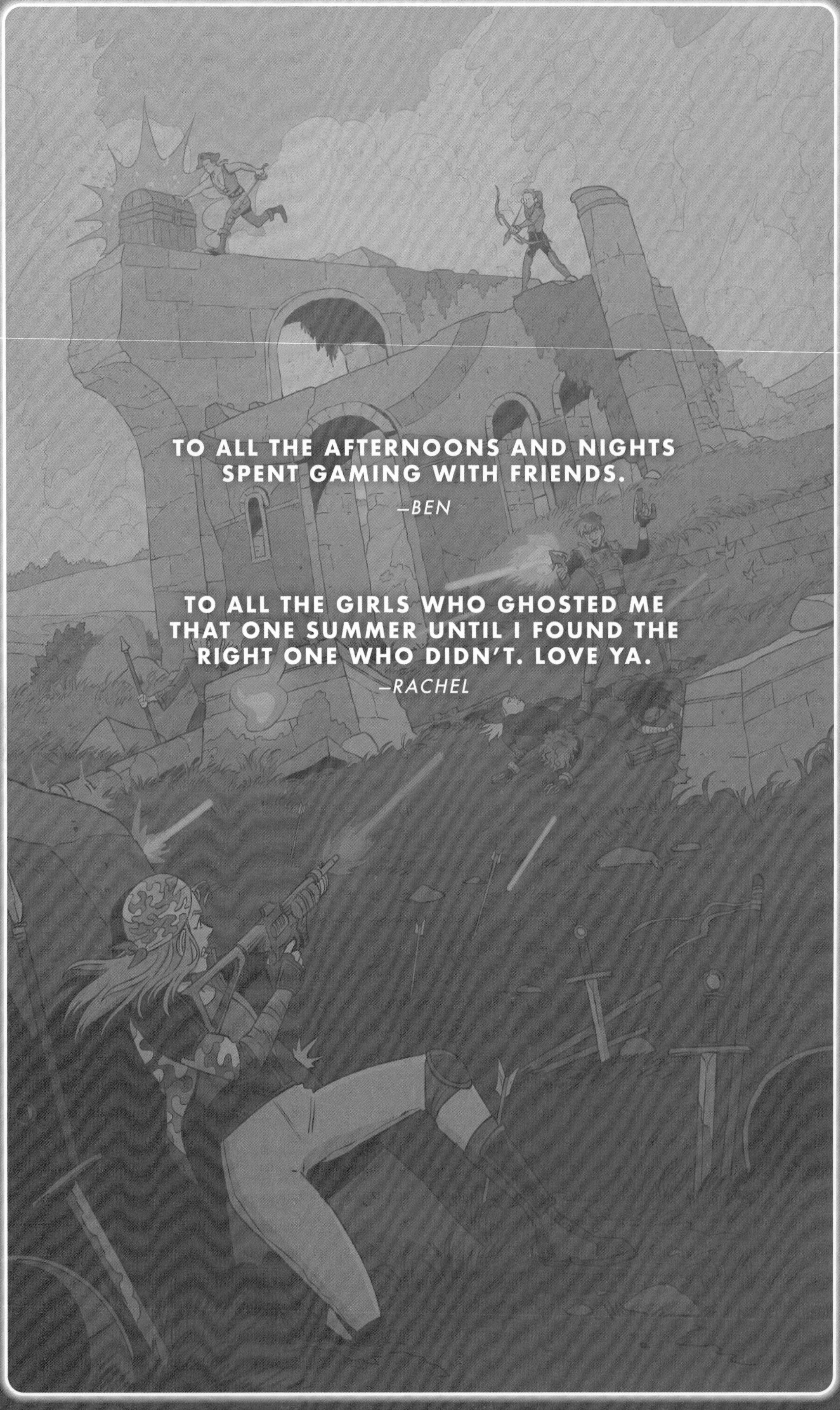

TO ALL THE AFTERNOONS AND NIGHTS SPENT GAMING WITH FRIENDS.

—BEN

TO ALL THE GIRLS WHO GHOSTED ME THAT ONE SUMMER UNTIL I FOUND THE RIGHT ONE WHO DIDN'T. LOVE YA.

—RACHEL

RENEGADE RULE
™

WRITTEN BY
BEN KAHN AND
RACHEL SILVERSTEIN

ART BY
SAM BECK

LETTERS BY
JIM CAMPBELL

LOGO DESIGN BY
TIM DANIEL

 DARK HORSE BOOKS

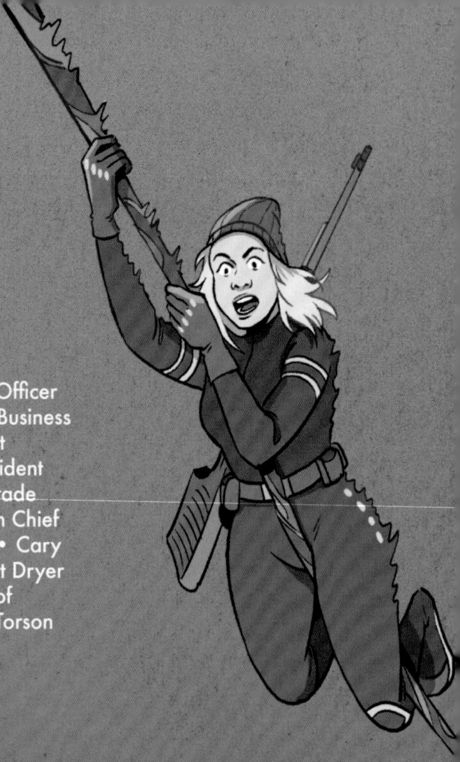

President and Publisher MIKE RICHARDSON
Editor JENNY BLENK
Designer BRENNAN THOME
Digital Art Technician ANN GRAY

Neil Hankerson Executive Vice President • Tom Weddle Chief Financial Officer • Randy Stradley Vice President of Publishing • Nick McWhorter Chief Business Development Officer • Dale LaFountain Chief Information Officer • Matt Parkinson Vice President of Marketing • Vanessa Todd-Holmes Vice President of Production and Scheduling • Mark Bernardi Vice President of Book Trade and Digital Sales • Ken Lizzi General Counsel • Dave Marshall Editor in Chief • Davey Estrada Editorial Director • Chris Warner Senior Books Editor • Cary Grazzini Director of Specialty Projects • Lia Ribacchi Art Director • Matt Dryer Director of Digital Art and Prepress • Michael Gombos Senior Director of Licensed Publications • Kari Yadro Director of Custom Programs • Kari Torson Director of International Licensing • Sean Brice Director of Trade Sales

Published by Dark Horse Books
A division of Dark Horse Comics LLC
10956 SE Main Street
Milwaukie, OR 97222

DarkHorse.com
Comic Shop Locator Service: Comicshoplocator.com

First edition: May 2021
eBOOK ISBN 978-1-50671-800-2
ISBN 978-1-50671-801-9

10 9 8 7 6 5 4 3 2 1
Printed in China

Library of Congress Cataloging-in-Publication Data

Names: Kahn, Ben (Comics writer), writer. | Silverstein, Rachel, writer. | Beck, Sam (Freelance artist), artist. | Campbell, Jim (Letterer), letterer.
Title: Renegade rule / written by Ben Kahn and Rachel Silverstein ; art by Sam Beck ; letters by Jim Campbell.
Description: First edition. | Milwaukie, OR : Dark Horse Books, 2021. | Summary: "The Manhattan Mist have beaten the odds to land themselves in the national championships for Renegade Rule, one of the hottest virtual reality games in existence. But they're in for competition fiercer than they ever imagined, and one team member's entire future could be at stake. Four queer female friends will have to play harder than ever against self-doubt, infighting, romantic distraction, and a slew of other world-class teams if they hope to become champions"– Provided by publisher.
Identifiers: LCCN 2020050801 (print) | LCCN 2020050802 (ebook) | ISBN 9781506718019 (paperback) | ISBN 9781506718002 (ebook)
Subjects: LCSH: Graphic novels.
Classification: LCC PN6727.K23 R46 2021 (print) | LCC PN6727.K23 (ebook) | DDC 741.5/973–dc23
LC record available at https://lccn.loc.gov/2020050801
LC ebook record available at https://lccn.loc.gov/2020050802

CHAPTER ONE

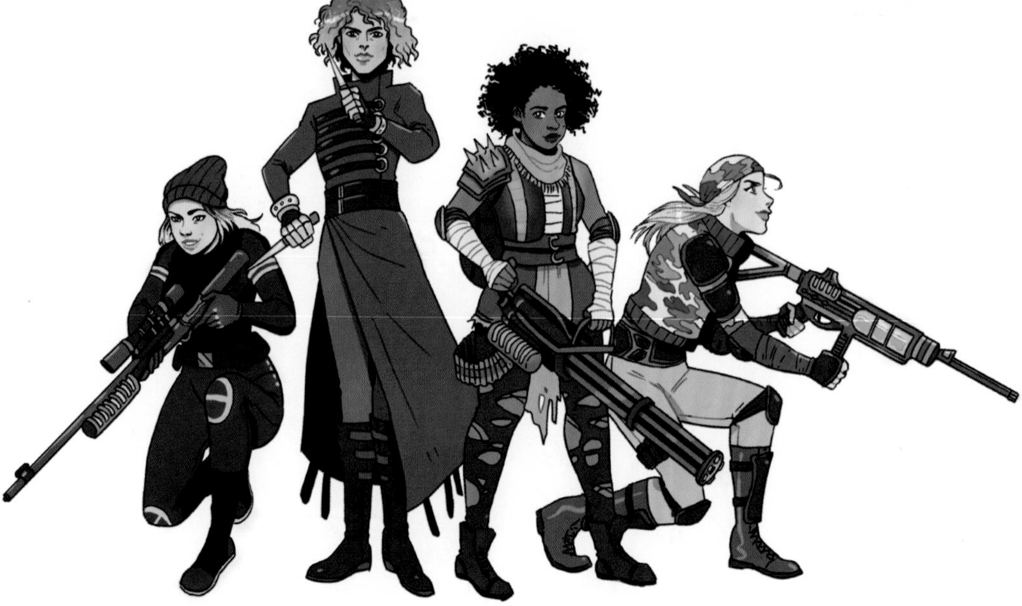

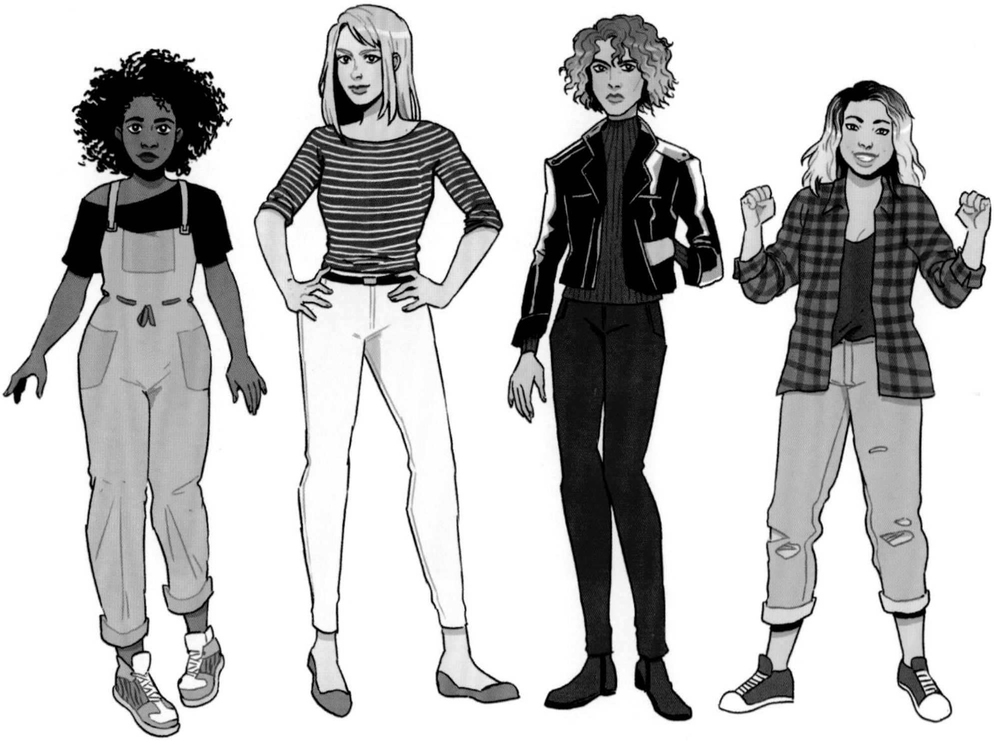

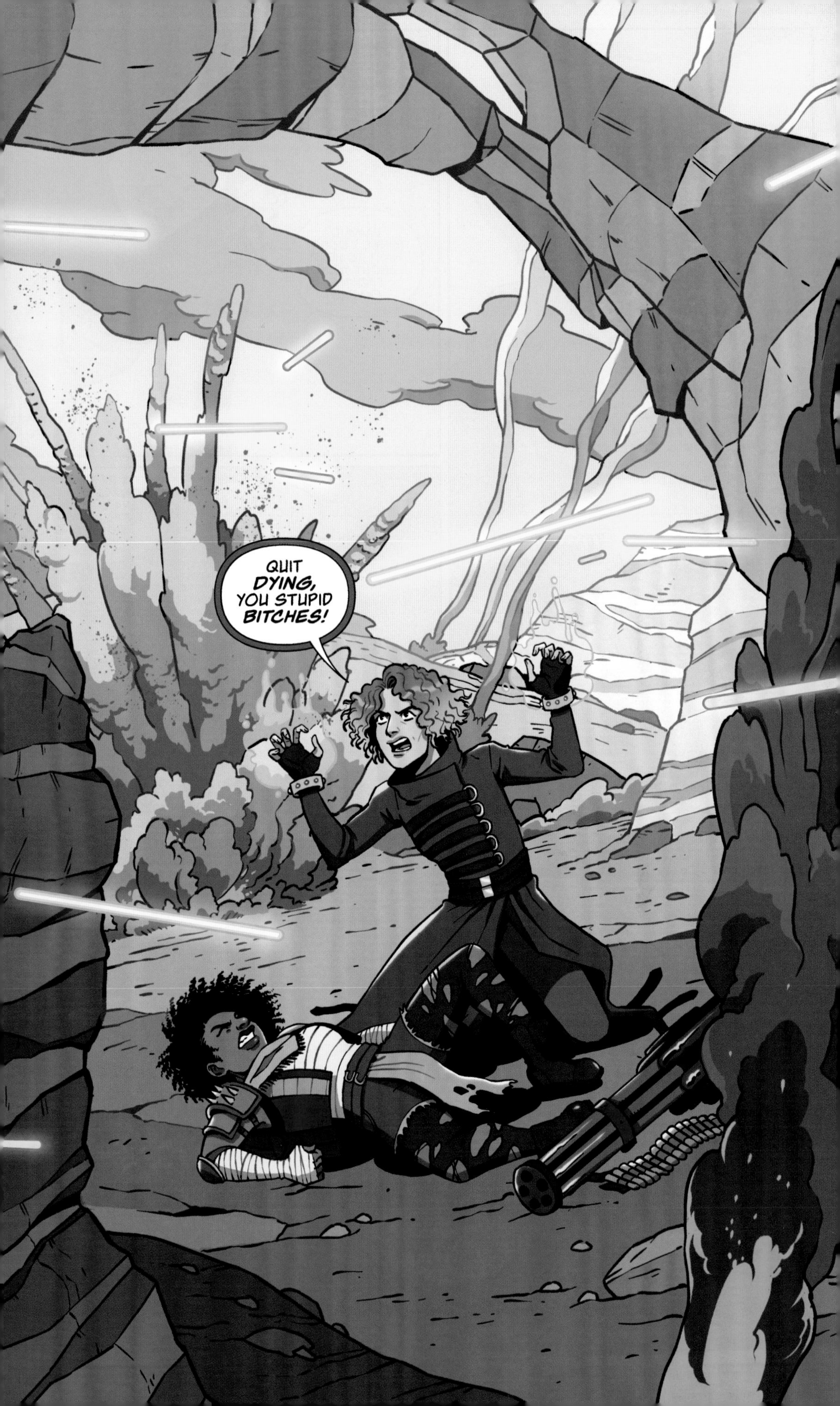
QUIT DYING, YOU STUPID BITCHES!

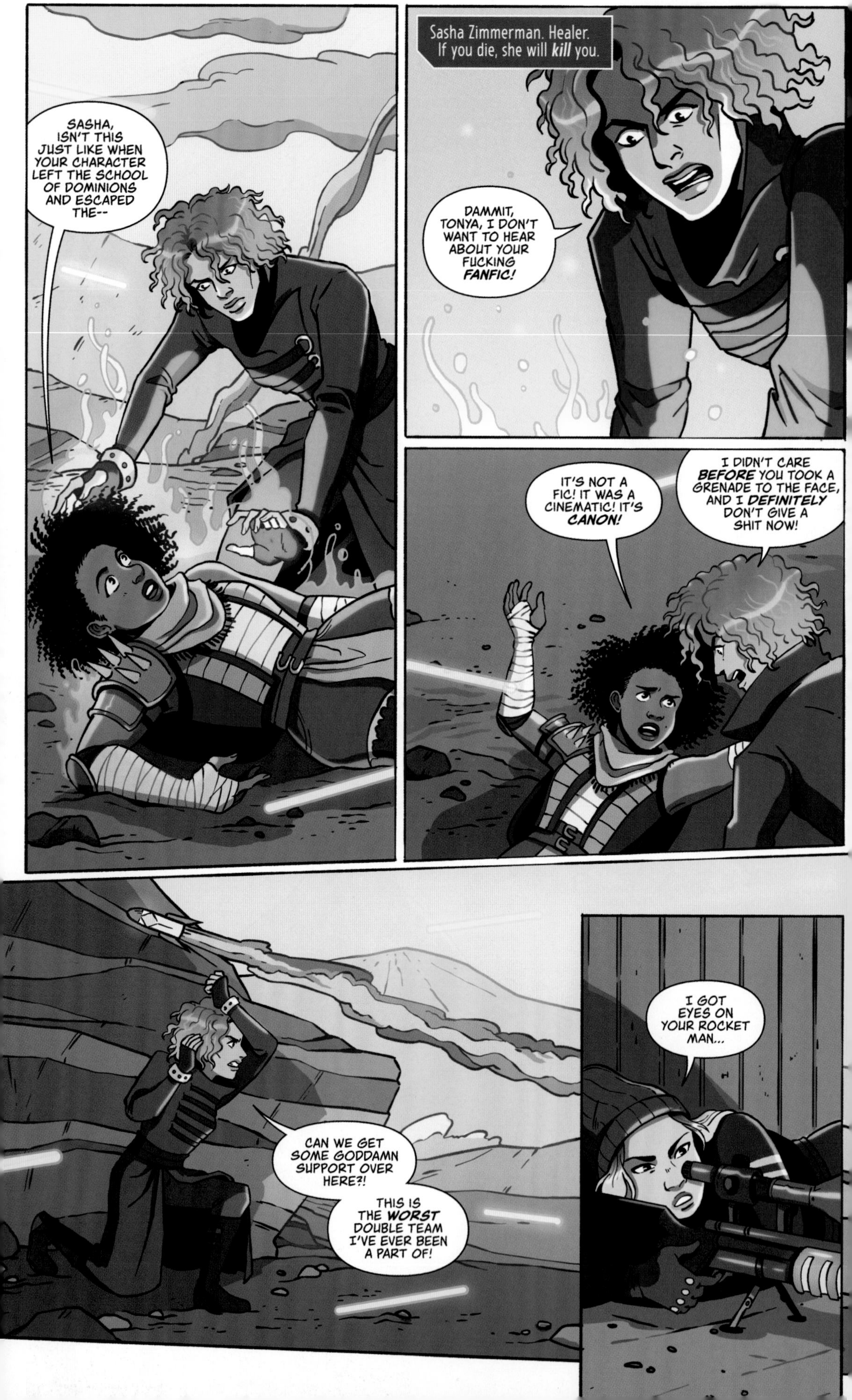
SASHA, ISN'T THIS JUST LIKE WHEN YOUR CHARACTER LEFT THE SCHOOL OF DOMINIONS AND ESCAPED THE--
Sasha Zimmerman. Healer. If you die, she will **kill** you.
DAMMIT, TONYA, I DON'T WANT TO HEAR ABOUT YOUR FUCKING ***FANFIC!***
IT'S NOT A FIC! IT WAS A CINEMATIC! IT'S ***CANON!***
I DIDN'T CARE ***BEFORE*** YOU TOOK A GRENADE TO THE FACE, AND I ***DEFINITELY*** DON'T GIVE A SHIT NOW!
CAN WE GET SOME GODDAMN SUPPORT OVER HERE?!
THIS IS THE ***WORST*** DOUBLE TEAM I'VE EVER BEEN A PART OF!
I GOT EYES ON YOUR ROCKET MAN...

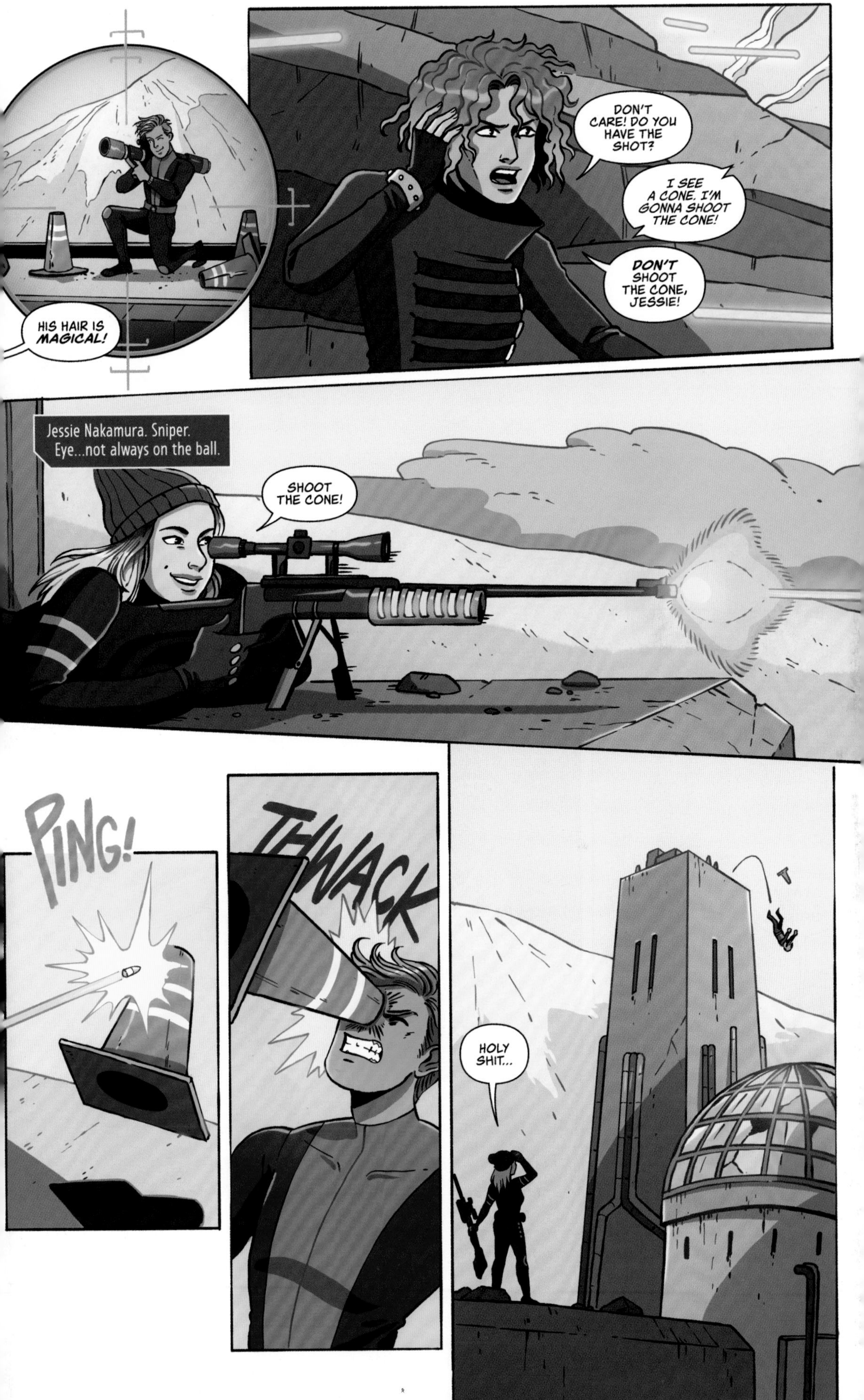
HIS HAIR IS MAGICAL!
DON'T CARE! DO YOU HAVE THE SHOT?
I SEE A CONE. I'M GONNA SHOOT THE CONE!
DON'T SHOOT THE CONE, JESSIE!
Jessie Nakamura. Sniper. Eye...not always on the ball.
SHOOT THE CONE!
PING!
THWACK
HOLY SHIT...

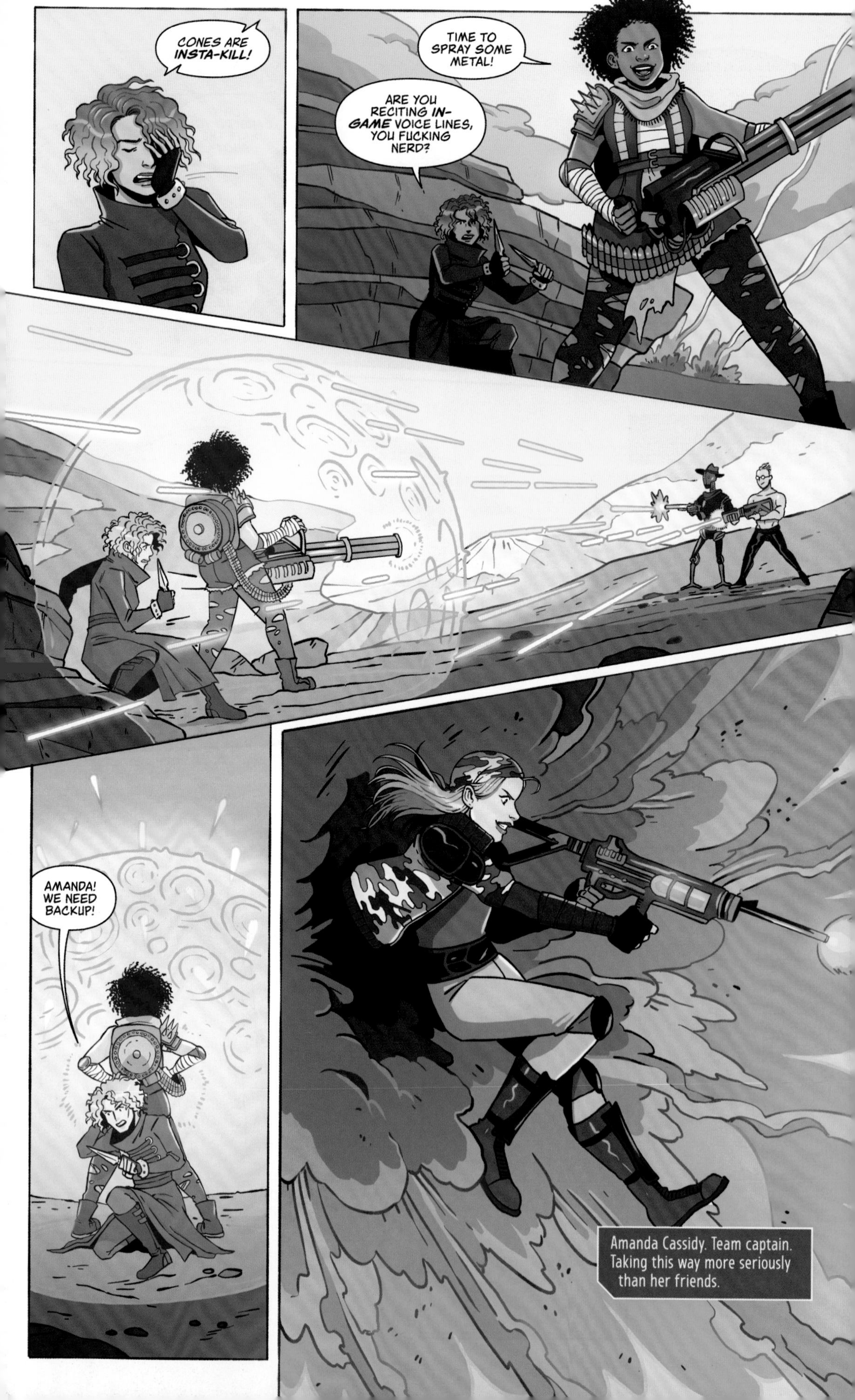
CONES ARE INSTA-KILL!
TIME TO SPRAY SOME METAL!
ARE YOU RECITING IN-GAME VOICE LINES, YOU FUCKING NERD?
AMANDA! WE NEED BACKUP!
Amanda Cassidy. Team captain. Taking this way more seriously than her friends.

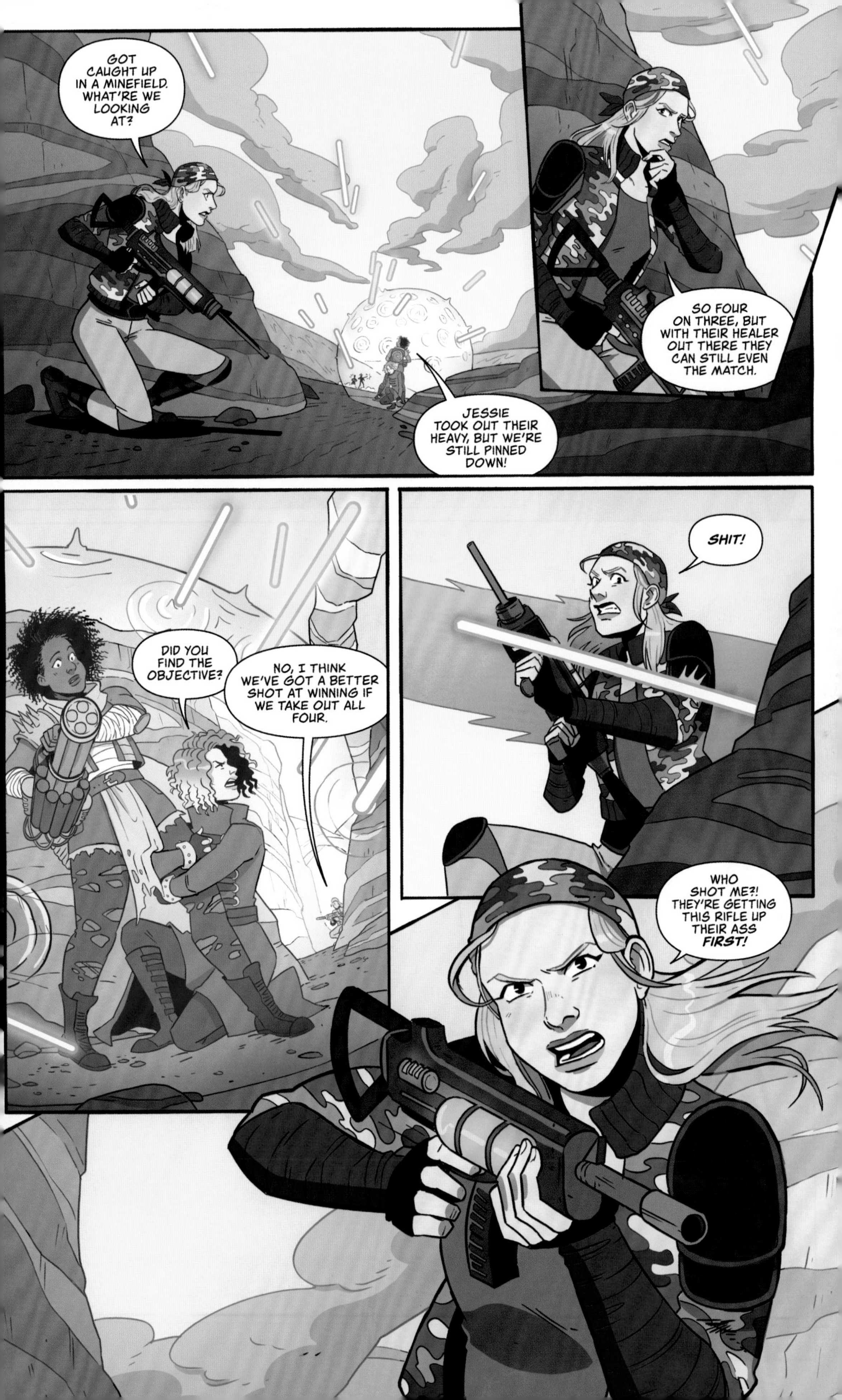
GOT CAUGHT UP IN A MINEFIELD. WHAT'RE WE LOOKING AT?
JESSIE TOOK OUT THEIR HEAVY, BUT WE'RE STILL PINNED DOWN!
SO FOUR ON THREE, BUT WITH THEIR HEALER OUT THERE THEY CAN STILL EVEN THE MATCH.
DID YOU FIND THE OBJECTIVE?
NO, I THINK WE'VE GOT A BETTER SHOT AT WINNING IF WE TAKE OUT ALL FOUR.
SHIT!
WHO SHOT ME?! THEY'RE GETTING THIS RIFLE UP THEIR ASS FIRST!

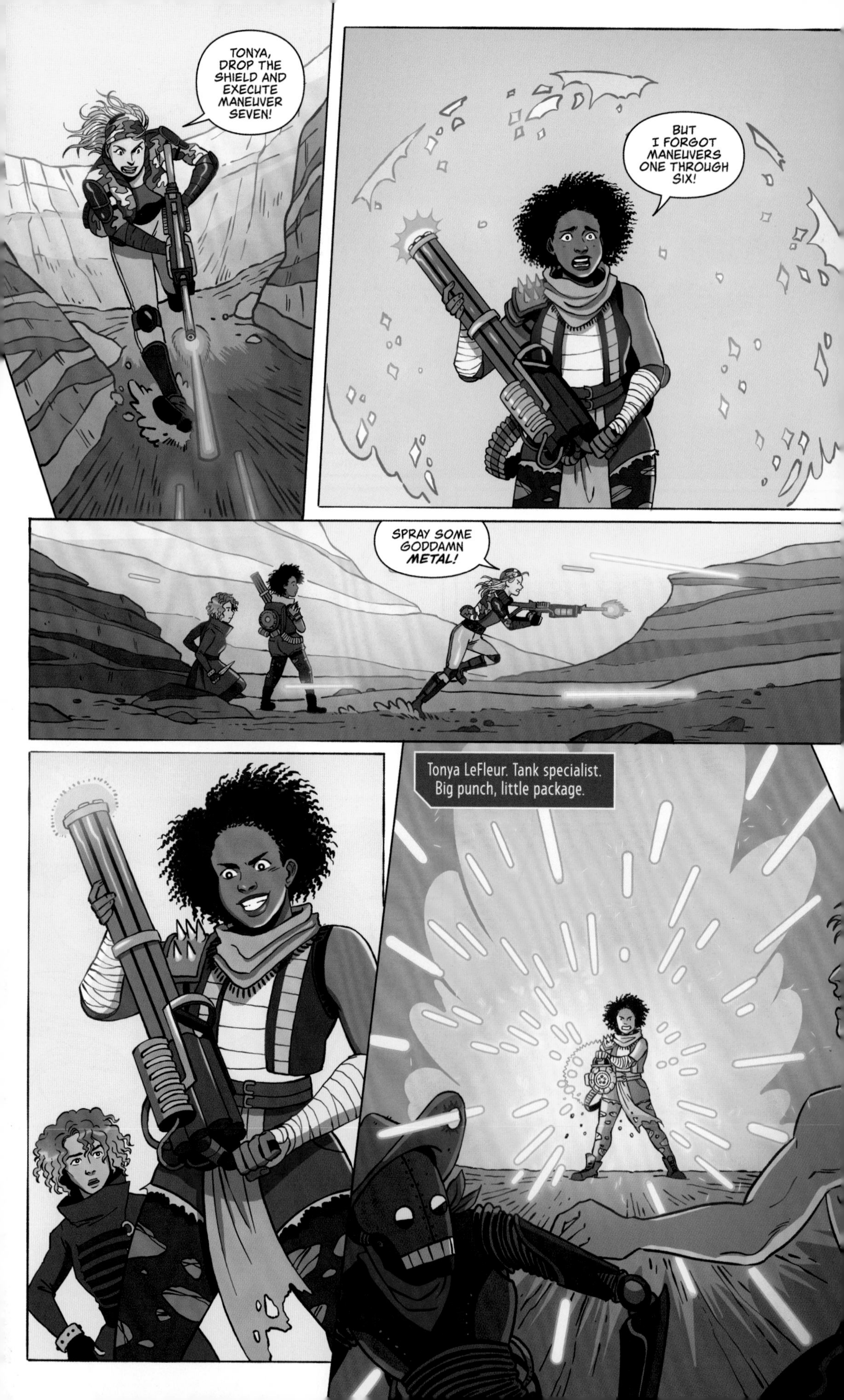
TONYA, DROP THE SHIELD AND EXECUTE MANEUVER SEVEN!
BUT I FORGOT MANEUVERS ONE THROUGH SIX!
SPRAY SOME GODDAMN *METAL!*
Tonya LeFleur. Tank specialist. Big punch, little package.

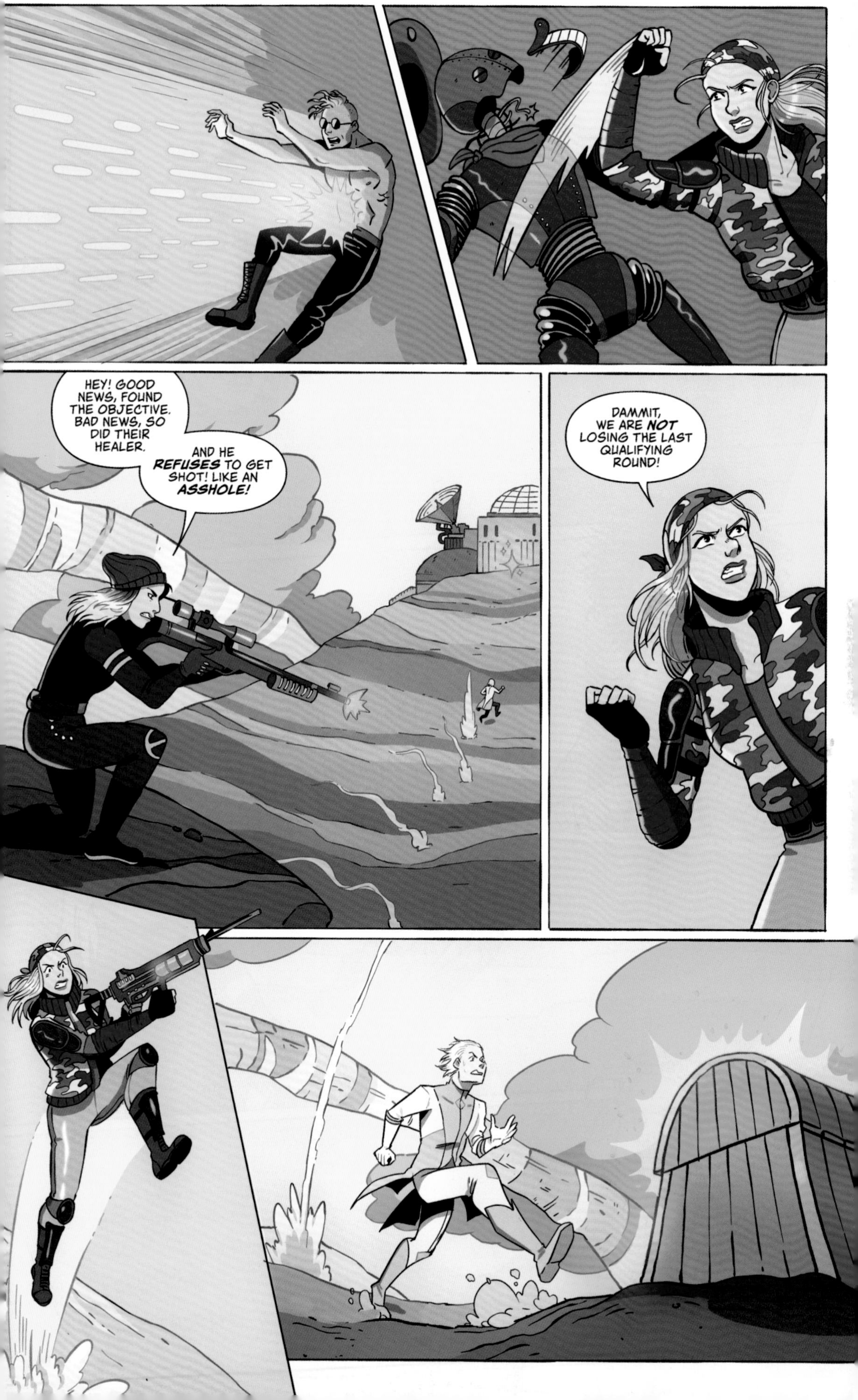
HEY! GOOD NEWS, FOUND THE OBJECTIVE. BAD NEWS, SO DID THEIR HEALER.
AND HE *REFUSES* TO GET SHOT! LIKE AN *ASSHOLE!*
DAMMIT, WE ARE *NOT* LOSING THE LAST QUALIFYING ROUND!

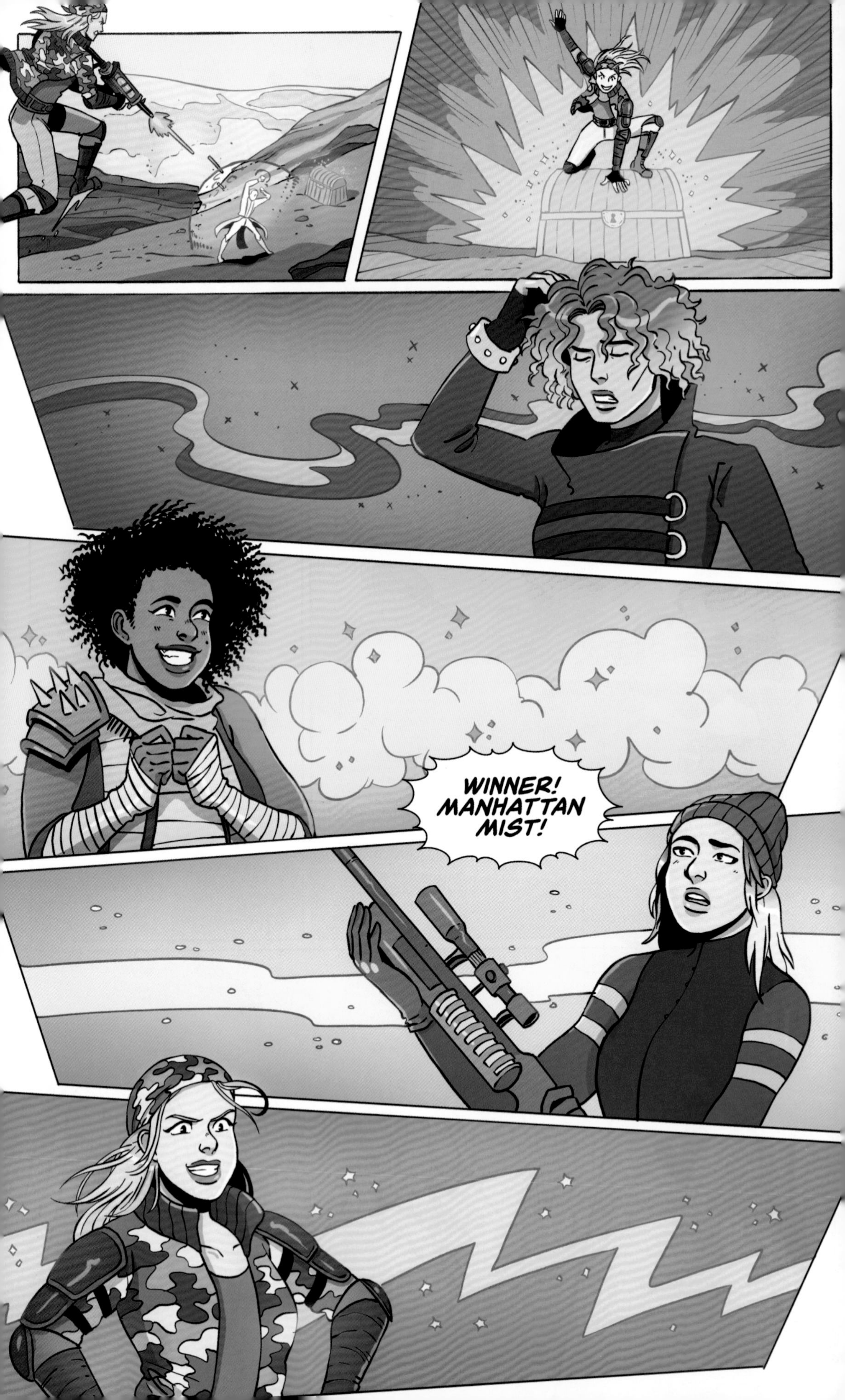
WINNER! MANHATTAN MIST!

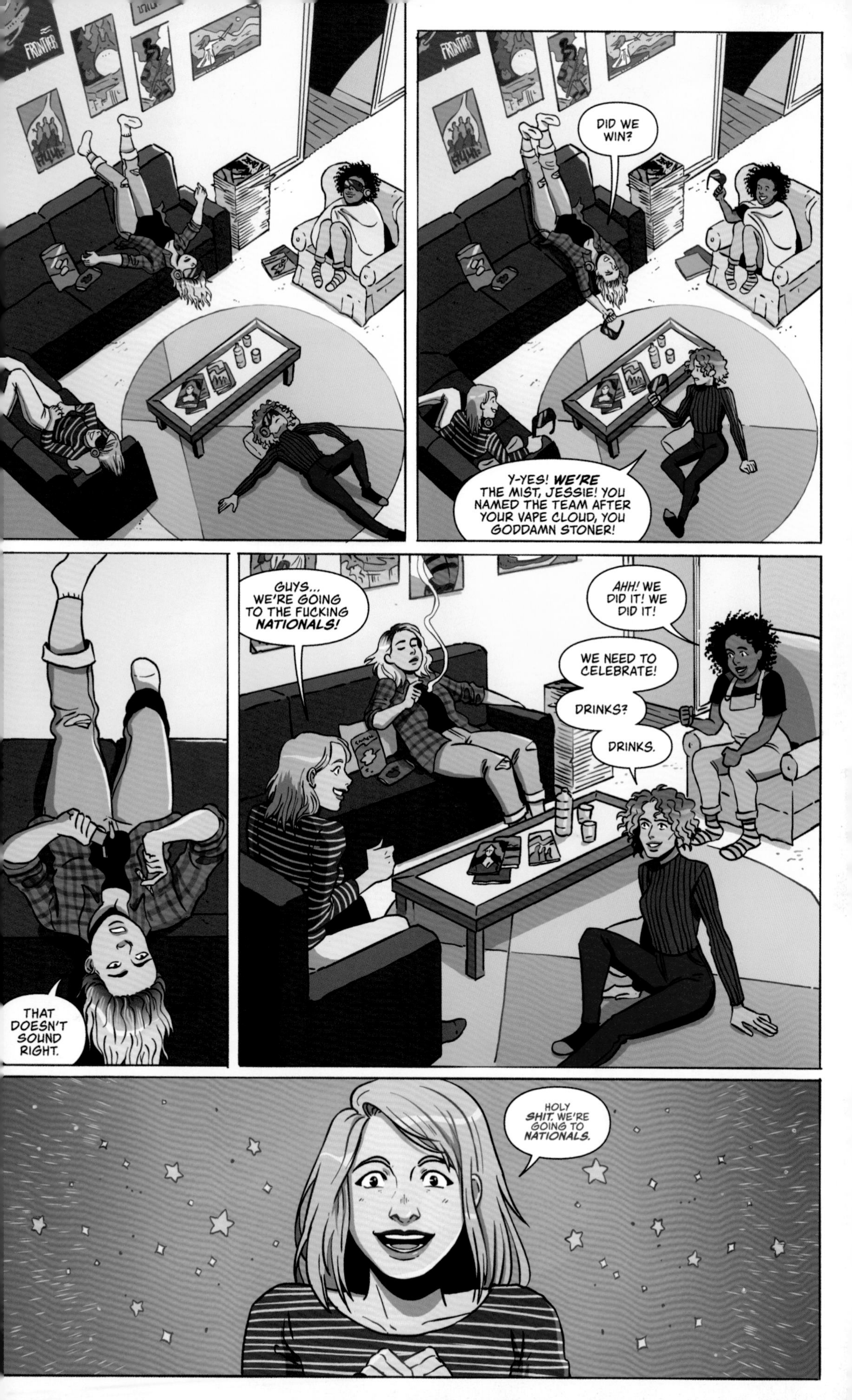
DID WE WIN?
Y-YES! WE'RE THE MIST, JESSIE! YOU NAMED THE TEAM AFTER YOUR VAPE CLOUD, YOU GODDAMN STONER!
THAT DOESN'T SOUND RIGHT.
GUYS... WE'RE GOING TO THE FUCKING NATIONALS!
AHH! WE DID IT! WE DID IT!
WE NEED TO CELEBRATE!
DRINKS?
DRINKS.
HOLY SHIT. WE'RE GOING TO NATIONALS.

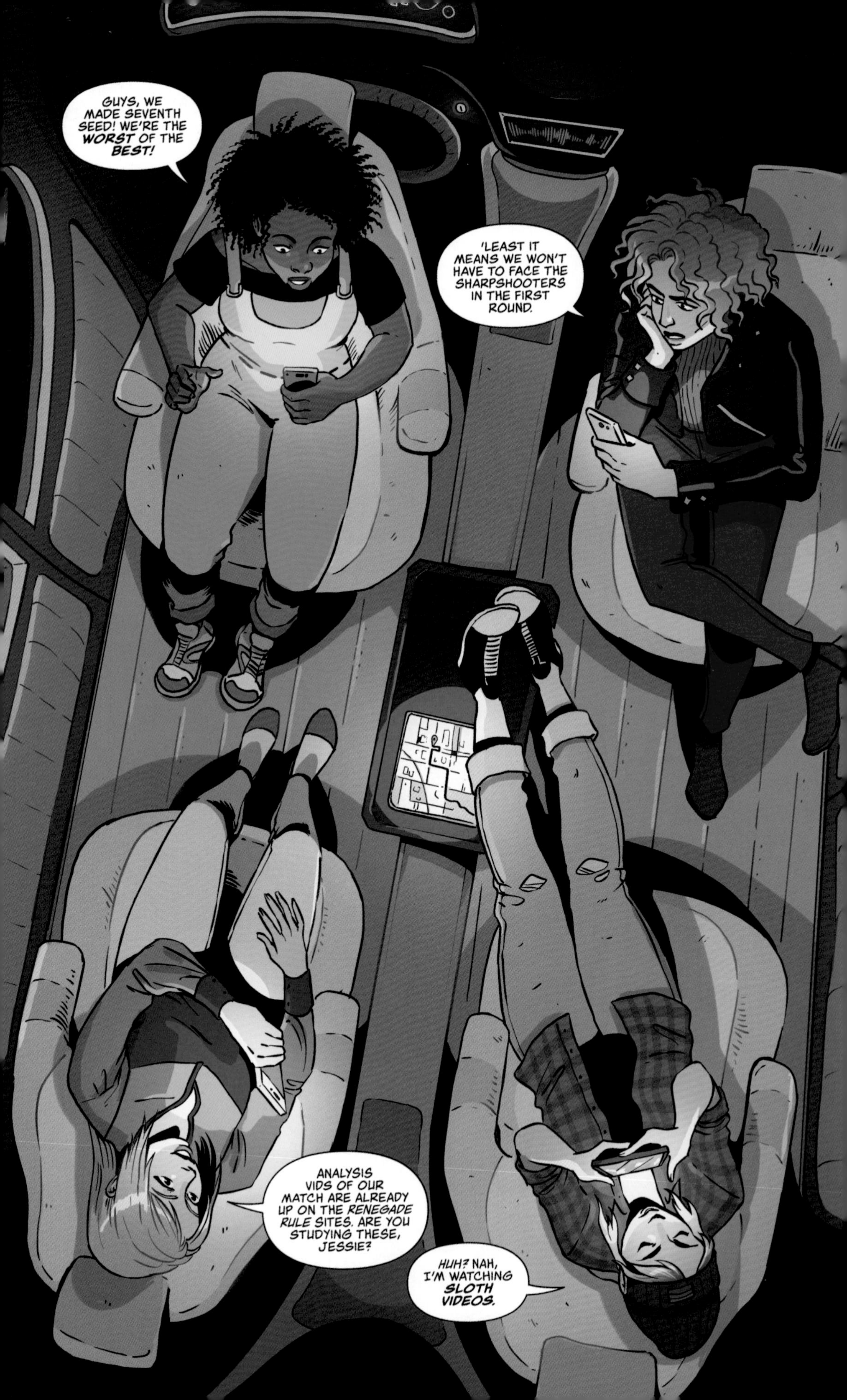
GUYS, WE MADE SEVENTH SEED! WE'RE THE *WORST* OF THE *BEST!*
'LEAST IT MEANS WE WON'T HAVE TO FACE THE SHARPSHOOTERS IN THE FIRST ROUND.
ANALYSIS VIDS OF OUR MATCH ARE ALREADY UP ON THE *RENEGADE RULE* SITES. ARE YOU STUDYING THESE, JESSIE?
HUH? NAH, I'M WATCHING ***SLOTH VIDEOS.***

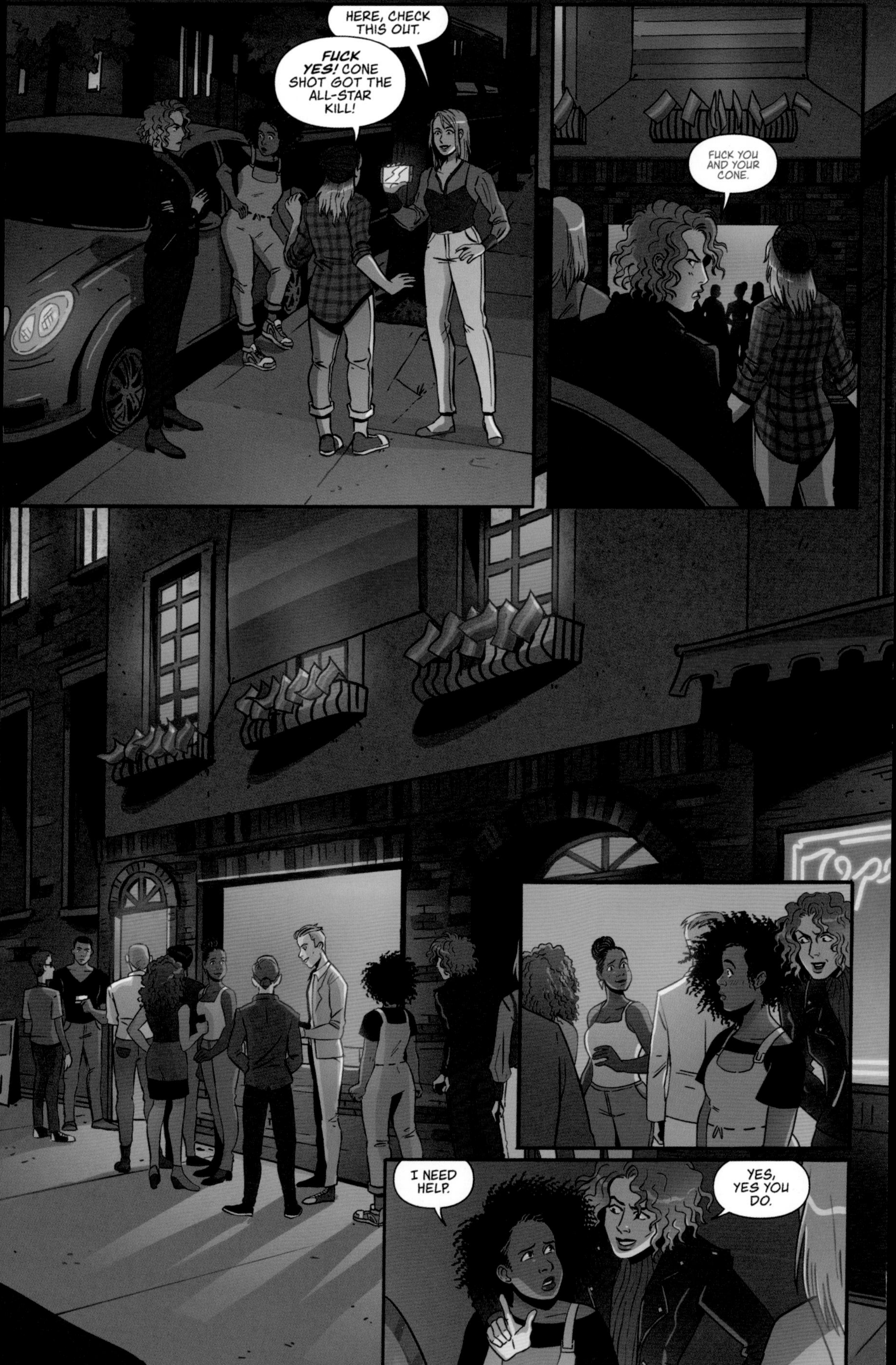
HERE, CHECK THIS OUT.
FUCK YES! CONE SHOT GOT THE ALL-STAR KILL!
FUCK YOU AND YOUR CONE.
I NEED HELP.
YES, YES YOU DO.

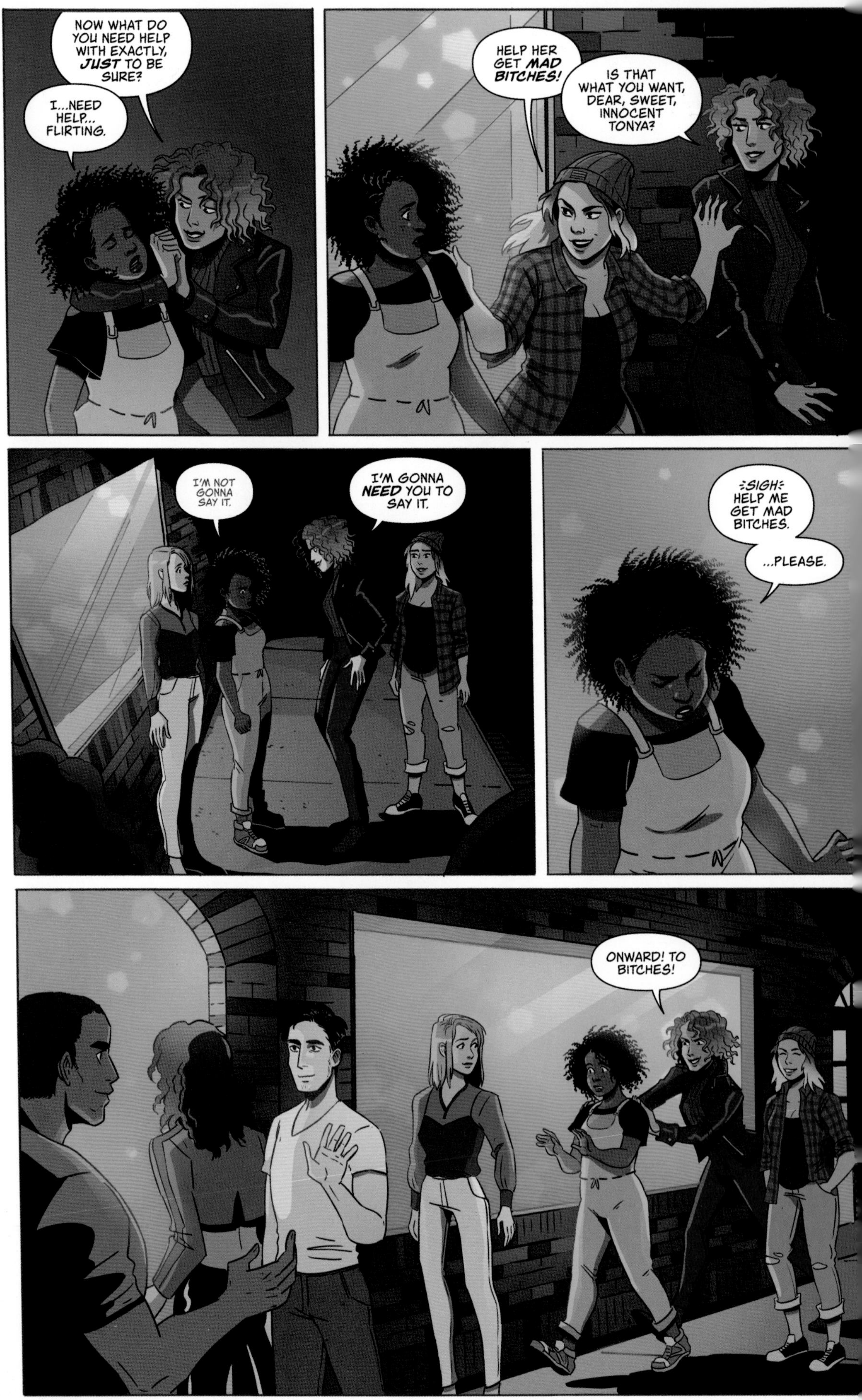
NOW WHAT DO YOU NEED HELP WITH EXACTLY, JUST TO BE SURE?
I...NEED HELP... FLIRTING.
HELP HER GET MAD BITCHES!
IS THAT WHAT YOU WANT, DEAR, SWEET, INNOCENT TONYA?
I'M NOT GONNA SAY IT.
I'M GONNA NEED YOU TO SAY IT.
SIGH HELP ME GET MAD BITCHES.
...PLEASE.
ONWARD! TO BITCHES!

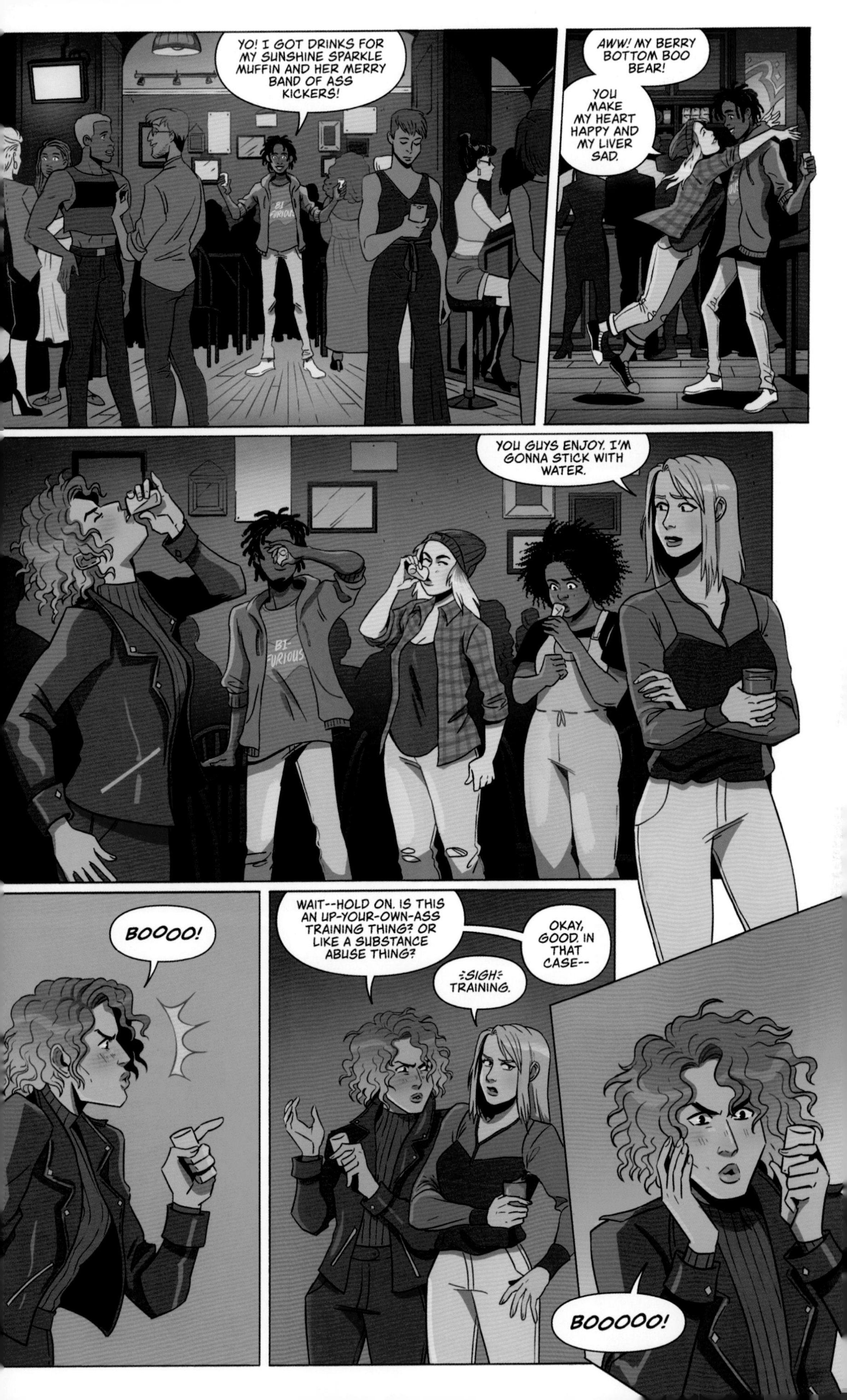

YO! I GOT DRINKS FOR MY SUNSHINE SPARKLE MUFFIN AND HER MERRY BAND OF ASS KICKERS!
BI FURIOUS
AWW! MY BERRY BOTTOM BOO BEAR!
YOU MAKE MY HEART HAPPY AND MY LIVER SAD.
YOU GUYS ENJOY. I'M GONNA STICK WITH WATER.
BI-FURIOUS
BOOOO!
WAIT--HOLD ON. IS THIS AN UP-YOUR-OWN-ASS TRAINING THING? OR LIKE A SUBSTANCE ABUSE THING?
SIGH TRAINING.
OKAY, GOOD. IN THAT CASE--
BOOOOO!

WHATEVER--EVERY-ONE HUDDLE UP. I WANNA MAKE A TOAST!

TO US! THE OL' COLLEGE DISASTER GAYS.

AND THEY SAID SKIPPING CLASS TO PLAY VIDEO GAMES WAS WASTING OUR FUTURES!

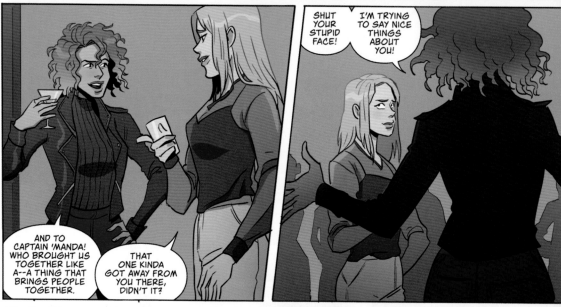

SHUT YOUR STUPID FACE!

I'M TRYING TO SAY NICE THINGS ABOUT YOU!

AND TO CAPTAIN 'MANDA! WHO BROUGHT US TOGETHER LIKE A--A THING THAT BRINGS PEOPLE TOGETHER.

THAT ONE KINDA GOT AWAY FROM YOU THERE, DIDN'T IT?

TONYA, YOU'RE MY BEST FRIEND. YOUR FANFIC IS WEIRD--

IT'S ROMANTIC! OUR CHARACTERS ARE IN LOVE!

THIS IS THE SHIT I'M TALKING ABOUT!

AND JESSIE...

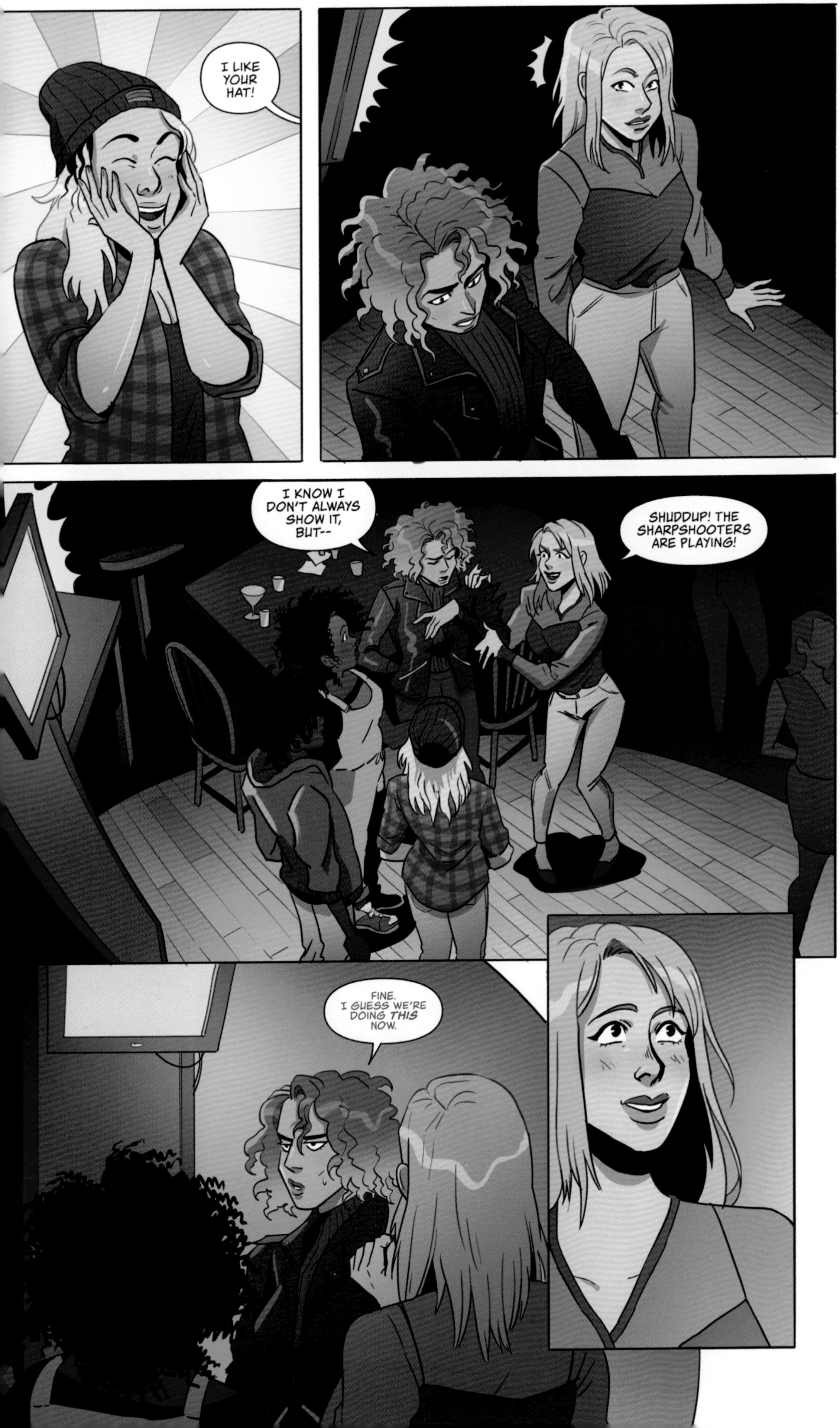
I LIKE YOUR HAT!
I KNOW I DON'T ALWAYS SHOW IT, BUT--
SHUDDUP! THE SHARPSHOOTERS ARE PLAYING!
FINE. I GUESS WE'RE DOING *THIS* NOW.

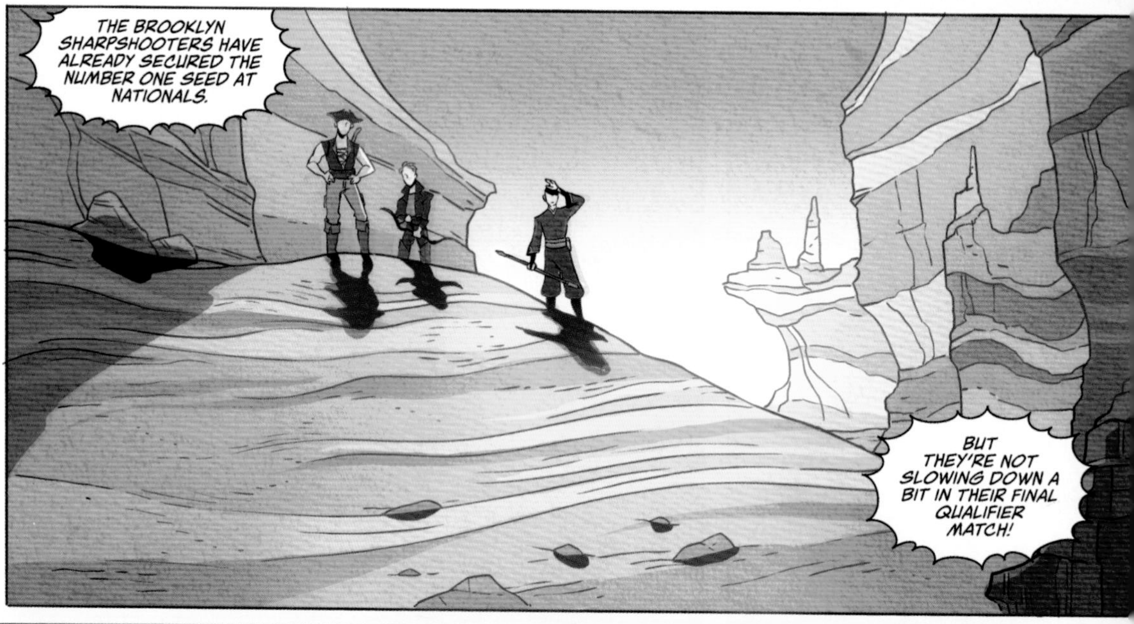
THE BROOKLYN SHARPSHOOTERS HAVE ALREADY SECURED THE NUMBER ONE SEED AT NATIONALS.
BUT THEY'RE NOT SLOWING DOWN A BIT IN THEIR FINAL QUALIFIER MATCH!

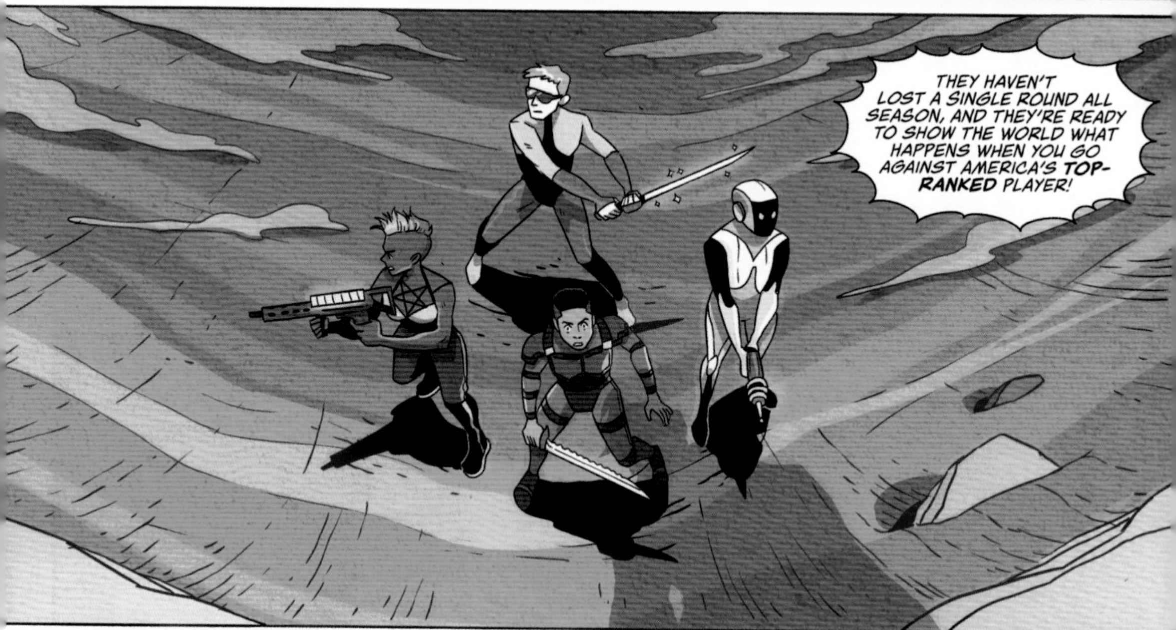
THEY HAVEN'T LOST A SINGLE ROUND ALL SEASON, AND THEY'RE READY TO SHOW THE WORLD WHAT HAPPENS WHEN YOU GO AGAINST AMERICA'S **TOP-RANKED** PLAYER!

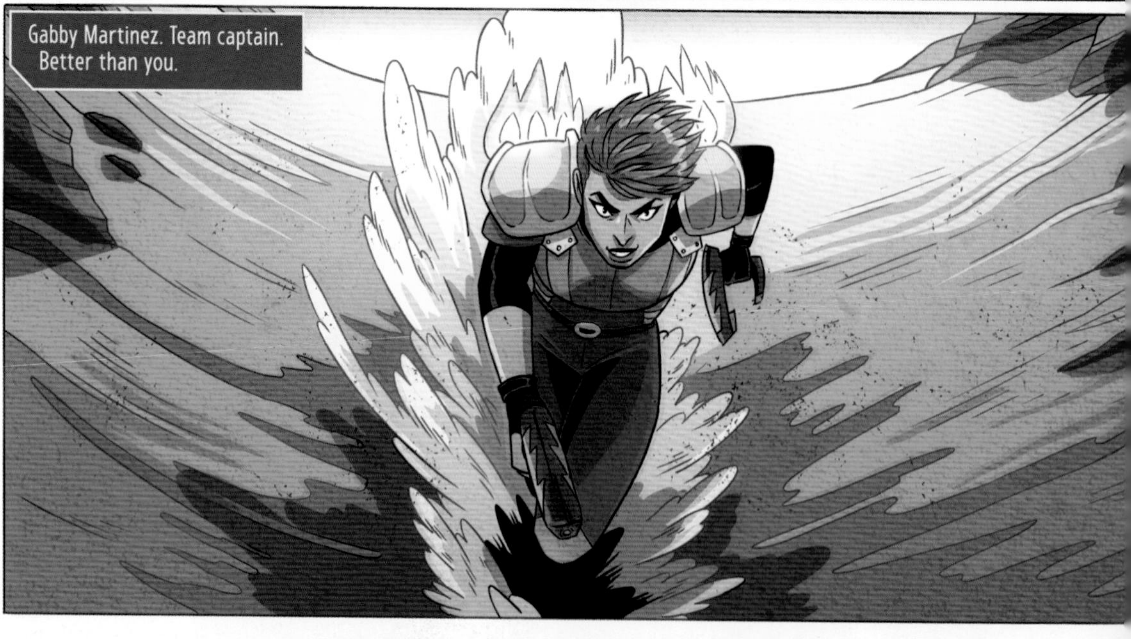
Gabby Martinez. Team captain.
Better than you.

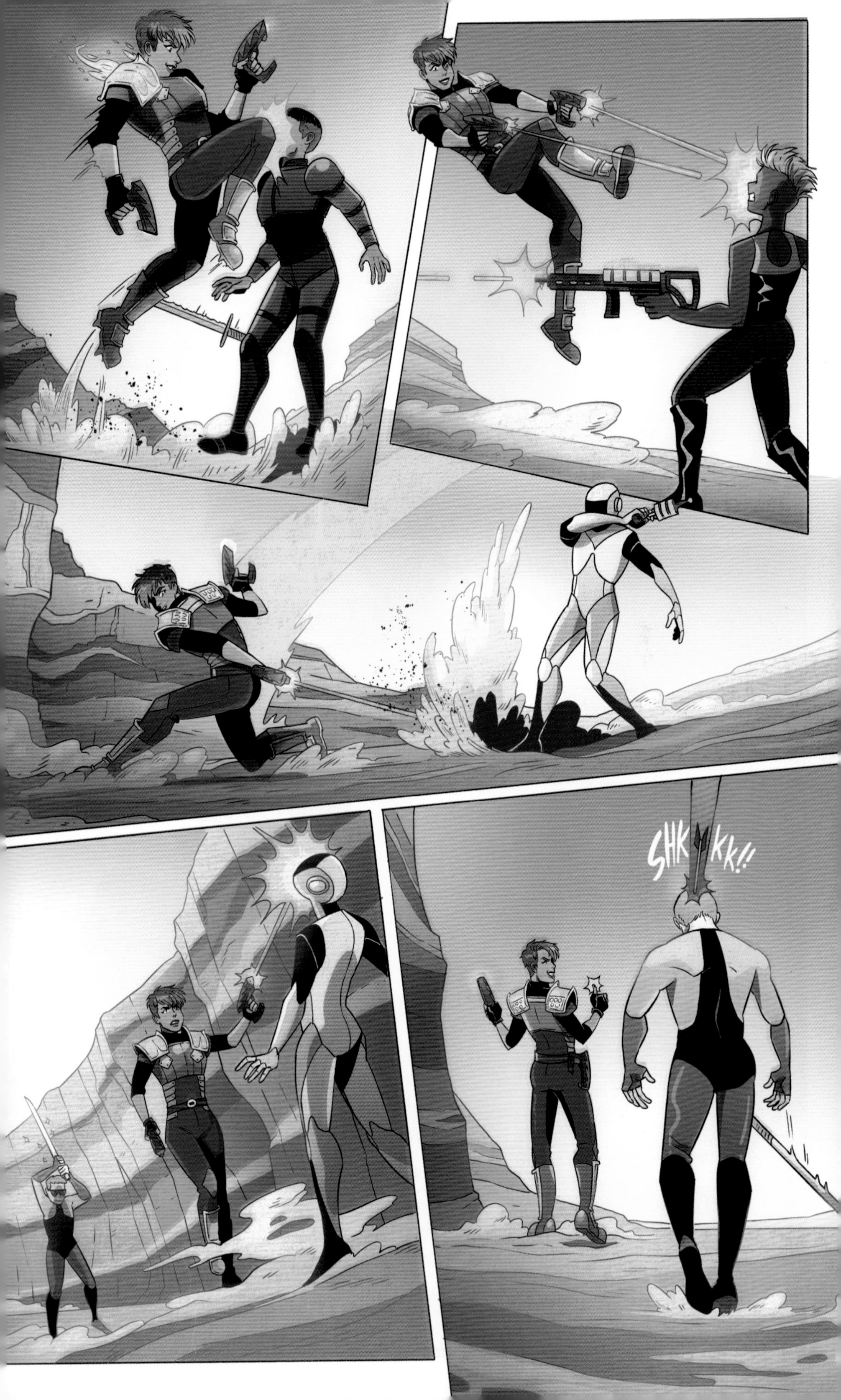
SHKKKK!!

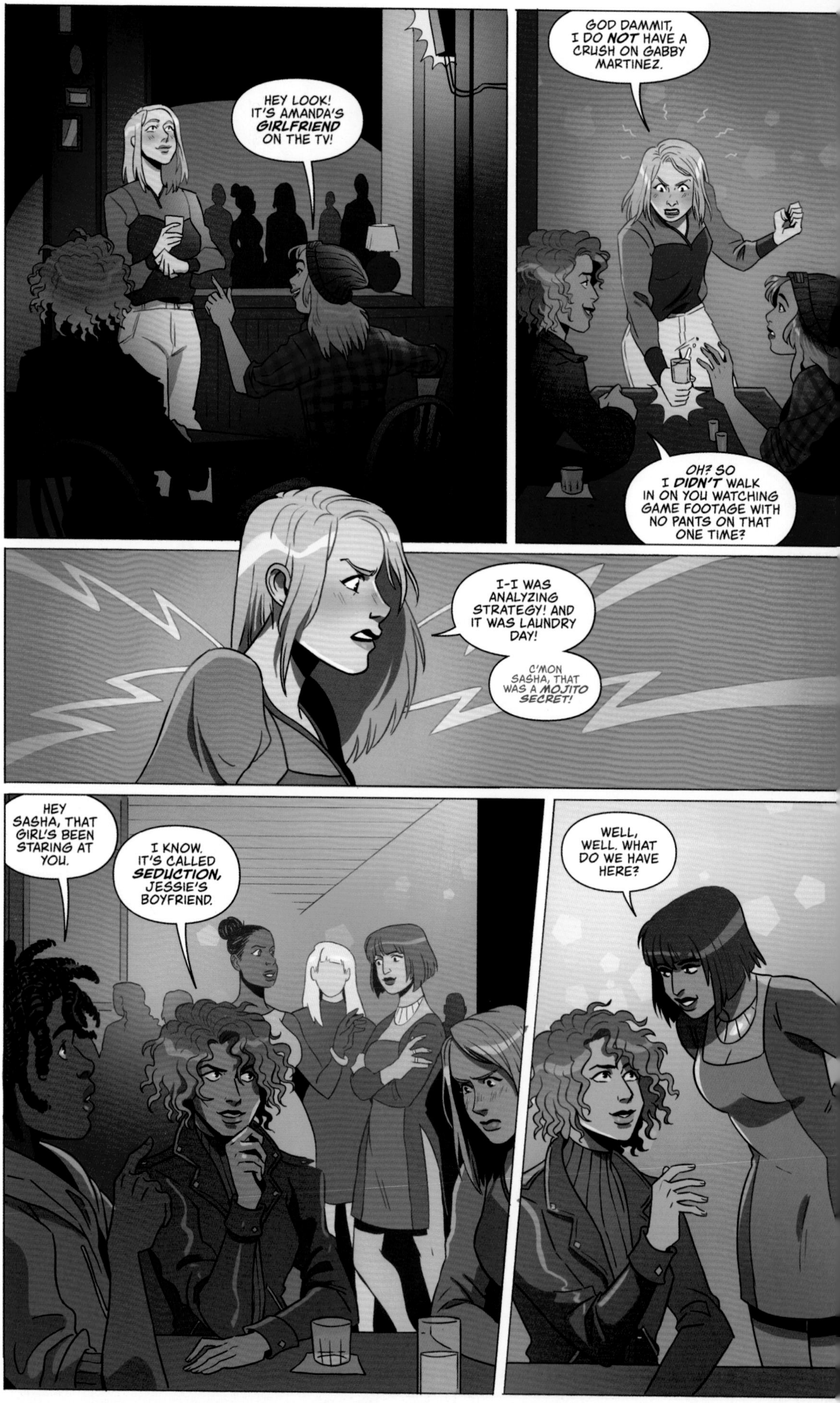
HEY LOOK! IT'S AMANDA'S GIRLFRIEND ON THE TV!
GOD DAMMIT, I DO NOT HAVE A CRUSH ON GABBY MARTINEZ.
OH? SO I DIDN'T WALK IN ON YOU WATCHING GAME FOOTAGE WITH NO PANTS ON THAT ONE TIME?
I-I WAS ANALYZING STRATEGY! AND IT WAS LAUNDRY DAY!
C'MON SASHA, THAT WAS A MOJITO SECRET!
HEY SASHA, THAT GIRL'S BEEN STARING AT YOU.
I KNOW. IT'S CALLED SEDUCTION, JESSIE'S BOYFRIEND.
WELL, WELL. WHAT DO WE HAVE HERE?

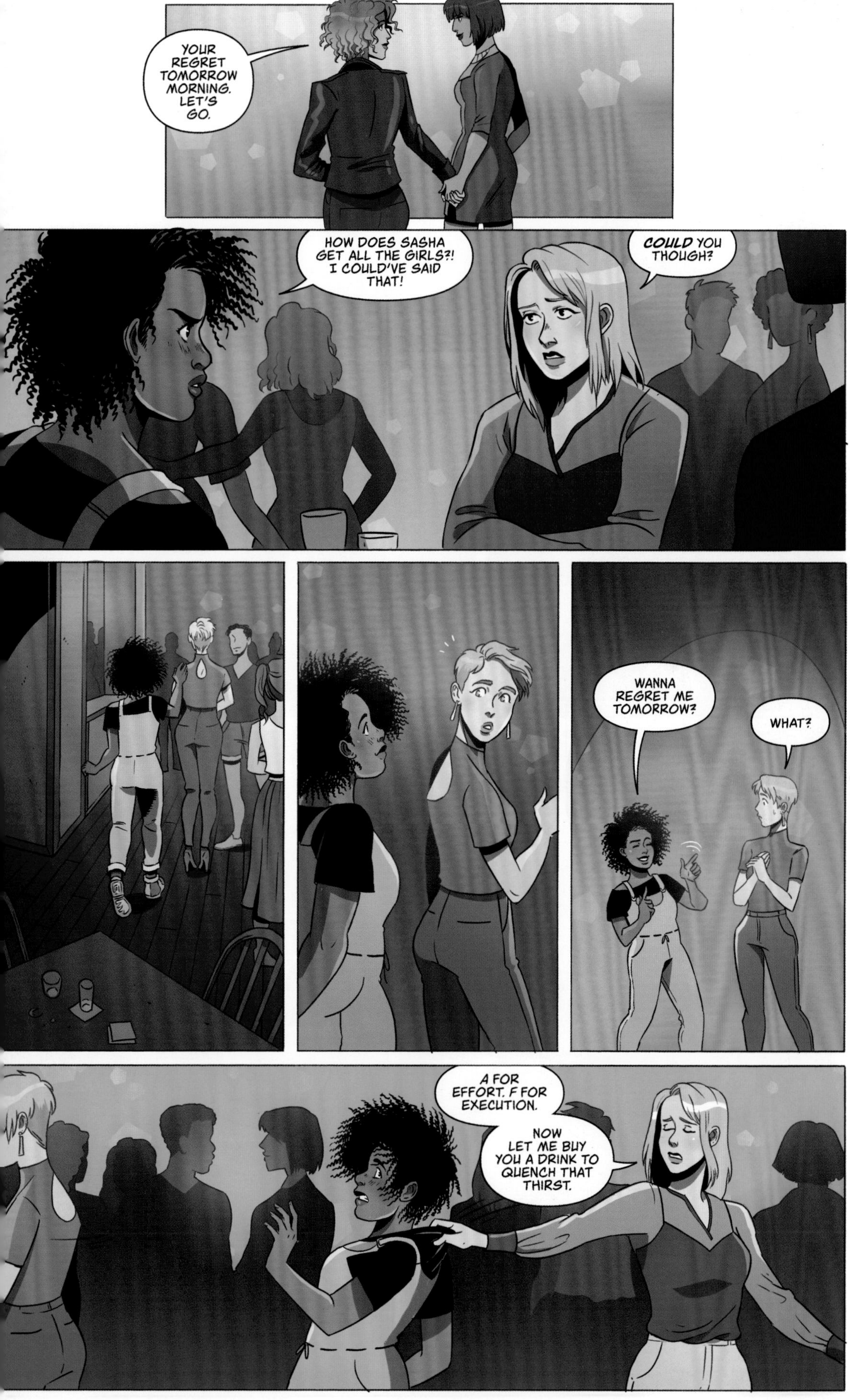
YOUR REGRET TOMORROW MORNING. LET'S GO.
HOW DOES SASHA GET ALL THE GIRLS?! I COULD'VE SAID THAT!
COULD YOU THOUGH?
WANNA REGRET ME TOMORROW?
WHAT?
A FOR EFFORT. F FOR EXECUTION.
NOW LET ME BUY YOU A DRINK TO QUENCH THAT THIRST.

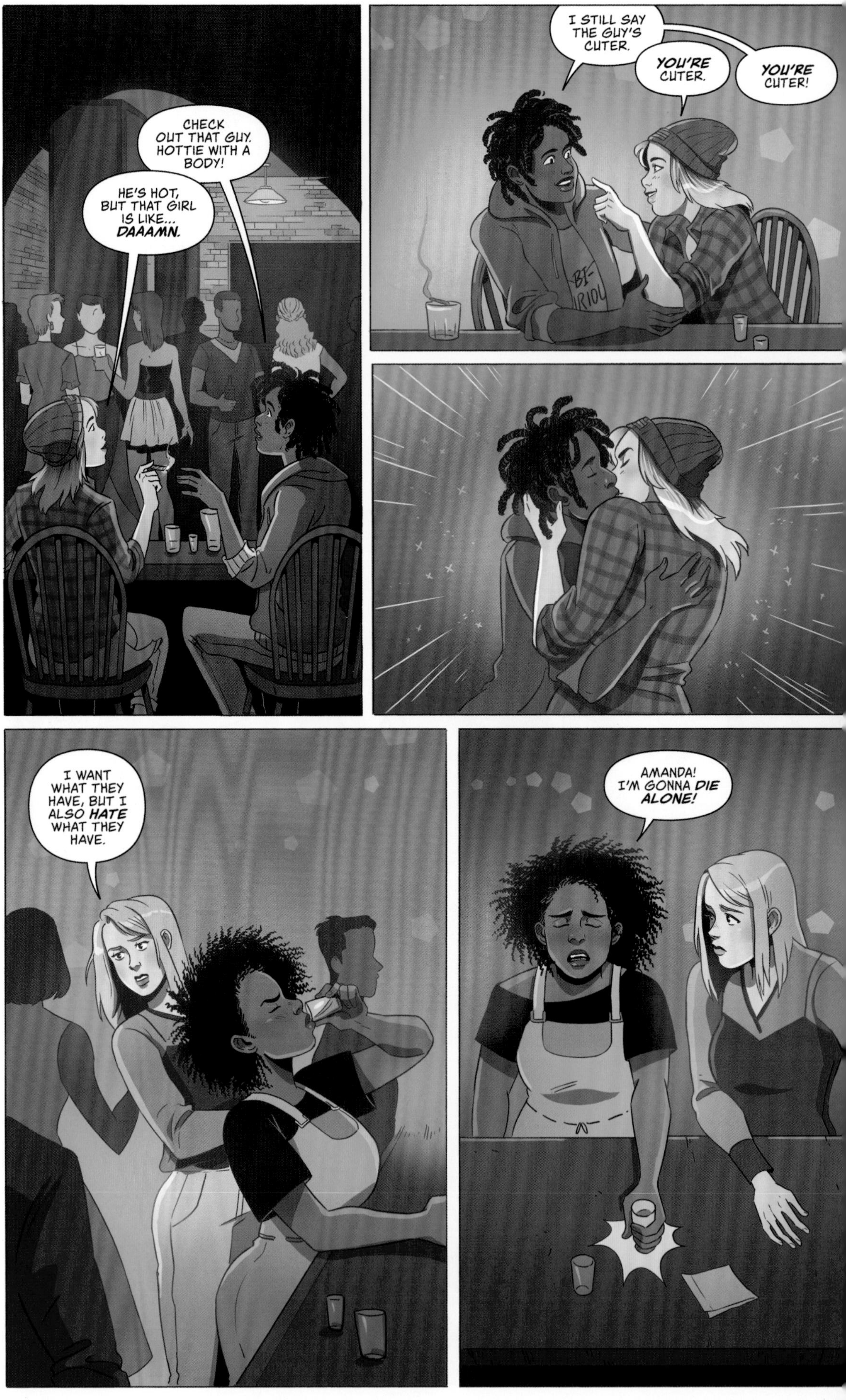
CHECK OUT THAT GUY. HOTTIE WITH A BODY!
HE'S HOT, BUT THAT GIRL IS LIKE... **DAAAMN.**
I STILL SAY THE GUY'S CUTER.
YOU'RE CUTER.
YOU'RE CUTER!
I WANT WHAT THEY HAVE, BUT I ALSO ***HATE*** WHAT THEY HAVE.
AMANDA! I'M GONNA ***DIE ALONE!***

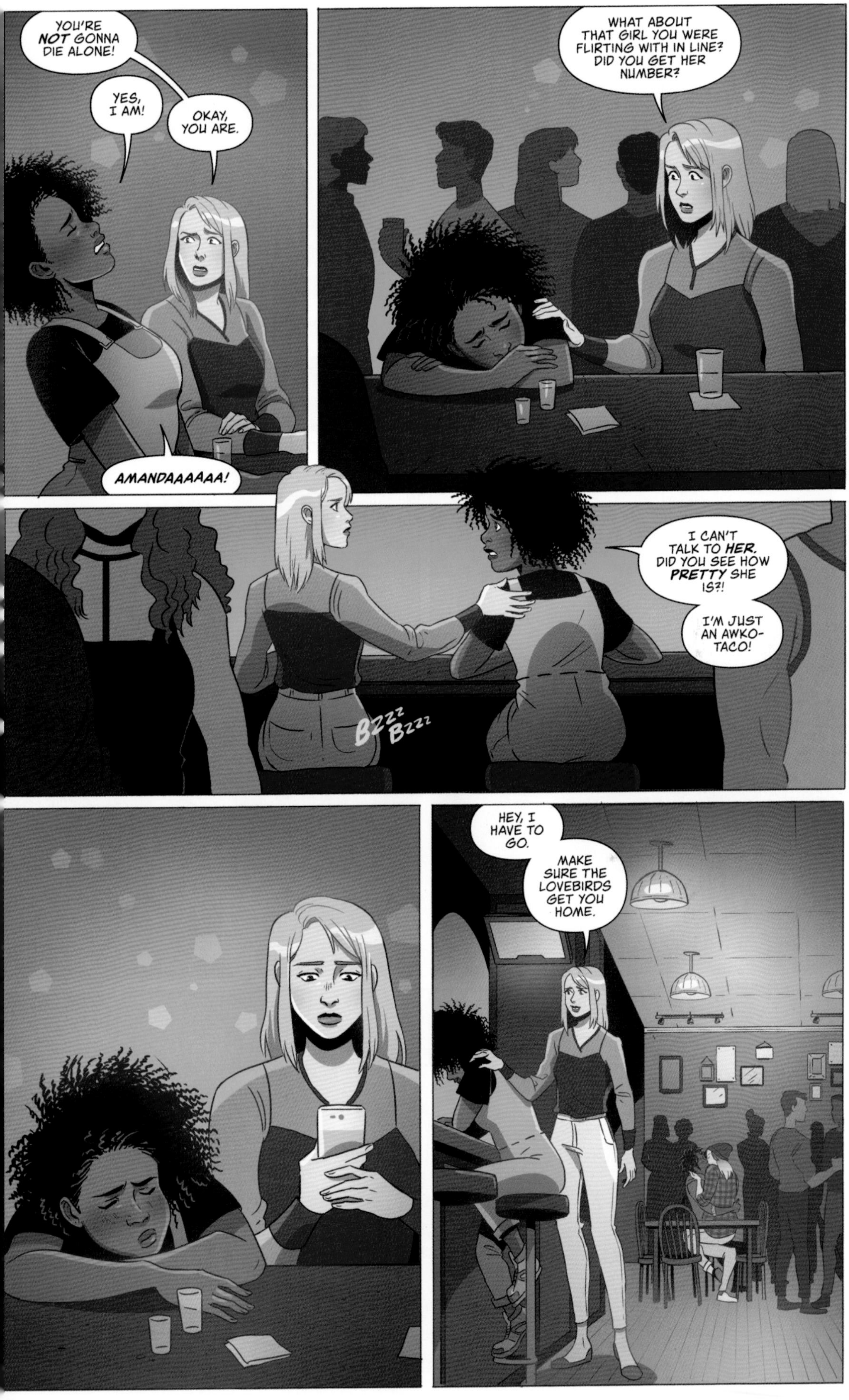
YOU'RE NOT GONNA DIE ALONE!
YES, I AM!
OKAY, YOU ARE.
AMANDAAAAAA!
WHAT ABOUT THAT GIRL YOU WERE FLIRTING WITH IN LINE? DID YOU GET HER NUMBER?
I CAN'T TALK TO HER. DID YOU SEE HOW PRETTY SHE IS?!
I'M JUST AN AWKO-TACO!
BZZZ BZZZ
HEY, I HAVE TO GO.
MAKE SURE THE LOVEBIRDS GET YOU HOME.

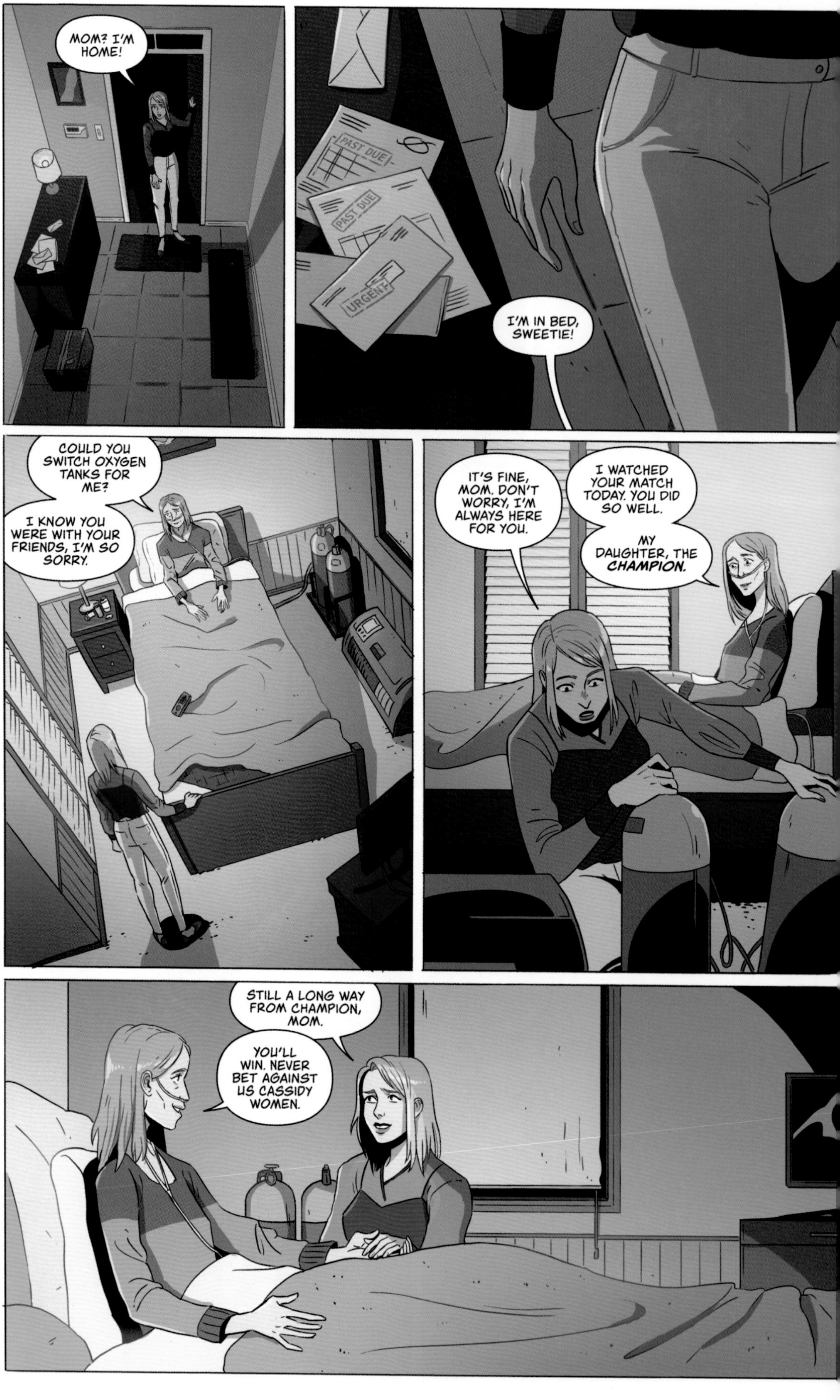
MOM? I'M HOME!
I'M IN BED, SWEETIE!
PAST DUE
PAST DUE
URGENT
COULD YOU SWITCH OXYGEN TANKS FOR ME?
I KNOW YOU WERE WITH YOUR FRIENDS, I'M SO SORRY.
IT'S FINE, MOM. DON'T WORRY, I'M ALWAYS HERE FOR YOU.
I WATCHED YOUR MATCH TODAY. YOU DID SO WELL.
MY DAUGHTER, THE **CHAMPION.**
STILL A LONG WAY FROM CHAMPION, MOM.
YOU'LL WIN. NEVER BET AGAINST US CASSIDY WOMEN.

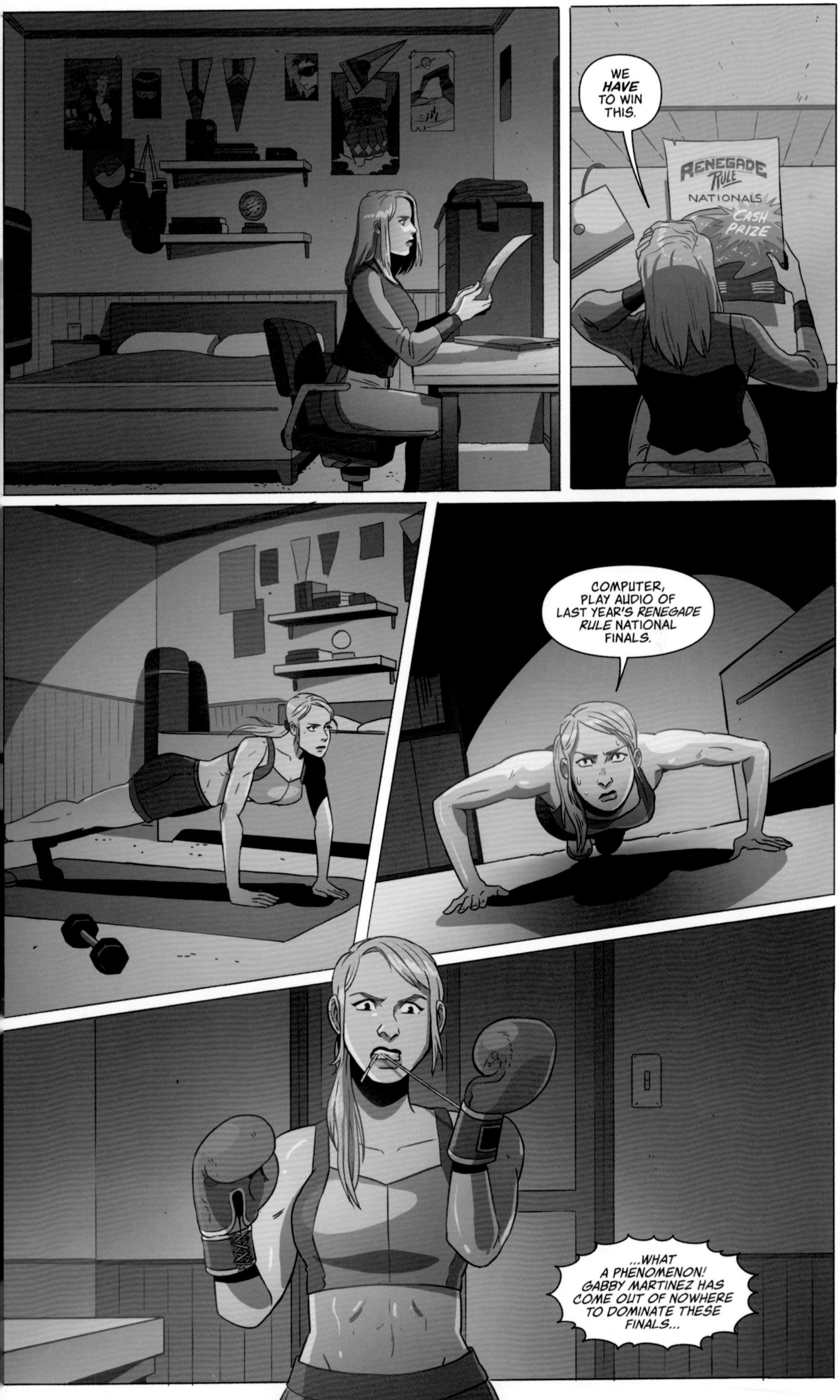

WE HAVE TO WIN THIS.
RENEGADE RULE
NATIONALS
CASH PRIZE
COMPUTER, PLAY AUDIO OF LAST YEAR'S RENEGADE RULE NATIONAL FINALS.
...WHAT A PHENOMENON! GABBY MARTINEZ HAS COME OUT OF NOWHERE TO DOMINATE THESE FINALS...

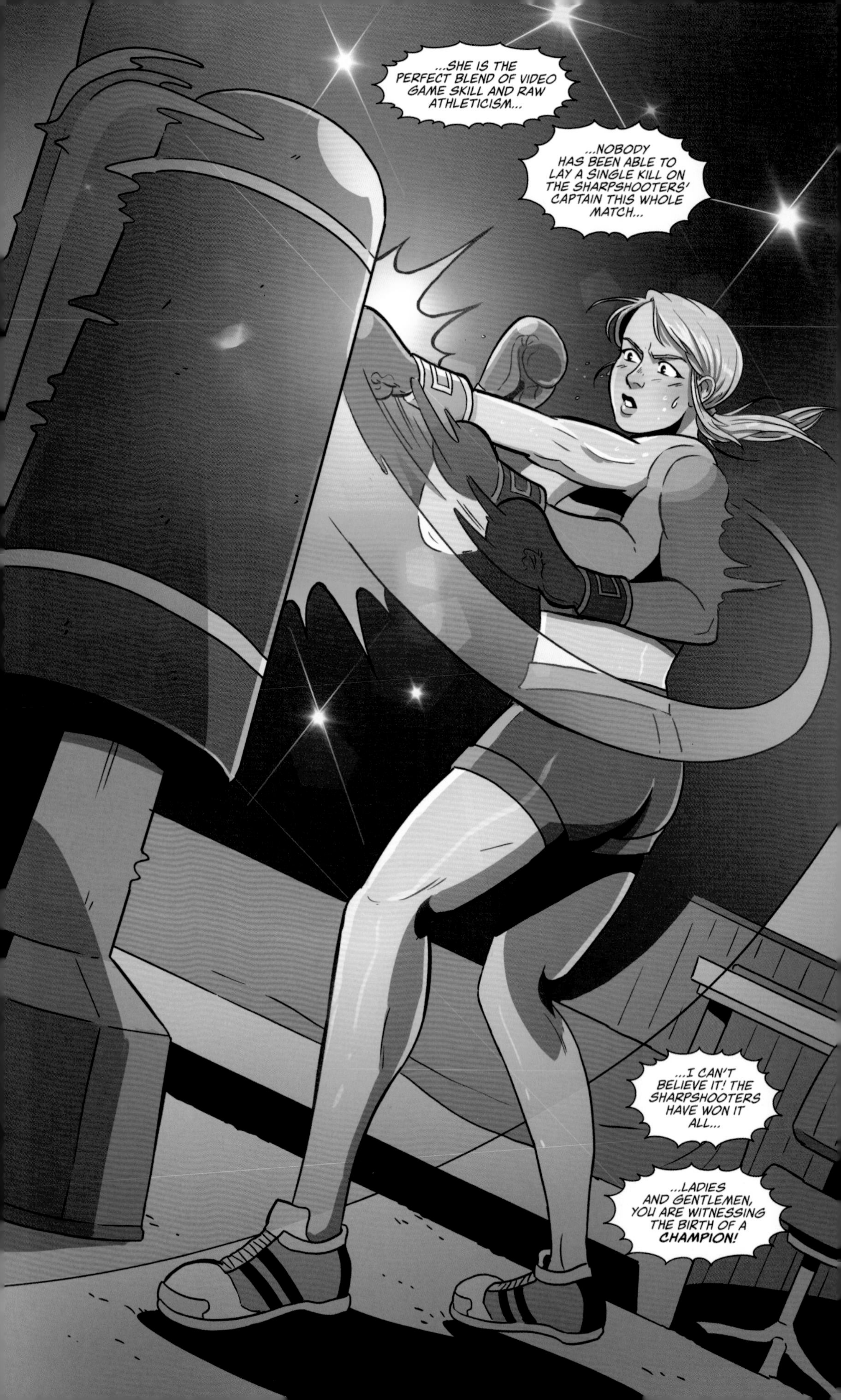
...SHE IS THE PERFECT BLEND OF VIDEO GAME SKILL AND RAW ATHLETICISM...
...NOBODY HAS BEEN ABLE TO LAY A SINGLE KILL ON THE SHARPSHOOTERS' CAPTAIN THIS WHOLE MATCH...
...I CAN'T BELIEVE IT! THE SHARPSHOOTERS HAVE WON IT ALL...
...LADIES AND GENTLEMEN, YOU ARE WITNESSING THE BIRTH OF A CHAMPION!

CHAPTER TWO

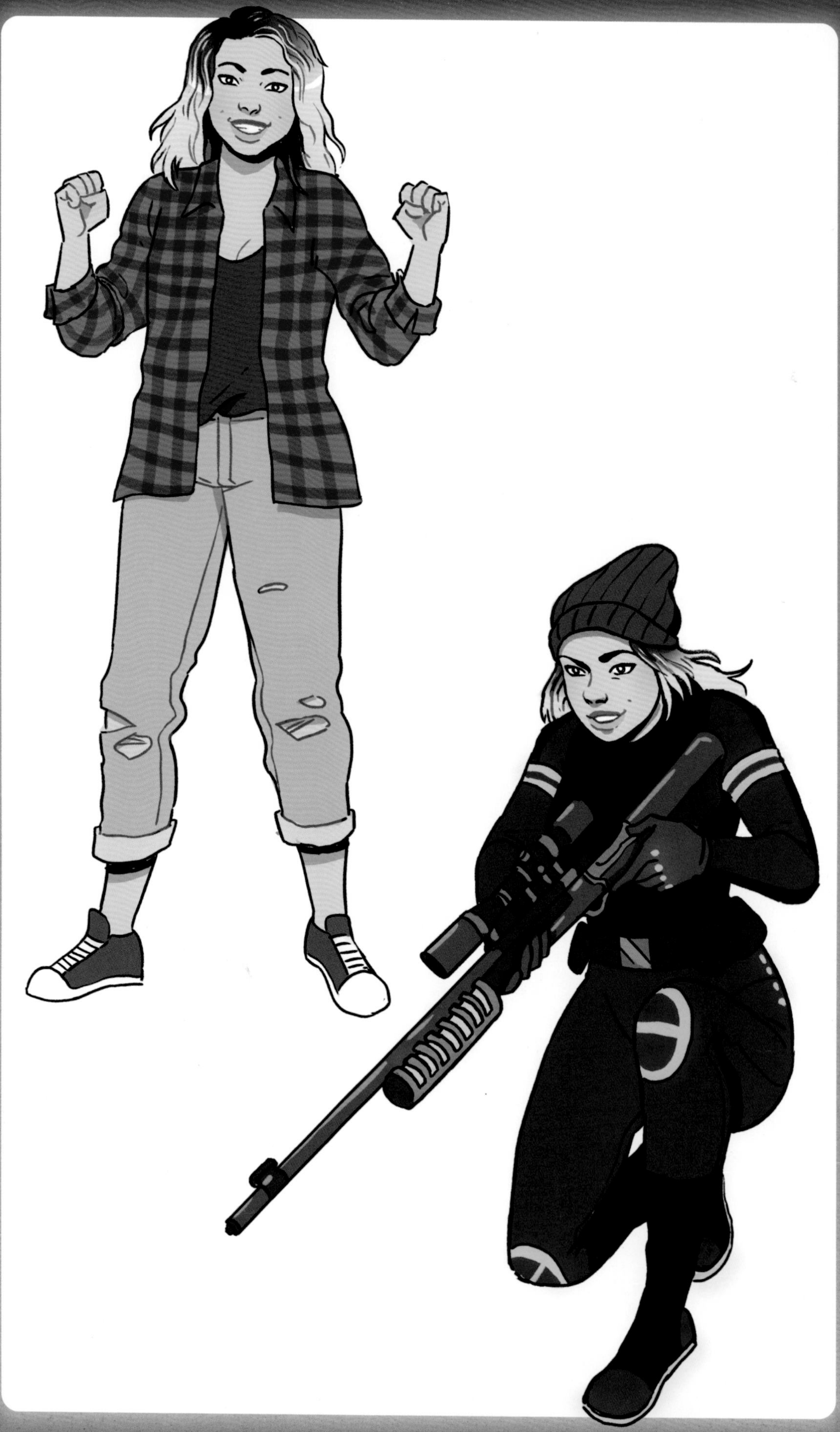

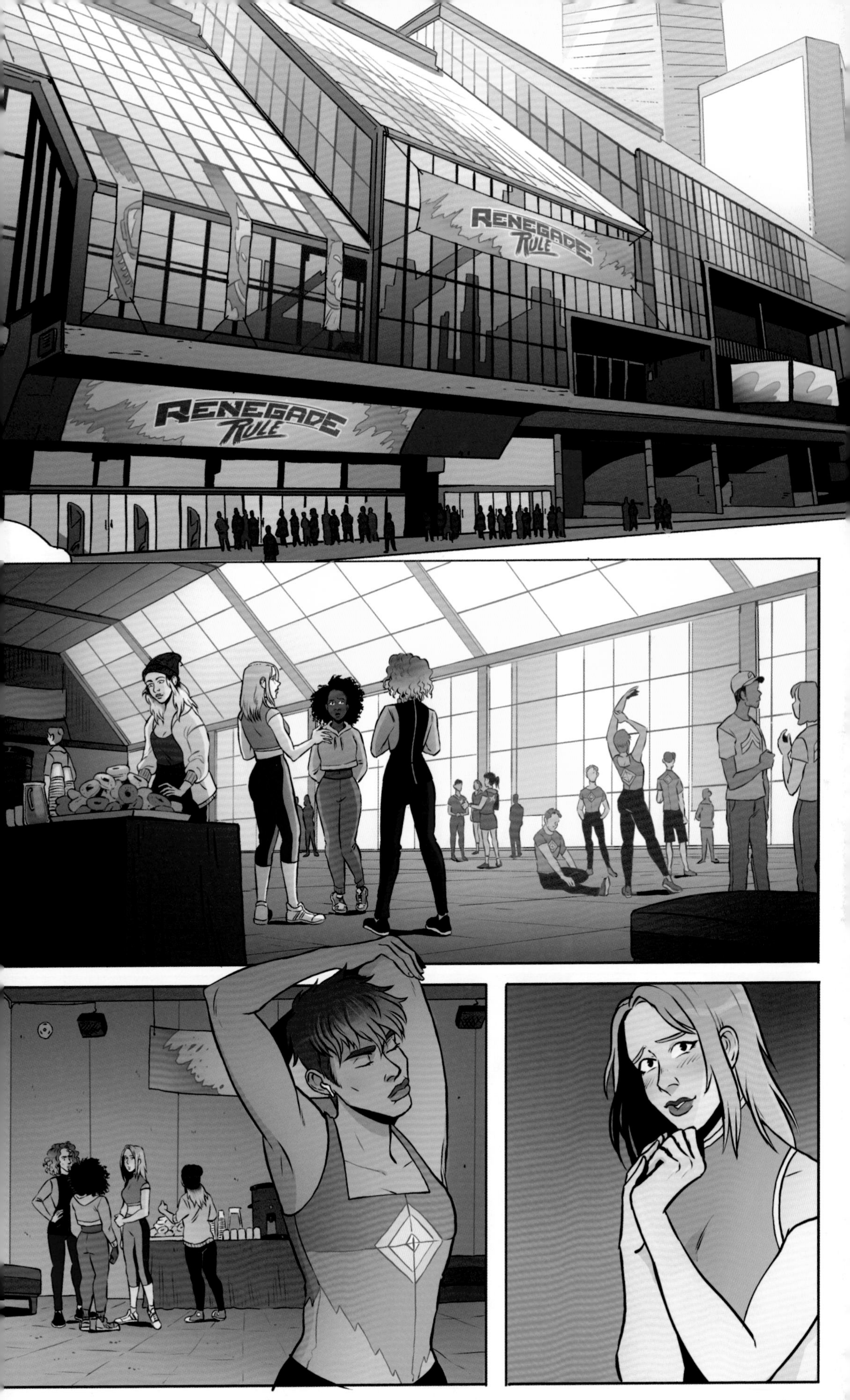
RENEGADE RULE
RENEGADE RULE

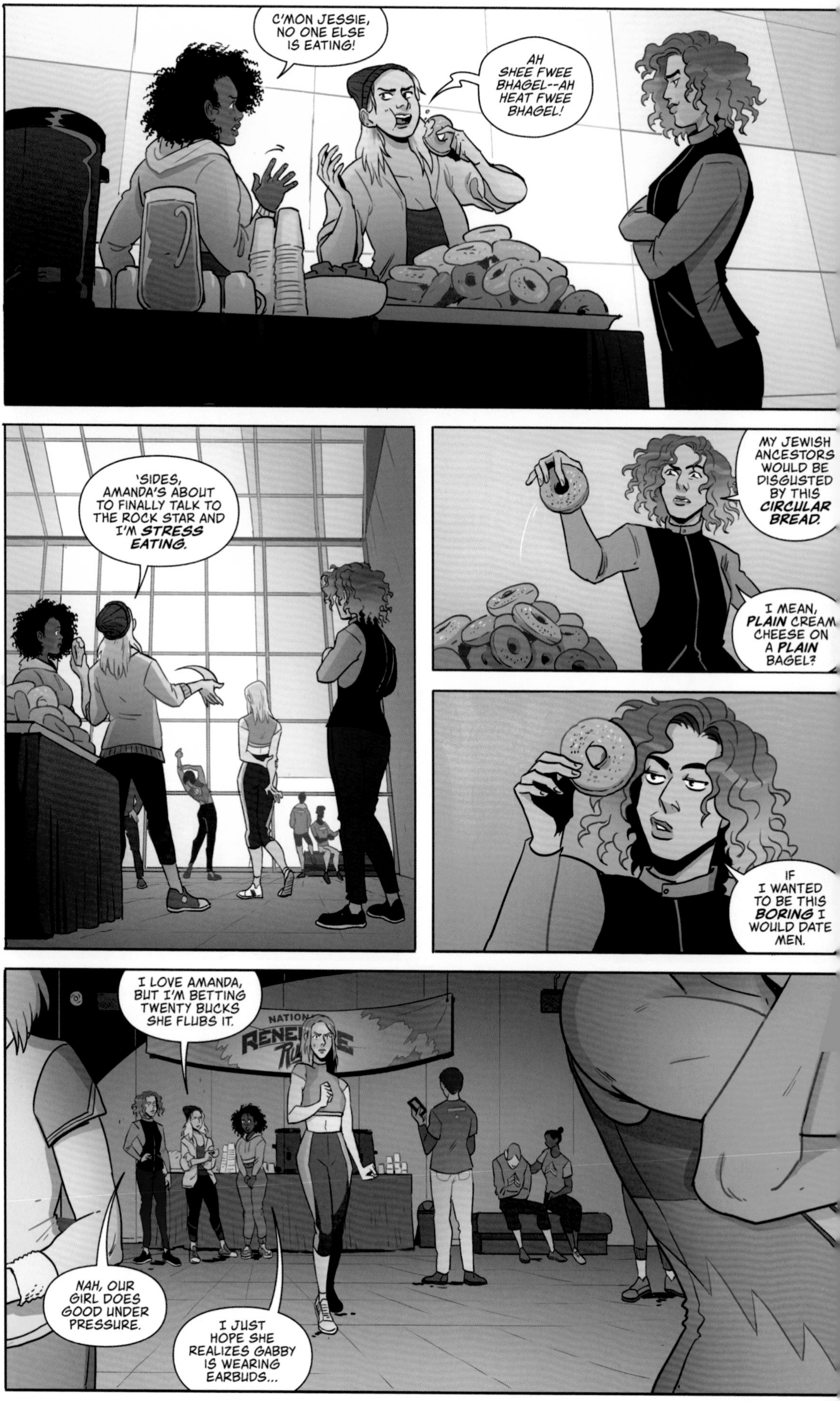
C'MON JESSIE, NO ONE ELSE IS EATING!
AH SHEE FWEE BHAGEL--AH HEAT FWEE BHAGEL!
'SIDES, AMANDA'S ABOUT TO FINALLY TALK TO THE ROCK STAR AND I'M *STRESS EATING.*
MY JEWISH ANCESTORS WOULD BE DISGUSTED BY THIS *CIRCULAR BREAD.*
I MEAN, *PLAIN* CREAM CHEESE ON A *PLAIN* BAGEL?
IF I WANTED TO BE THIS *BORING* I WOULD DATE MEN.
I LOVE AMANDA, BUT I'M BETTING TWENTY BUCKS SHE FLUBS IT.
NAH, OUR GIRL DOES GOOD UNDER PRESSURE.
I JUST HOPE SHE REALIZES GABBY IS WEARING EARBUDS...

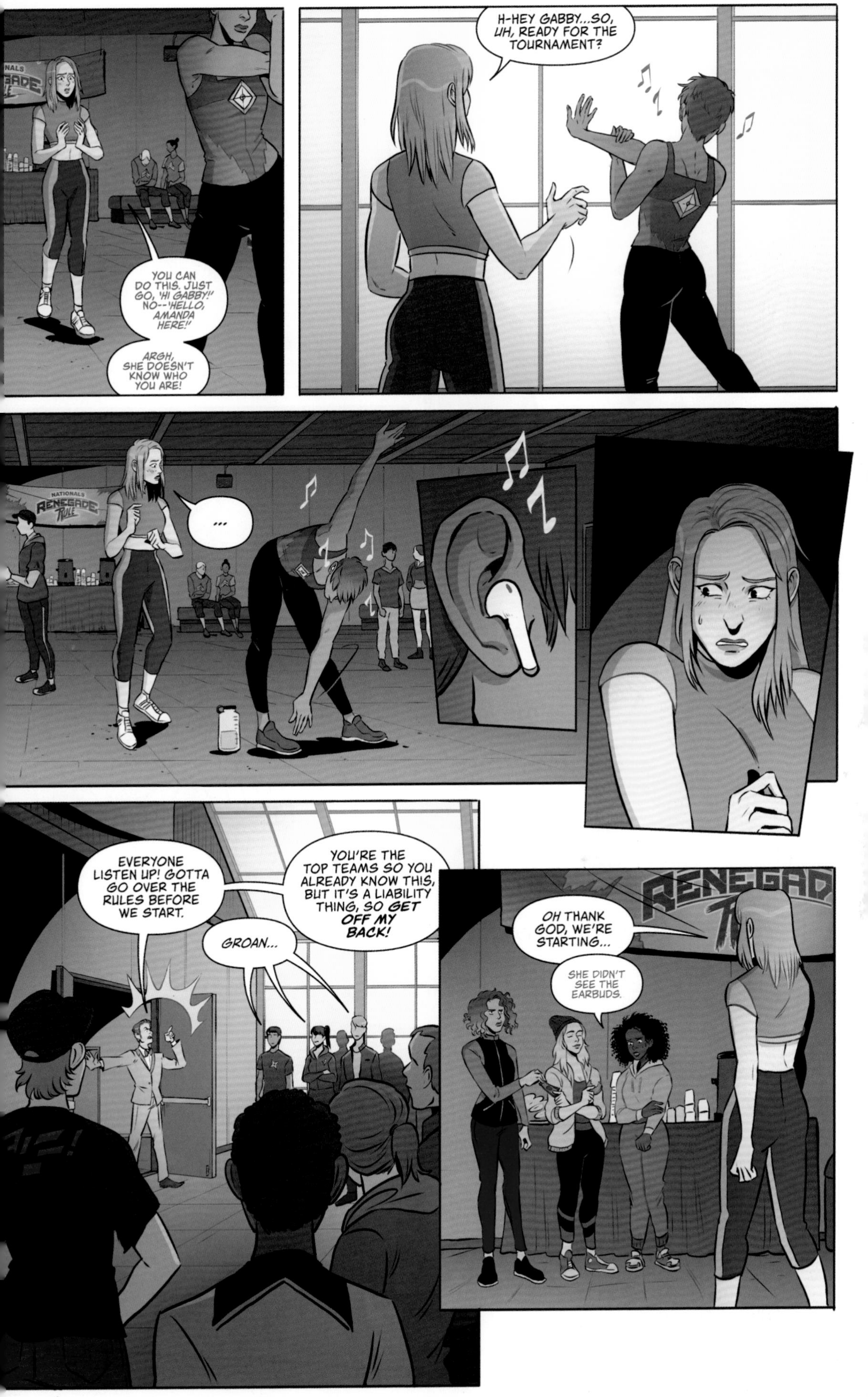
NATIONALS
RENEGADE RULE
YOU CAN DO THIS. JUST GO, 'HI GABBY!' NO--'HELLO, AMANDA HERE!'
ARGH, SHE DOESN'T KNOW WHO YOU ARE!
H-HEY GABBY...SO, UH, READY FOR THE TOURNAMENT?
...
EVERYONE LISTEN UP! GOTTA GO OVER THE RULES BEFORE WE START.
YOU'RE THE TOP TEAMS SO YOU ALREADY KNOW THIS, BUT IT'S A LIABILITY THING, SO GET OFF MY BACK!
GROAN...
OH THANK GOD, WE'RE STARTING...
SHE DIDN'T SEE THE EARBUDS.

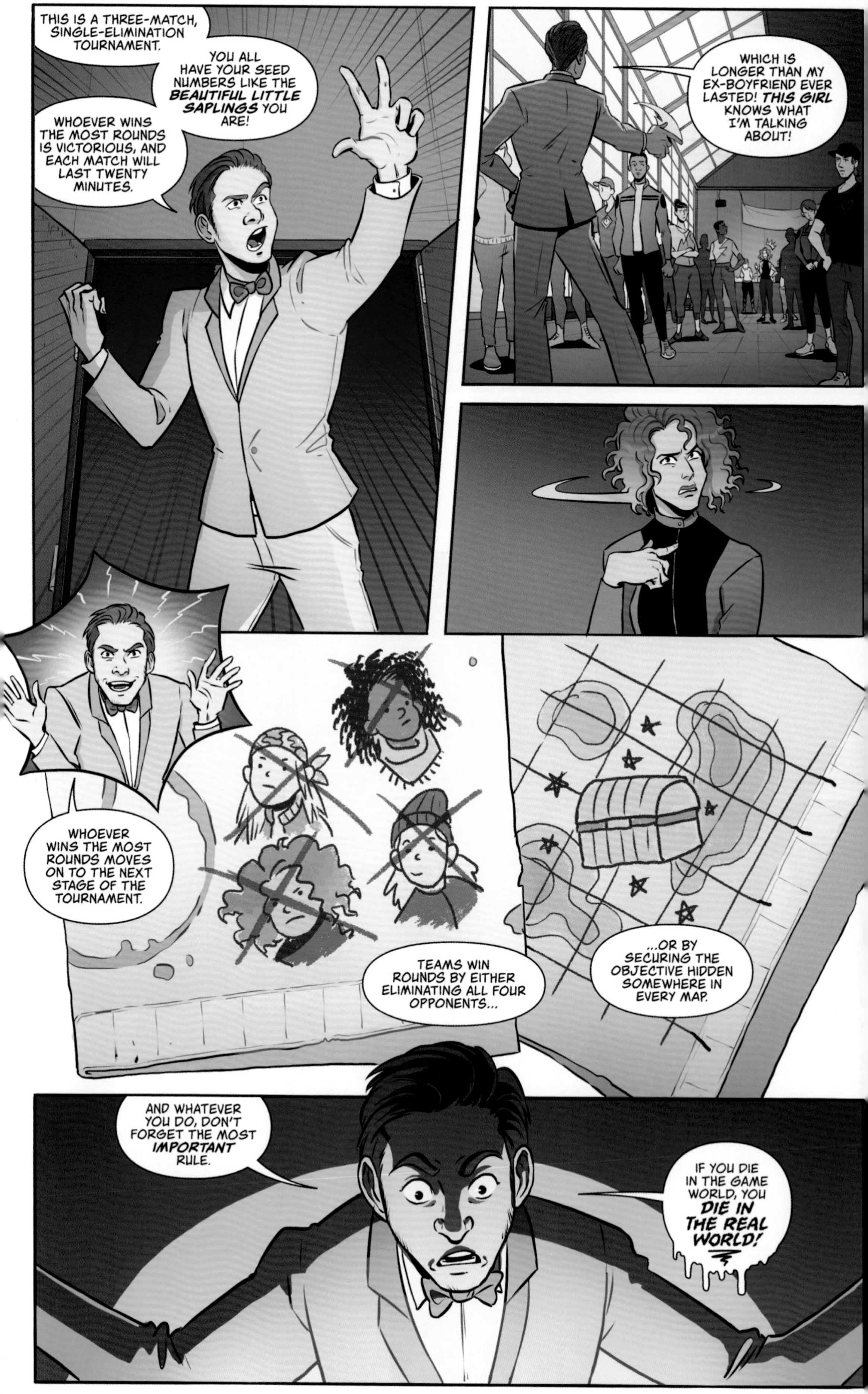

THIS IS A THREE-MATCH, SINGLE-ELIMINATION TOURNAMENT.
YOU ALL HAVE YOUR SEED NUMBERS LIKE THE **BEAUTIFUL LITTLE SAPLINGS** YOU ARE!
WHOEVER WINS THE MOST ROUNDS IS VICTORIOUS, AND EACH MATCH WILL LAST TWENTY MINUTES.
WHICH IS LONGER THAN MY EX-BOYFRIEND EVER LASTED! **THIS GIRL** KNOWS WHAT I'M TALKING ABOUT!
WHOEVER WINS THE MOST ROUNDS MOVES ON TO THE NEXT STAGE OF THE TOURNAMENT.
TEAMS WIN ROUNDS BY EITHER ELIMINATING ALL FOUR OPPONENTS...
...OR BY SECURING THE OBJECTIVE HIDDEN SOMEWHERE IN EVERY MAP.
AND WHATEVER YOU DO, DON'T FORGET THE MOST **IMPORTANT** RULE.
IF YOU DIE IN THE GAME WORLD, YOU **DIE IN THE REAL WORLD!**

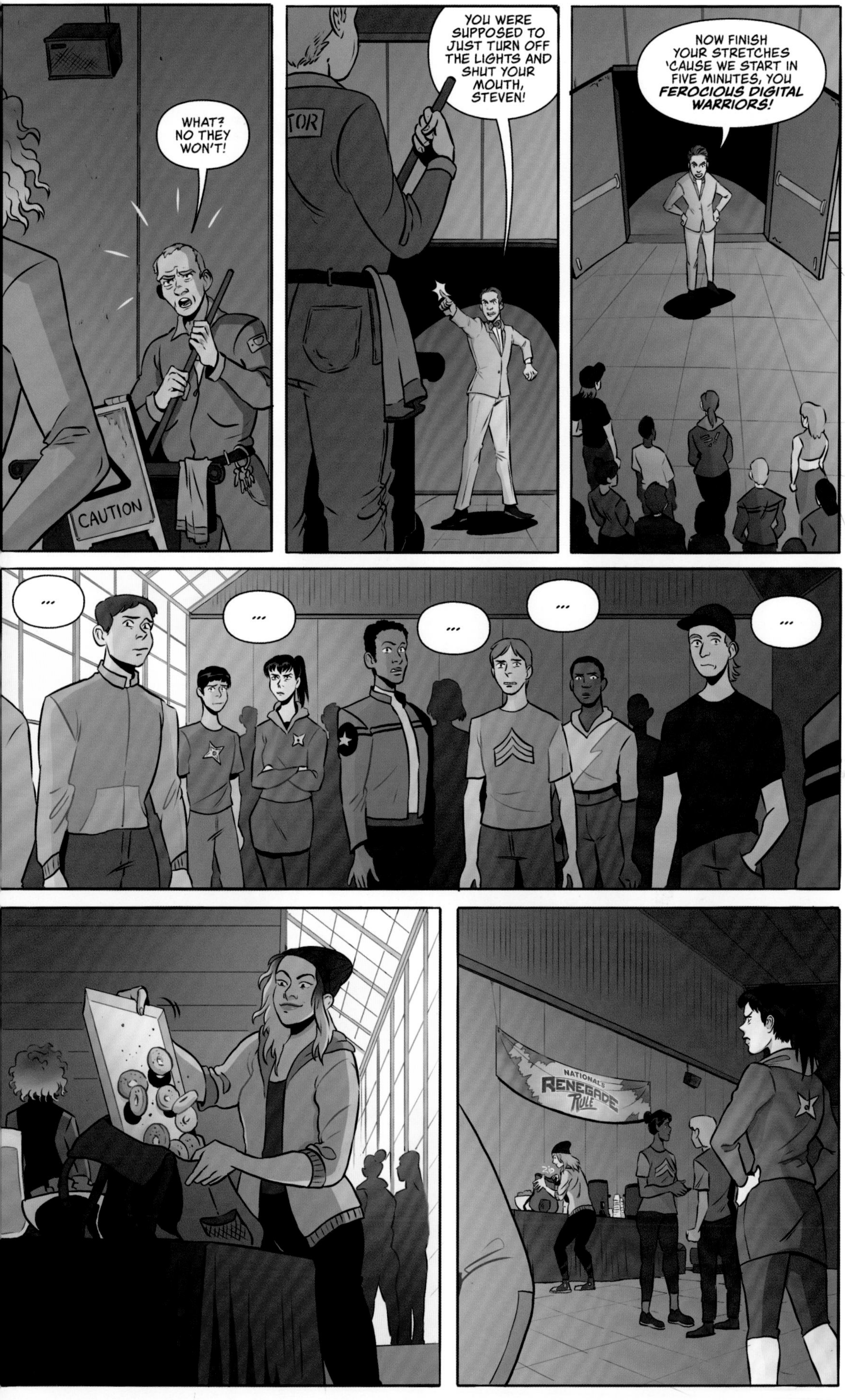
WHAT?
NO THEY WON'T!
YOU WERE SUPPOSED TO JUST TURN OFF THE LIGHTS AND SHUT YOUR MOUTH, STEVEN!
TOR
NOW FINISH YOUR STRETCHES 'CAUSE WE START IN FIVE MINUTES, YOU ***FEROCIOUS DIGITAL WARRIORS!***
CAUTION
...
...
...
...
...
...
NATIONALS
RENEGADE RULE
ZIP

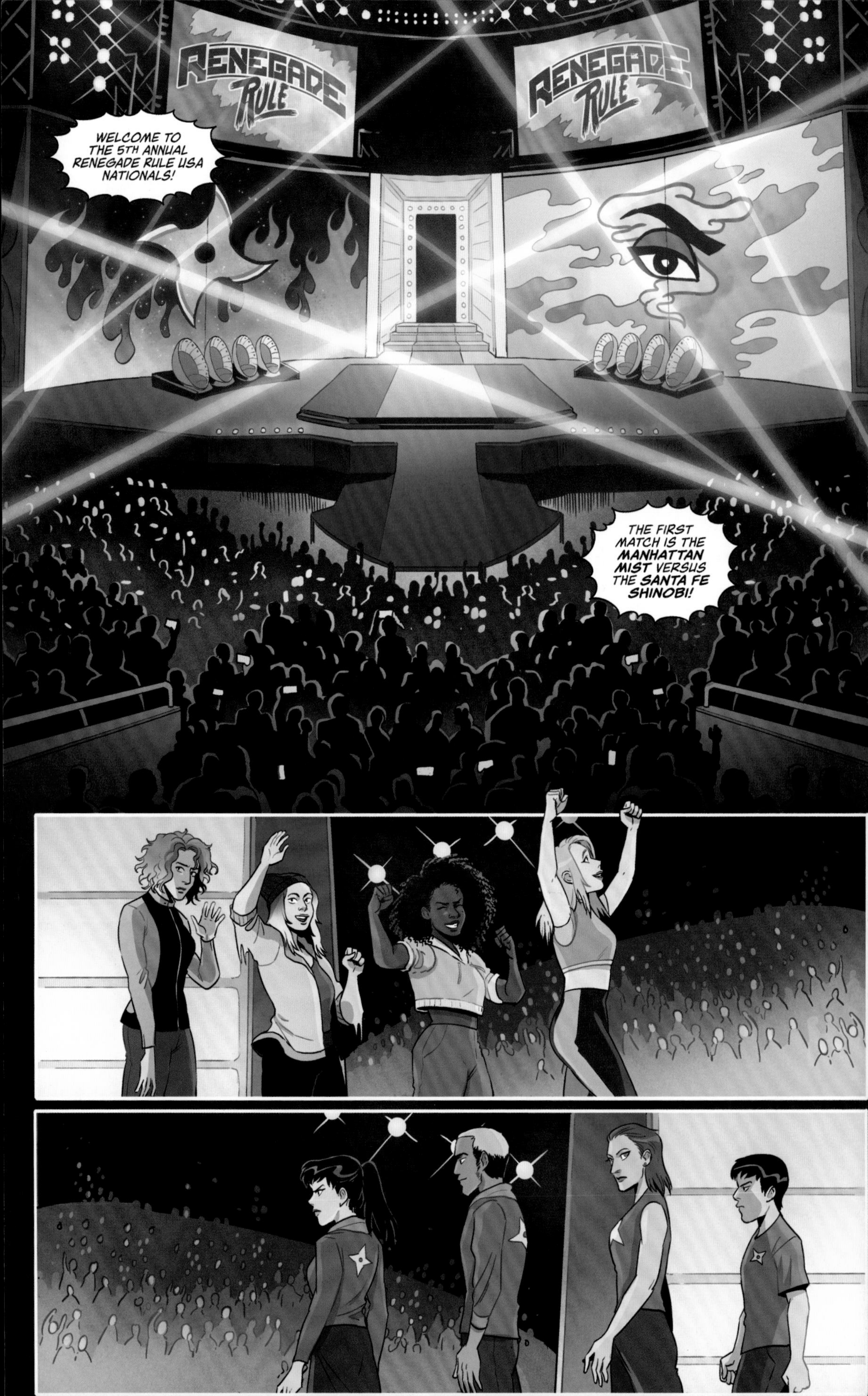
RENEGADE RULE
RENEGADE RULE
WELCOME TO THE 5TH ANNUAL RENEGADE RULE USA NATIONALS!
THE FIRST MATCH IS THE MANHATTAN MIST VERSUS THE SANTA FE SHINOBI!

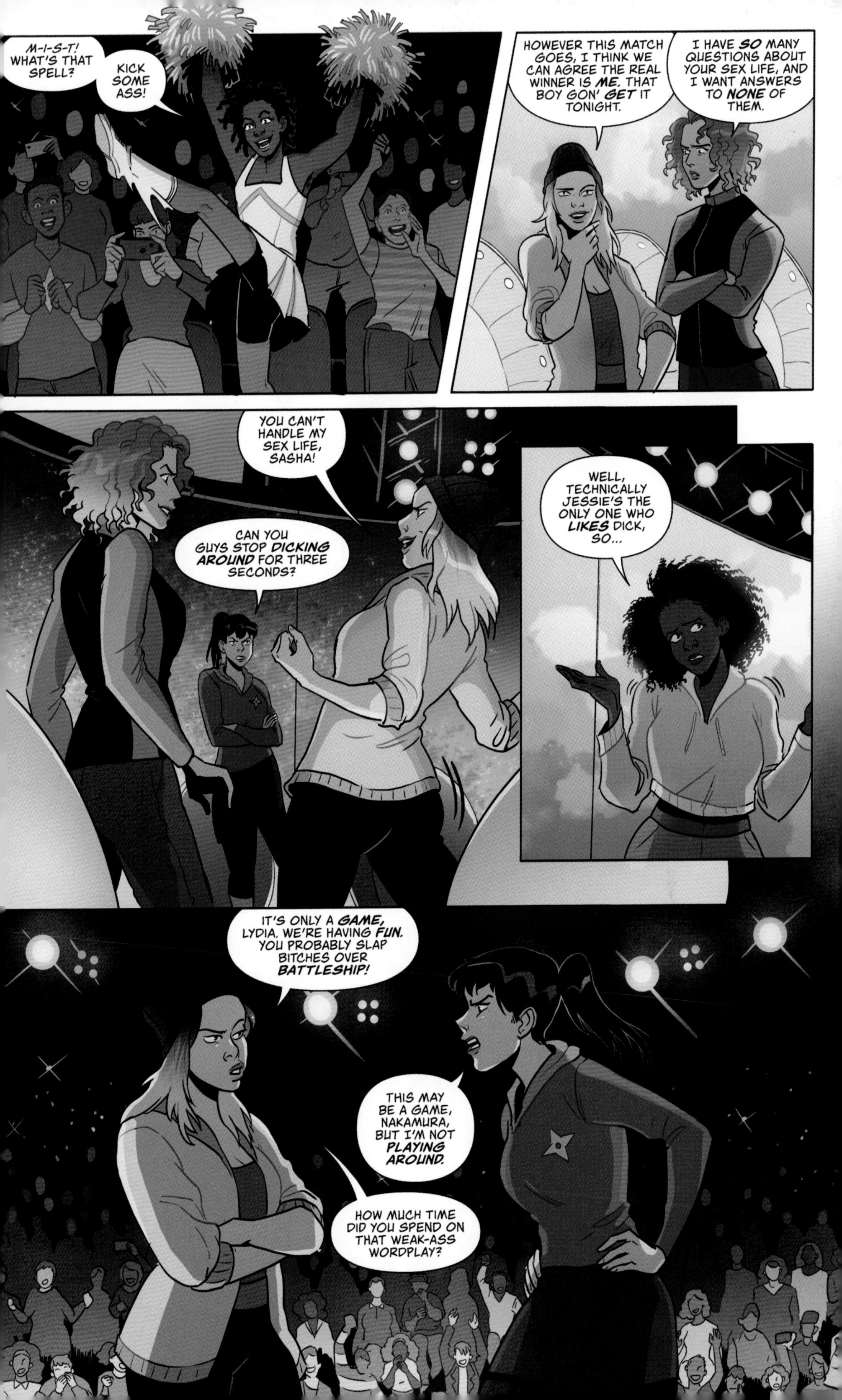

M-I-S-T! WHAT'S THAT SPELL?
KICK SOME ASS!
HOWEVER THIS MATCH GOES, I THINK WE CAN AGREE THE REAL WINNER IS ME. THAT BOY GON' GET IT TONIGHT.
I HAVE SO MANY QUESTIONS ABOUT YOUR SEX LIFE, AND I WANT ANSWERS TO NONE OF THEM.
YOU CAN'T HANDLE MY SEX LIFE, SASHA!
CAN YOU GUYS STOP DICKING AROUND FOR THREE SECONDS?
WELL, TECHNICALLY JESSIE'S THE ONLY ONE WHO LIKES DICK, SO...
IT'S ONLY A GAME, LYDIA. WE'RE HAVING FUN. YOU PROBABLY SLAP BITCHES OVER BATTLESHIP!
THIS MAY BE A GAME, NAKAMURA, BUT I'M NOT PLAYING AROUND.
HOW MUCH TIME DID YOU SPEND ON THAT WEAK-ASS WORDPLAY?

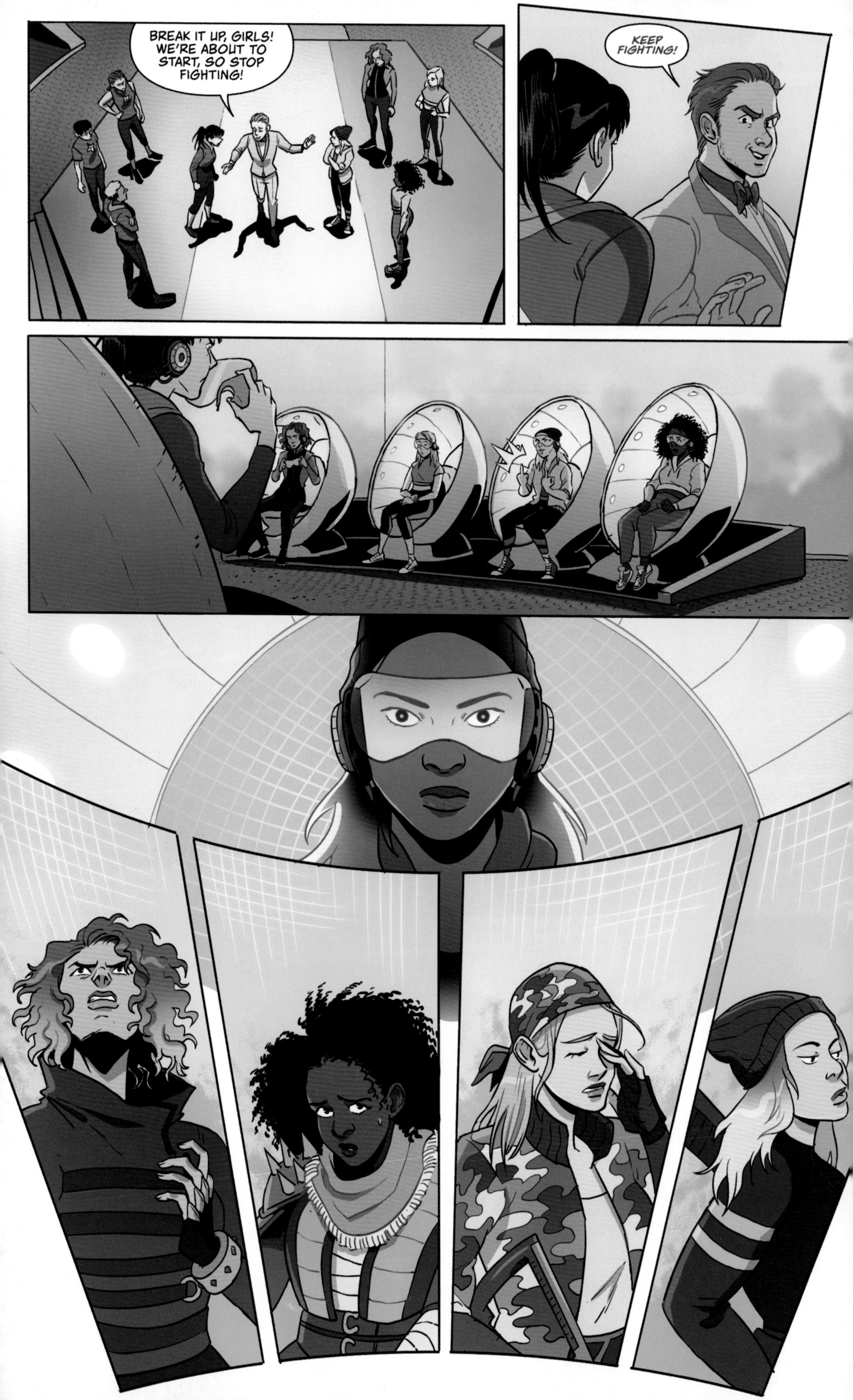
BREAK IT UP, GIRLS! WE'RE ABOUT TO START, SO STOP FIGHTING!
KEEP FIGHTING!

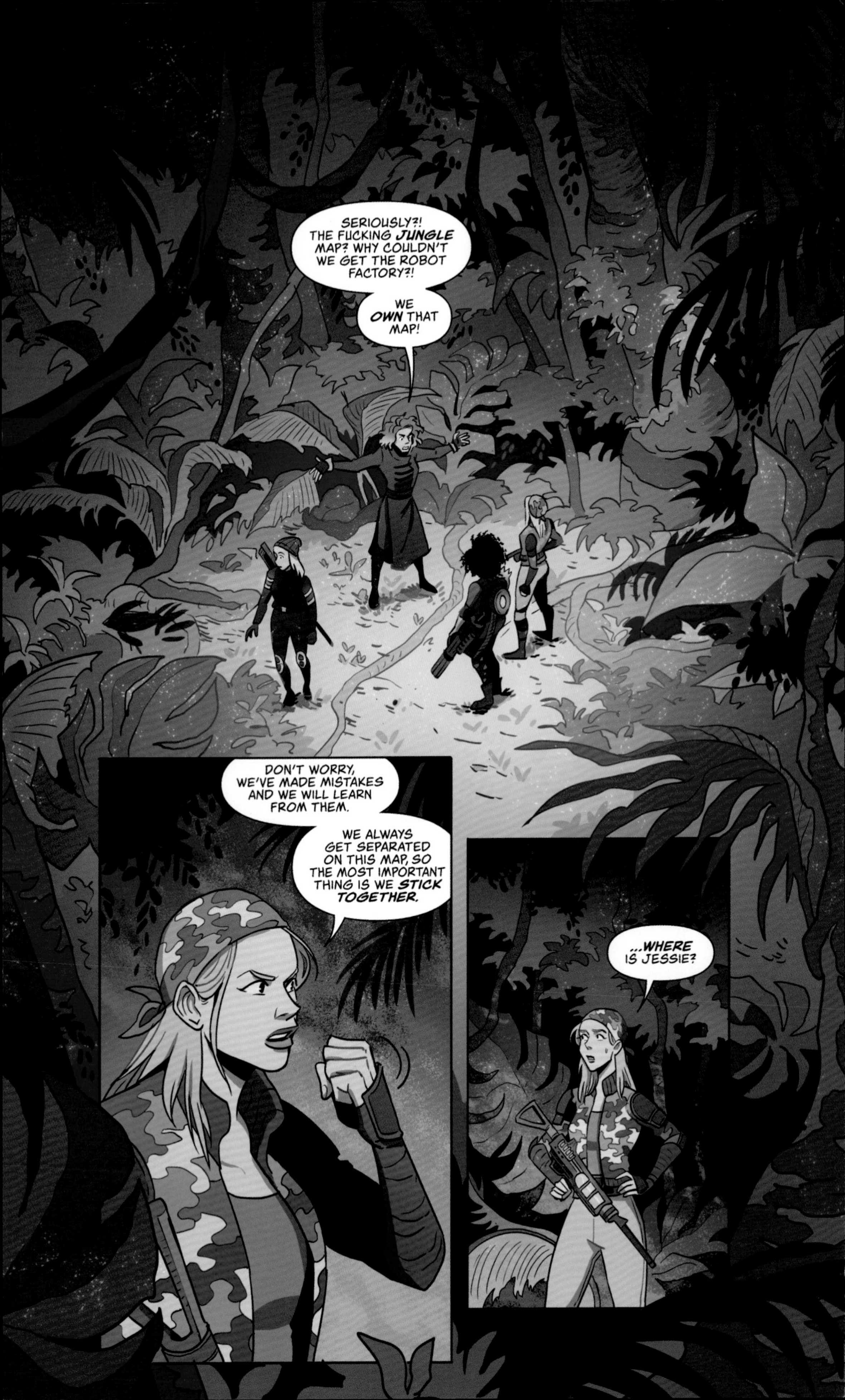
SERIOUSLY?! THE FUCKING JUNGLE MAP? WHY COULDN'T WE GET THE ROBOT FACTORY?!
WE OWN THAT MAP!
DON'T WORRY, WE'VE MADE MISTAKES AND WE WILL LEARN FROM THEM.
WE ALWAYS GET SEPARATED ON THIS MAP, SO THE MOST IMPORTANT THING IS WE STICK TOGETHER.
...WHERE IS JESSIE?

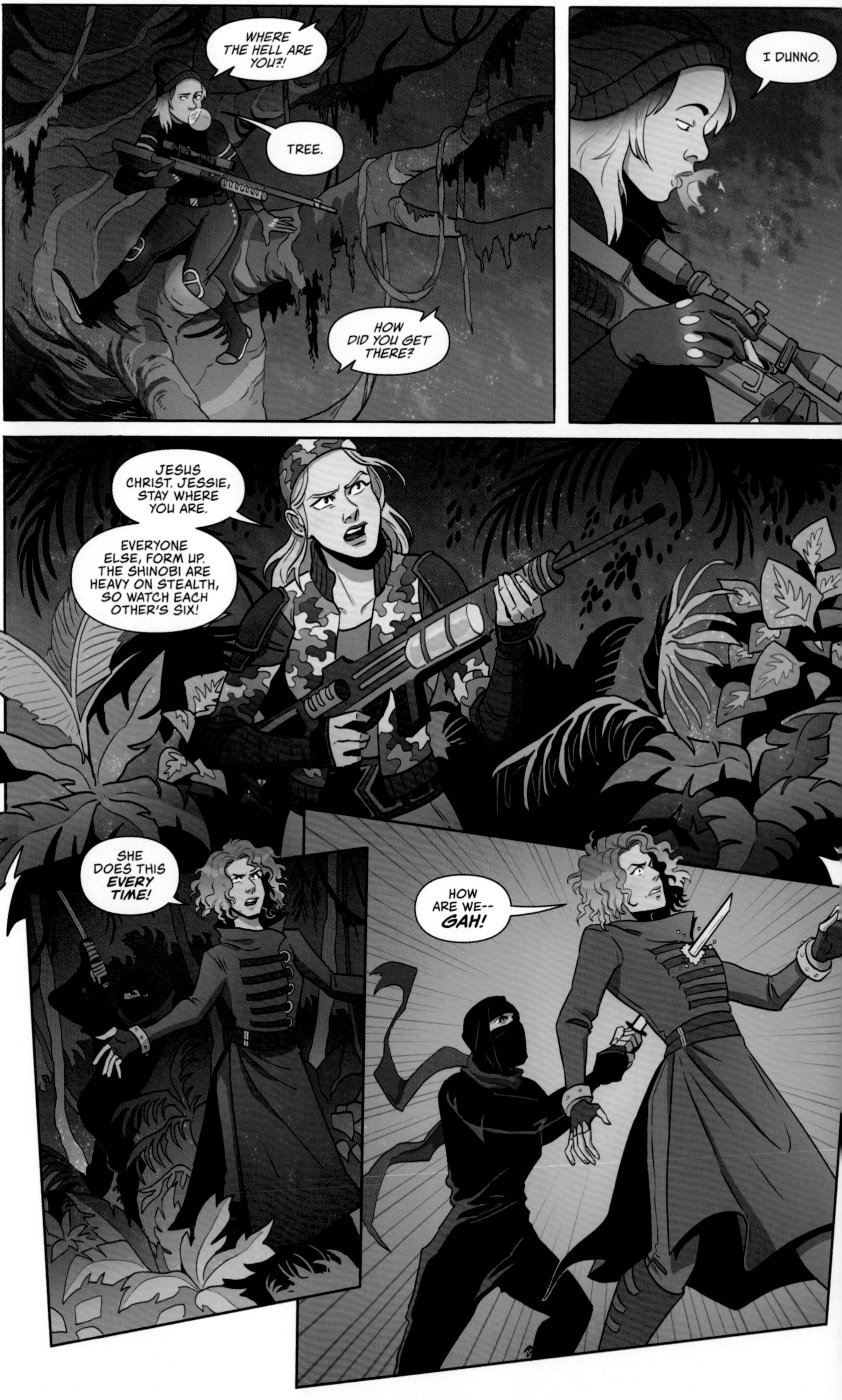
WHERE THE HELL ARE YOU?!
TREE.
HOW DID YOU GET THERE?
I DUNNO.
JESUS CHRIST. JESSIE, STAY WHERE YOU ARE.
EVERYONE ELSE, FORM UP. THE SHINOBI ARE HEAVY ON STEALTH, SO WATCH EACH OTHER'S SIX!
SHE DOES THIS EVERY TIME!
HOW ARE WE-- GAH!

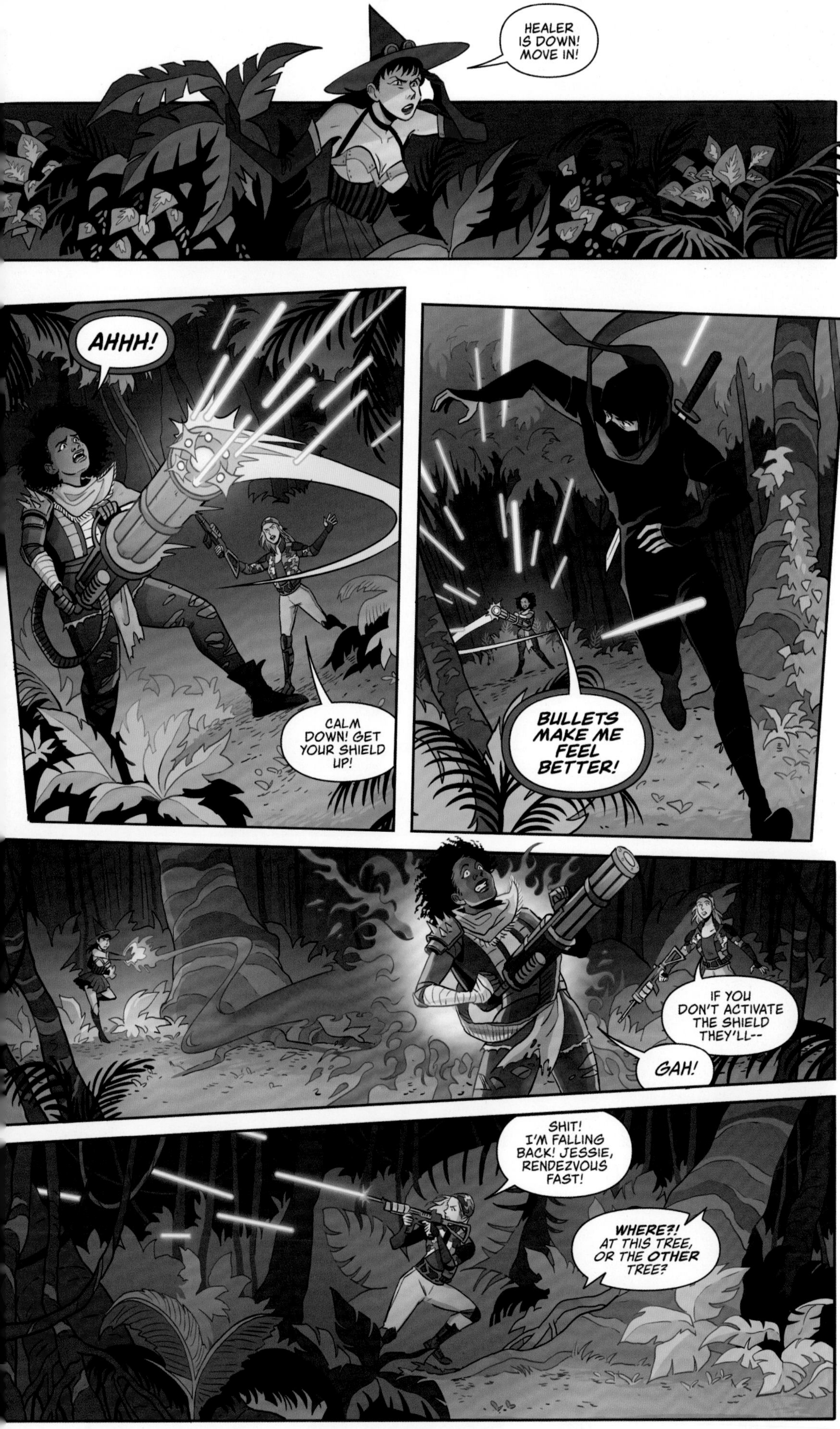

HEALER IS DOWN! MOVE IN!
AHHH!
CALM DOWN! GET YOUR SHIELD UP!
BULLETS MAKE ME FEEL BETTER!
IF YOU DON'T ACTIVATE THE SHIELD THEY'LL--
GAH!
SHIT! I'M FALLING BACK! JESSIE, RENDEZVOUS FAST!
WHERE?! AT THIS TREE, OR THE OTHER TREE?

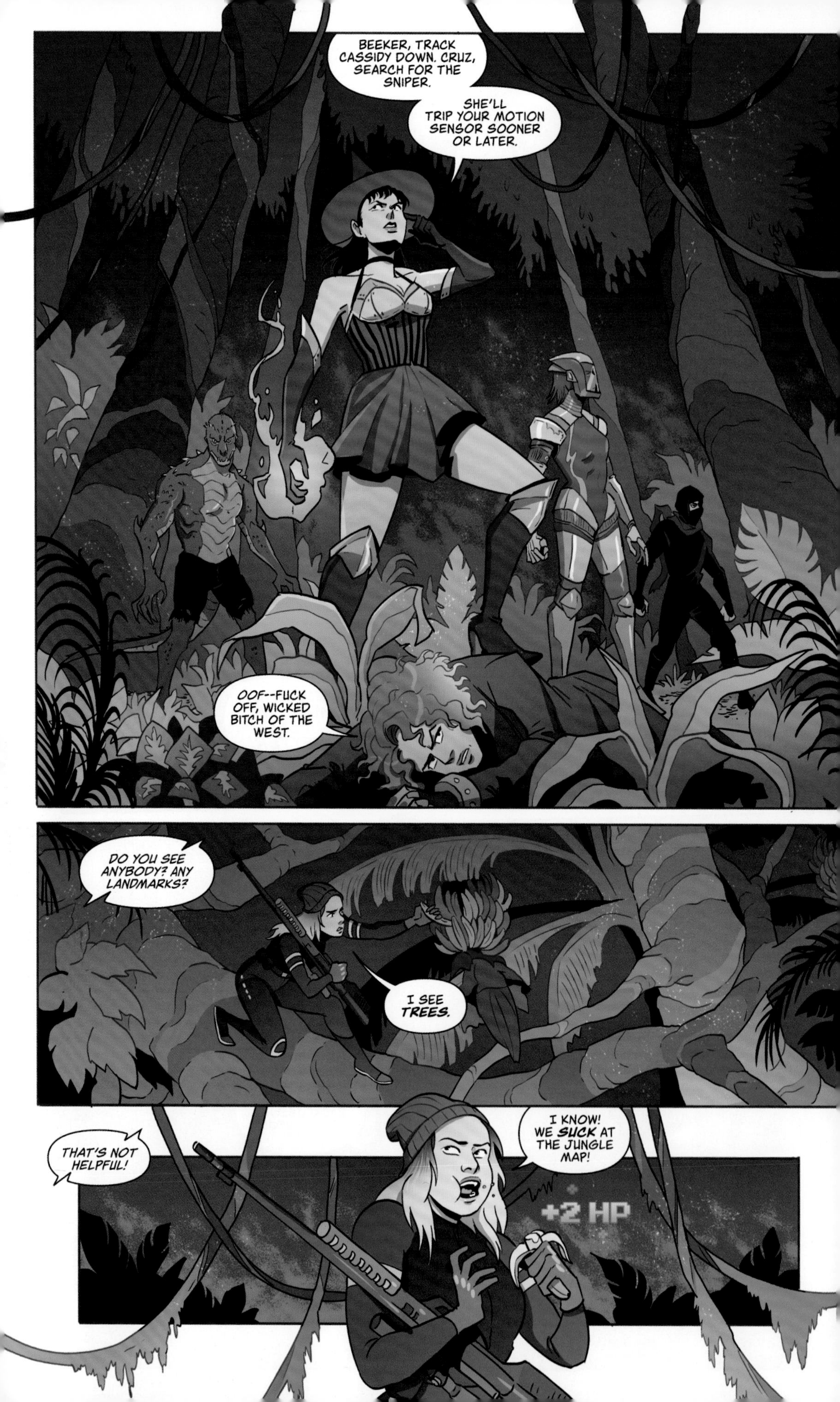
BEEKER, TRACK CASSIDY DOWN. CRUZ, SEARCH FOR THE SNIPER.
SHE'LL TRIP YOUR MOTION SENSOR SOONER OR LATER.
OOF--FUCK OFF, WICKED BITCH OF THE WEST.
DO YOU SEE ANYBODY? ANY LANDMARKS?
I SEE TREES.
THAT'S NOT HELPFUL!
I KNOW! WE SUCK AT THE JUNGLE MAP!
+2 HP

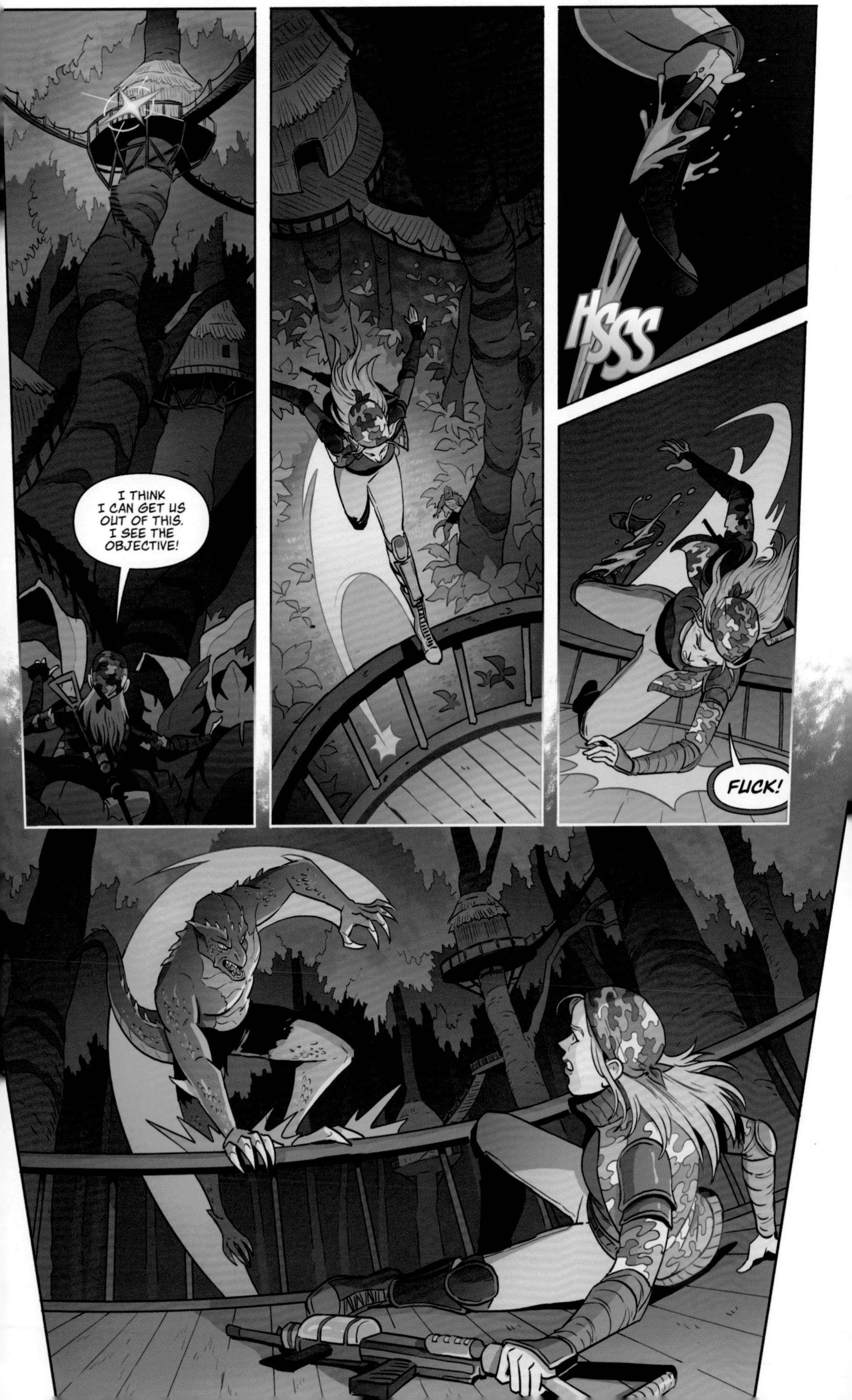
I THINK I CAN GET US OUT OF THIS. I SEE THE OBJECTIVE!
HSSS
FUCK!

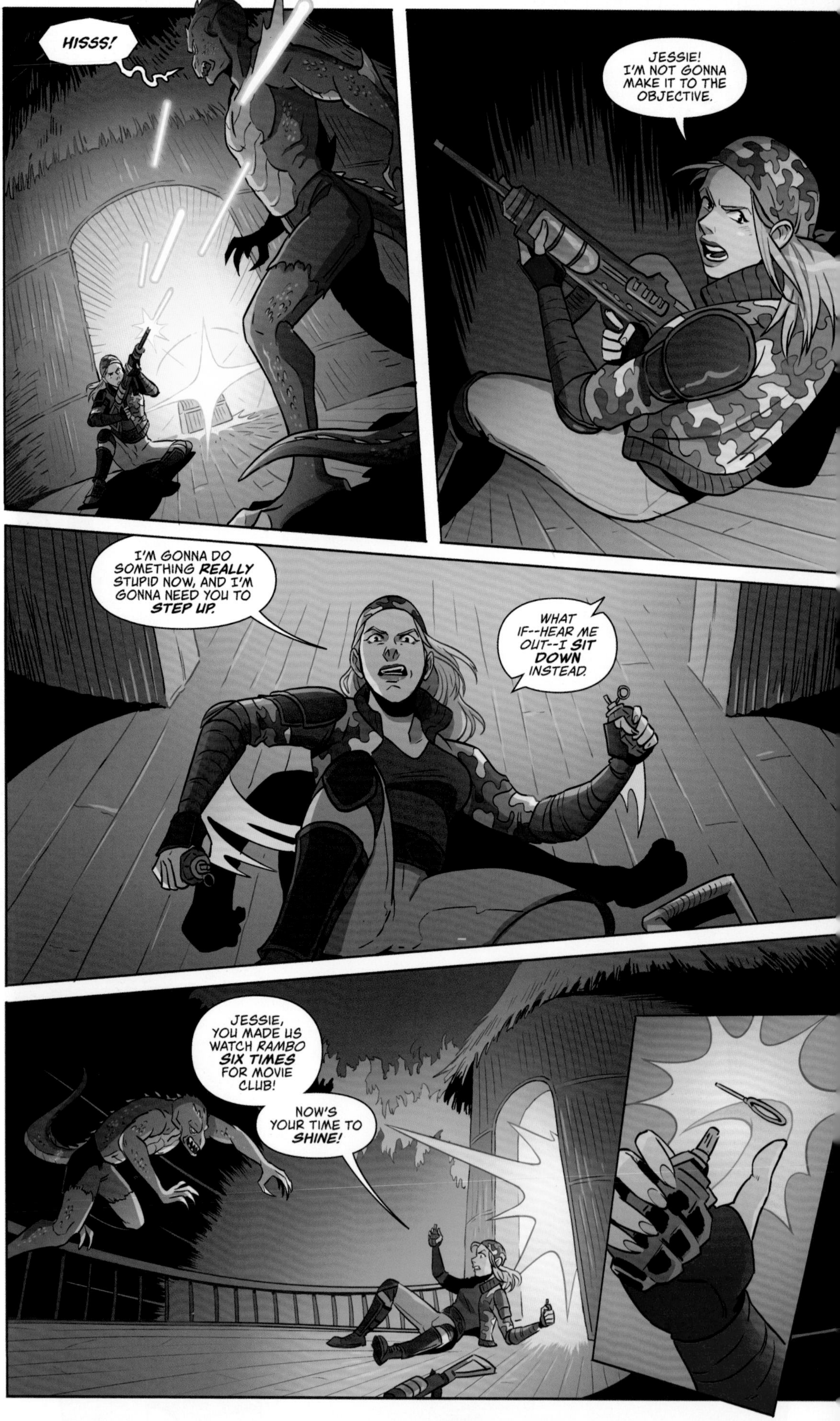

HISSS!
JESSIE! I'M NOT GONNA MAKE IT TO THE OBJECTIVE.
I'M GONNA DO SOMETHING REALLY STUPID NOW, AND I'M GONNA NEED YOU TO STEP UP.
WHAT IF--HEAR ME OUT--I SIT DOWN INSTEAD.
JESSIE, YOU MADE US WATCH RAMBO SIX TIMES FOR MOVIE CLUB!
NOW'S YOUR TIME TO SHINE!

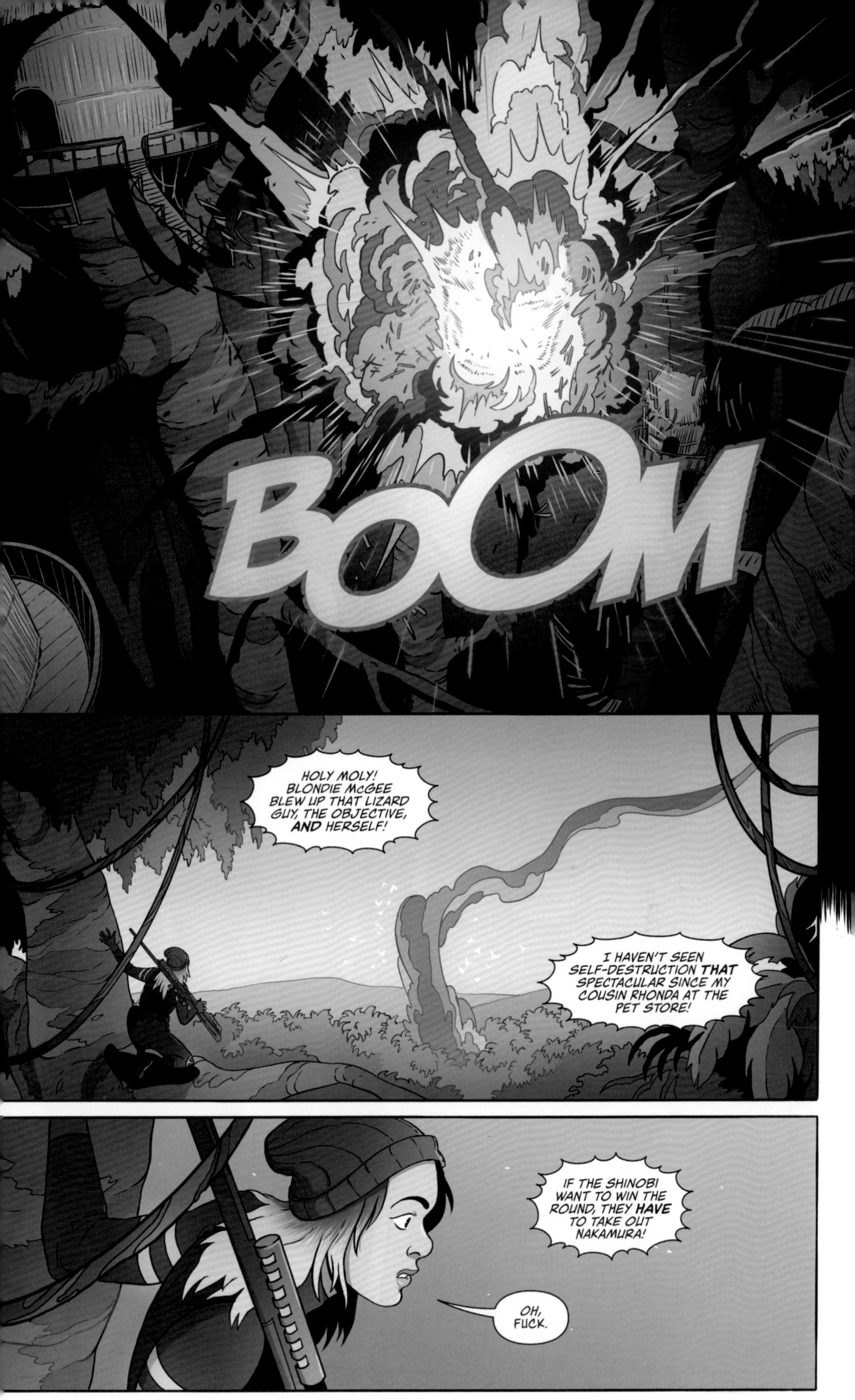
BOOM
HOLY MOLY! BLONDIE McGEE BLEW UP THAT LIZARD GUY, THE OBJECTIVE, AND HERSELF!
I HAVEN'T SEEN SELF-DESTRUCTION THAT SPECTACULAR SINCE MY COUSIN RHONDA AT THE PET STORE!
IF THE SHINOBI WANT TO WIN THE ROUND, THEY HAVE TO TAKE OUT NAKAMURA!
OH, FUCK.

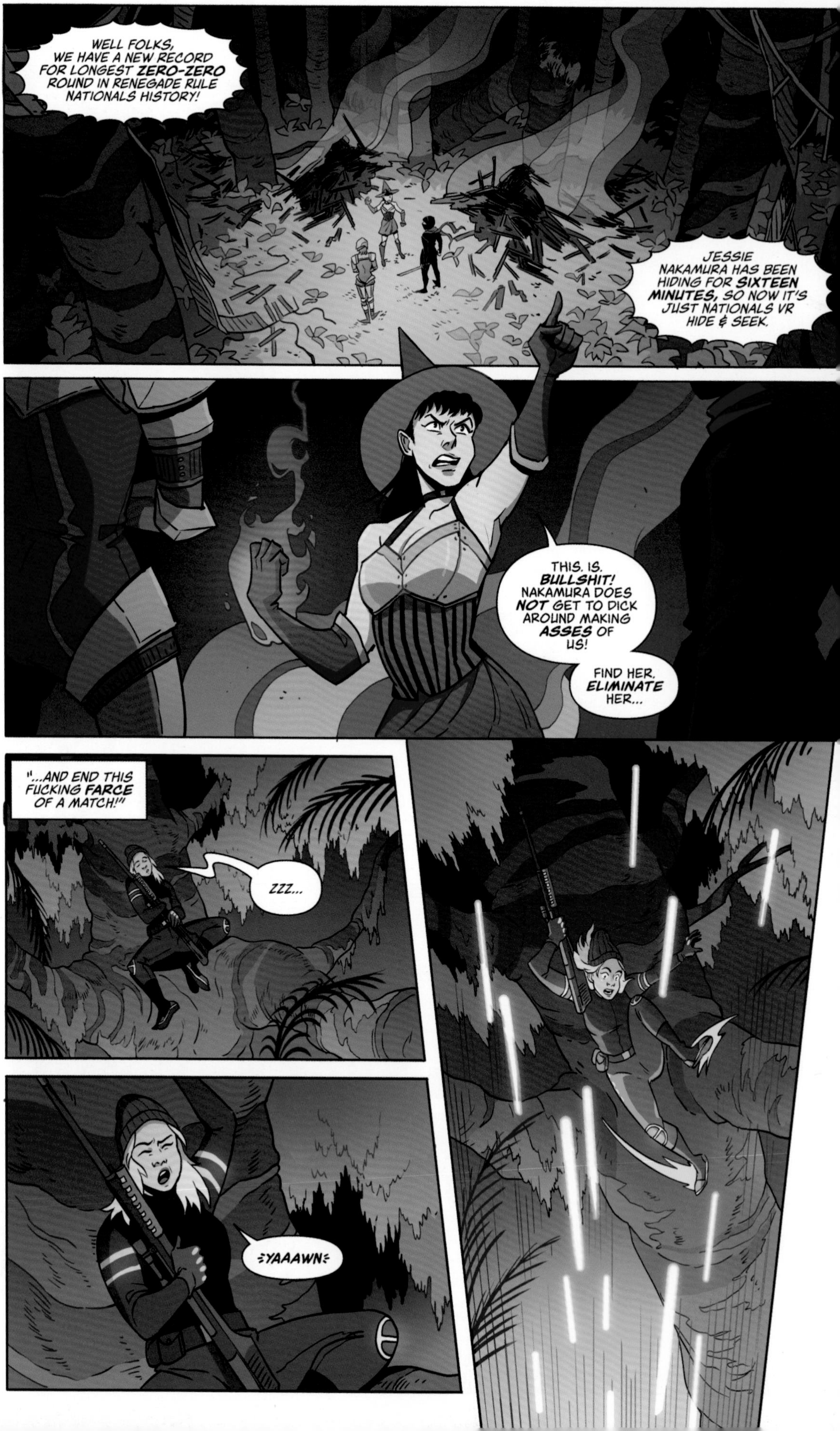
WELL FOLKS, WE HAVE A NEW RECORD FOR LONGEST ZERO-ZERO ROUND IN RENEGADE RULE NATIONALS HISTORY!
JESSIE NAKAMURA HAS BEEN HIDING FOR SIXTEEN MINUTES, SO NOW IT'S JUST NATIONALS VR HIDE & SEEK.
THIS. IS. BULLSHIT! NAKAMURA DOES NOT GET TO DICK AROUND MAKING ASSES OF US!
FIND HER. ELIMINATE HER...
"...AND END THIS FUCKING FARCE OF A MATCH!"
ZZZ...
YAAAWN

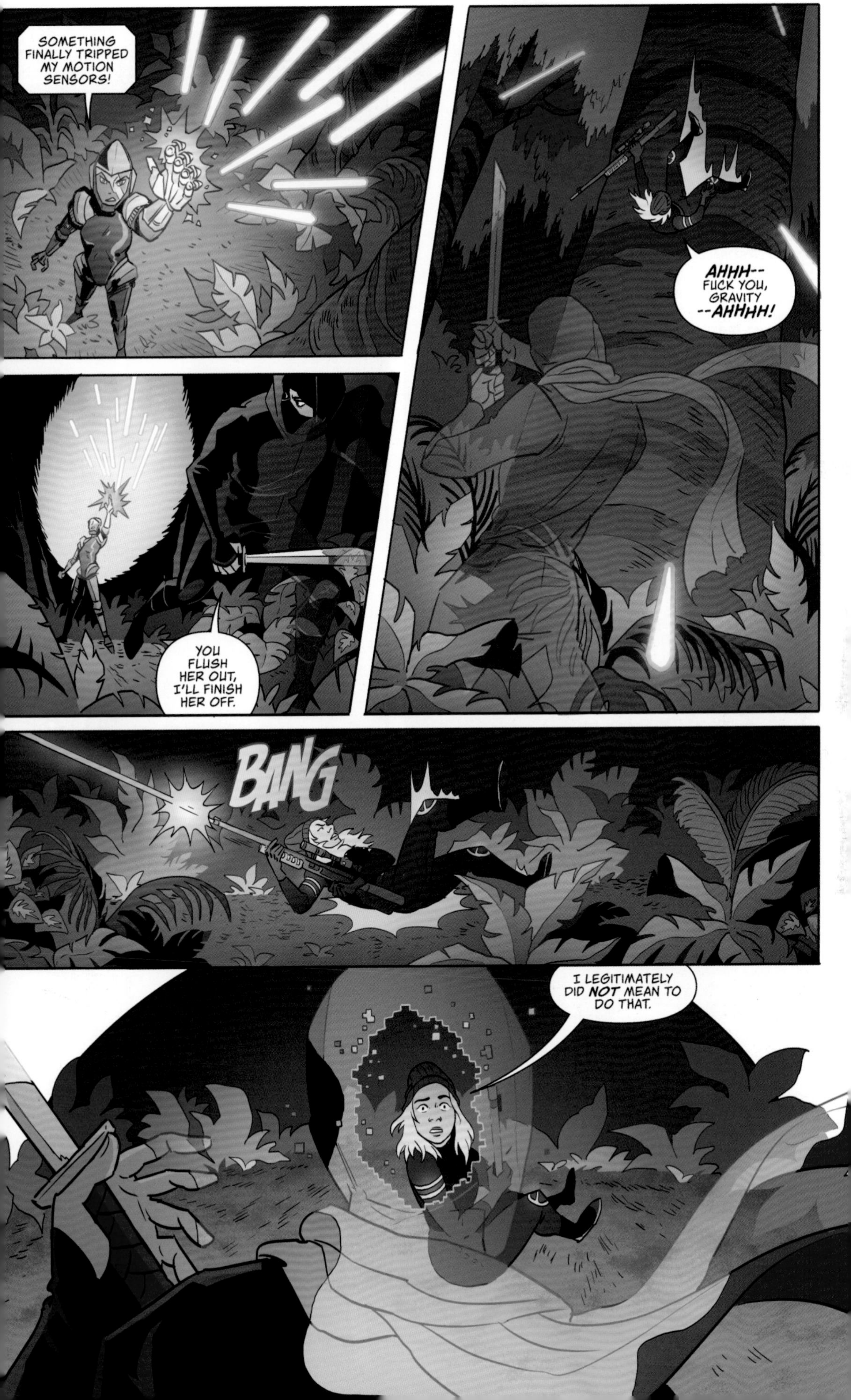

SOMETHING FINALLY TRIPPED MY MOTION SENSORS!
AHHH-- FUCK YOU, GRAVITY --AHHHH!
YOU FLUSH HER OUT, I'LL FINISH HER OFF.
BANG
I LEGITIMATELY DID NOT MEAN TO DO THAT.

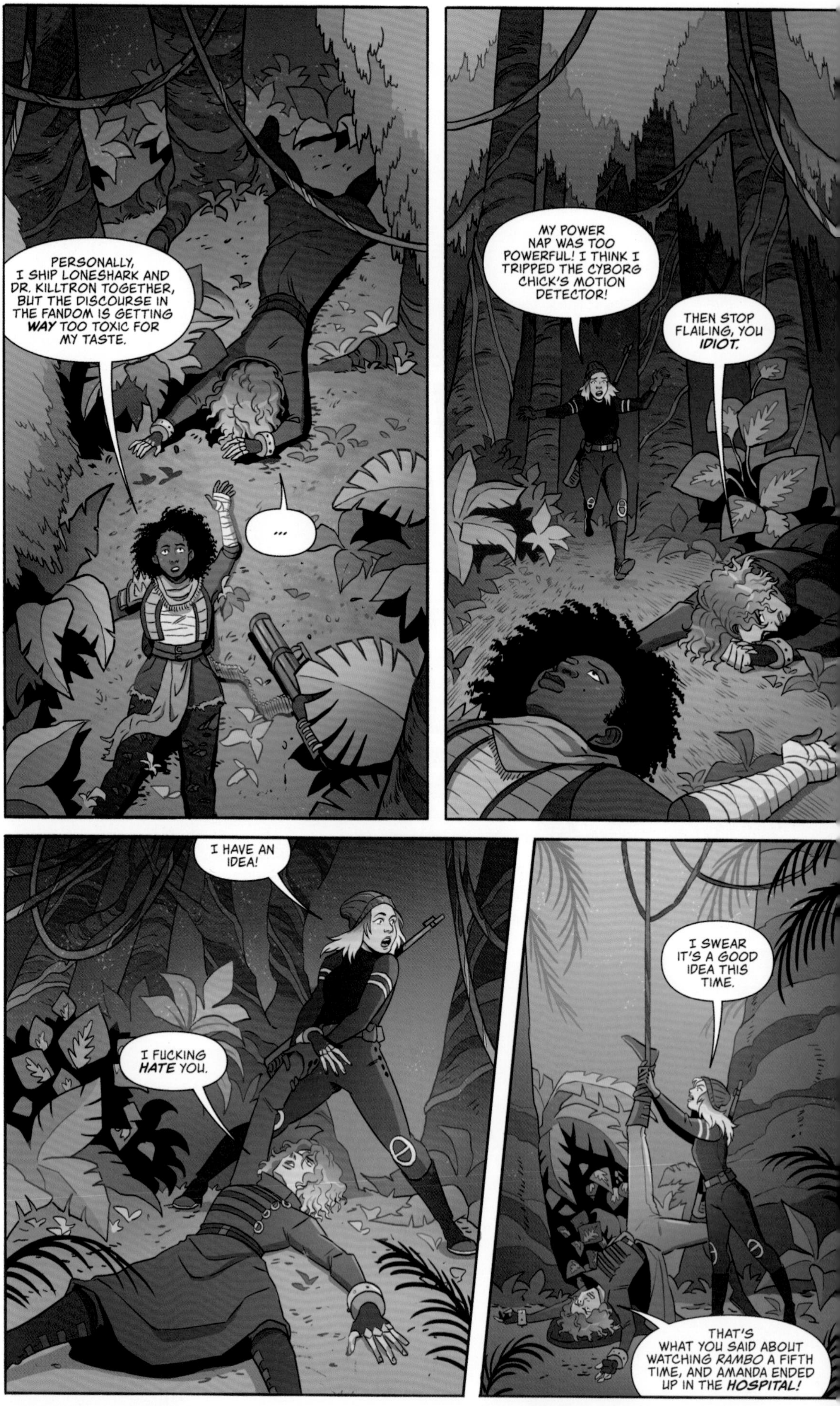
PERSONALLY, I SHIP LONESHARK AND DR. KILLTRON TOGETHER, BUT THE DISCOURSE IN THE FANDOM IS GETTING *WAY* TOO TOXIC FOR MY TASTE.
...
MY POWER NAP WAS TOO POWERFUL! I THINK I TRIPPED THE CYBORG CHICK'S MOTION DETECTOR!
THEN STOP FLAILING, YOU *IDIOT.*
I HAVE AN IDEA!
I FUCKING *HATE* YOU.
I SWEAR IT'S A GOOD IDEA THIS TIME.
THAT'S WHAT YOU SAID ABOUT WATCHING *RAMBO* A FIFTH TIME, AND AMANDA ENDED UP IN THE *HOSPITAL!*

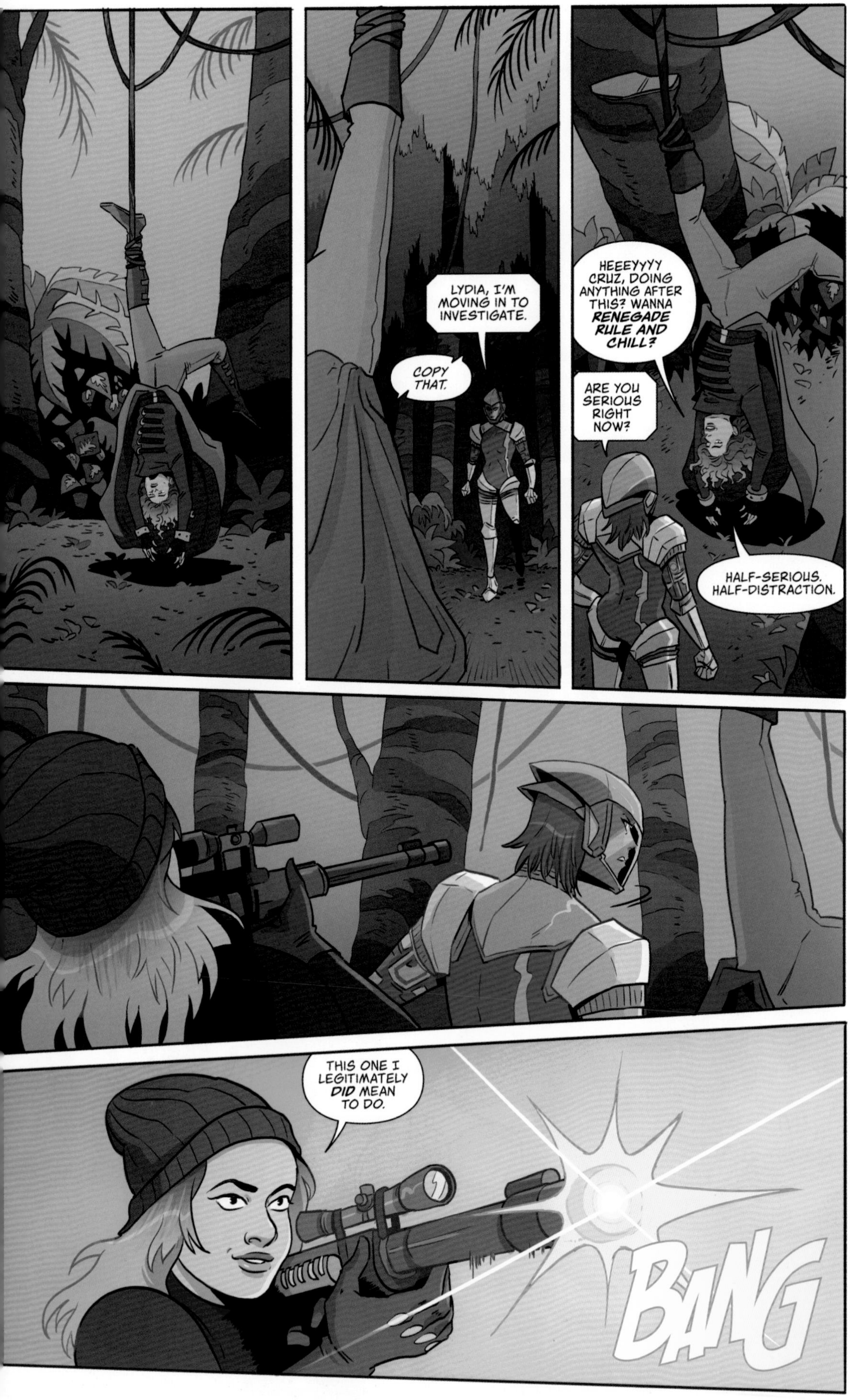
LYDIA, I'M MOVING IN TO INVESTIGATE.
COPY THAT.
HEEEYYYY CRUZ, DOING ANYTHING AFTER THIS? WANNA RENEGADE RULE AND CHILL?
ARE YOU SERIOUS RIGHT NOW?
HALF-SERIOUS. HALF-DISTRACTION.
THIS ONE I LEGITIMATELY DID MEAN TO DO.
BANG

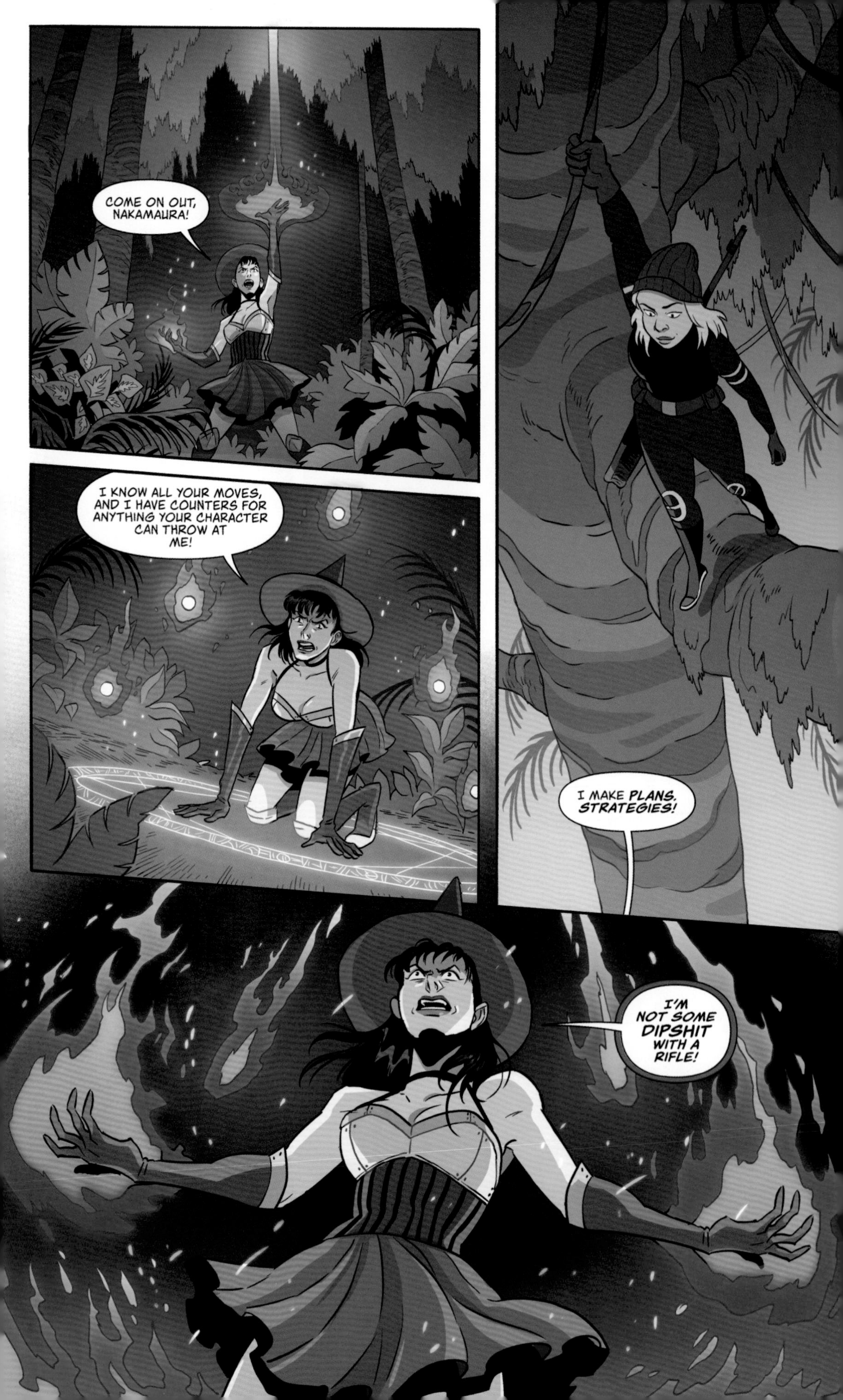
COME ON OUT, NAKAMAURA!
I KNOW ALL YOUR MOVES, AND I HAVE COUNTERS FOR ANYTHING YOUR CHARACTER CAN THROW AT ME!
I MAKE PLANS. STRATEGIES!
I'M NOT SOME DIPSHIT WITH A RIFLE!

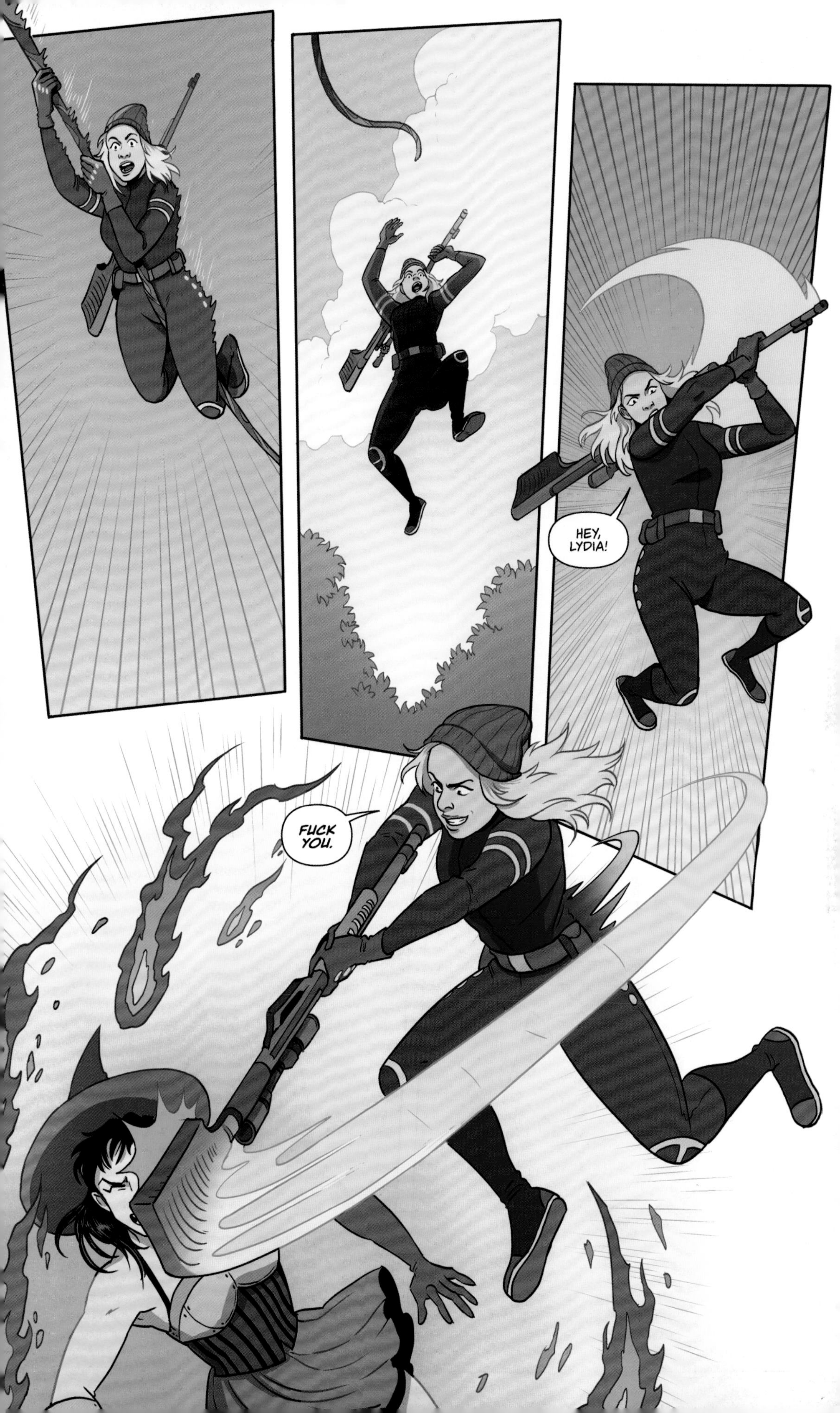
HEY, LYDIA!
FUCK YOU.

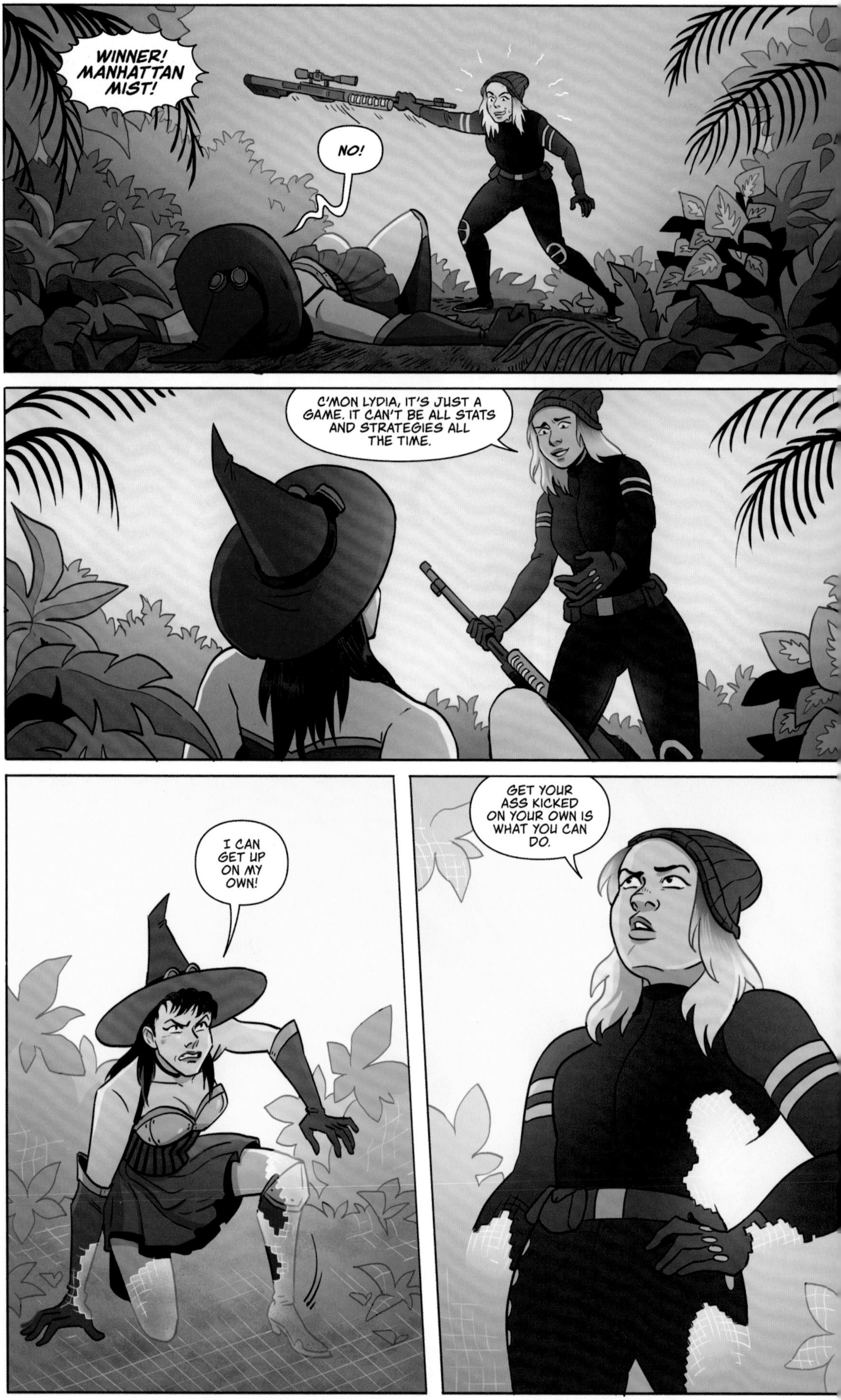
WINNER! MANHATTAN MIST!
NO!
C'MON LYDIA, IT'S JUST A GAME. IT CAN'T BE ALL STATS AND STRATEGIES ALL THE TIME.
I CAN GET UP ON MY OWN!
GET YOUR ASS KICKED ON YOUR OWN IS WHAT YOU CAN DO.

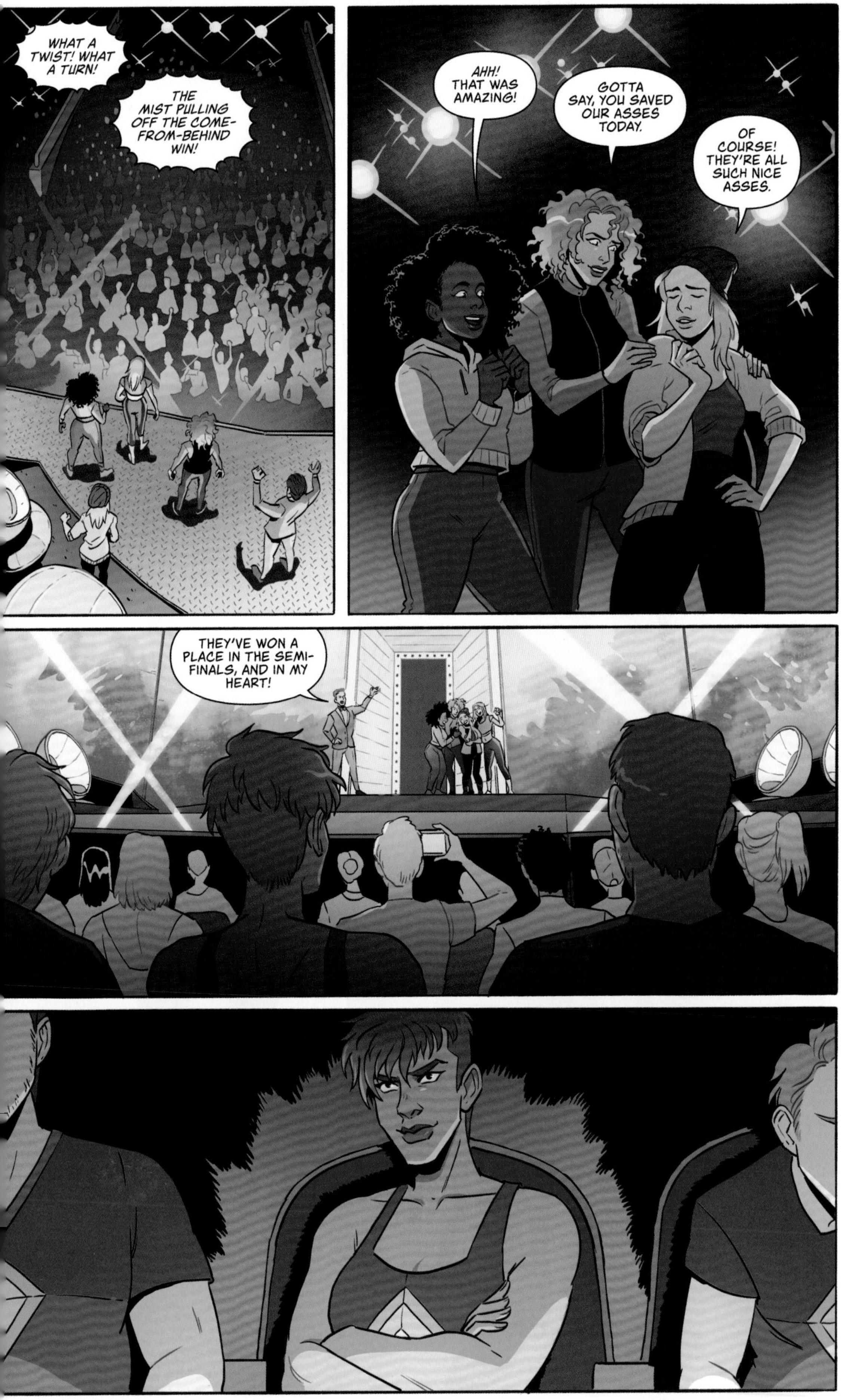
WHAT A TWIST! WHAT A TURN!
THE MIST PULLING OFF THE COME-FROM-BEHIND WIN!
AHH! THAT WAS AMAZING!
GOTTA SAY, YOU SAVED OUR ASSES TODAY.
OF COURSE! THEY'RE ALL SUCH NICE ASSES.
THEY'VE WON A PLACE IN THE SEMI-FINALS, AND IN MY HEART!

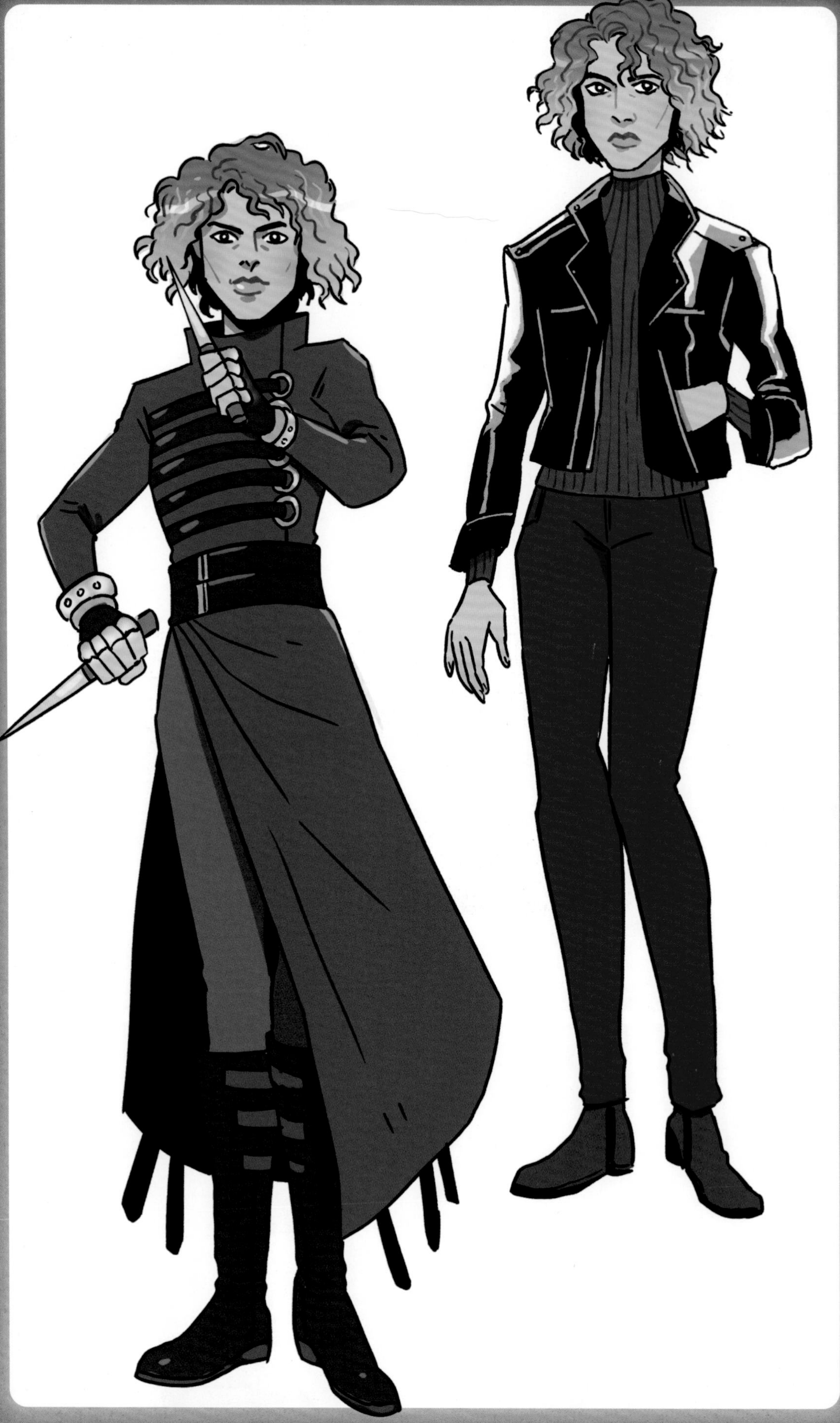

CHAPTER THREE

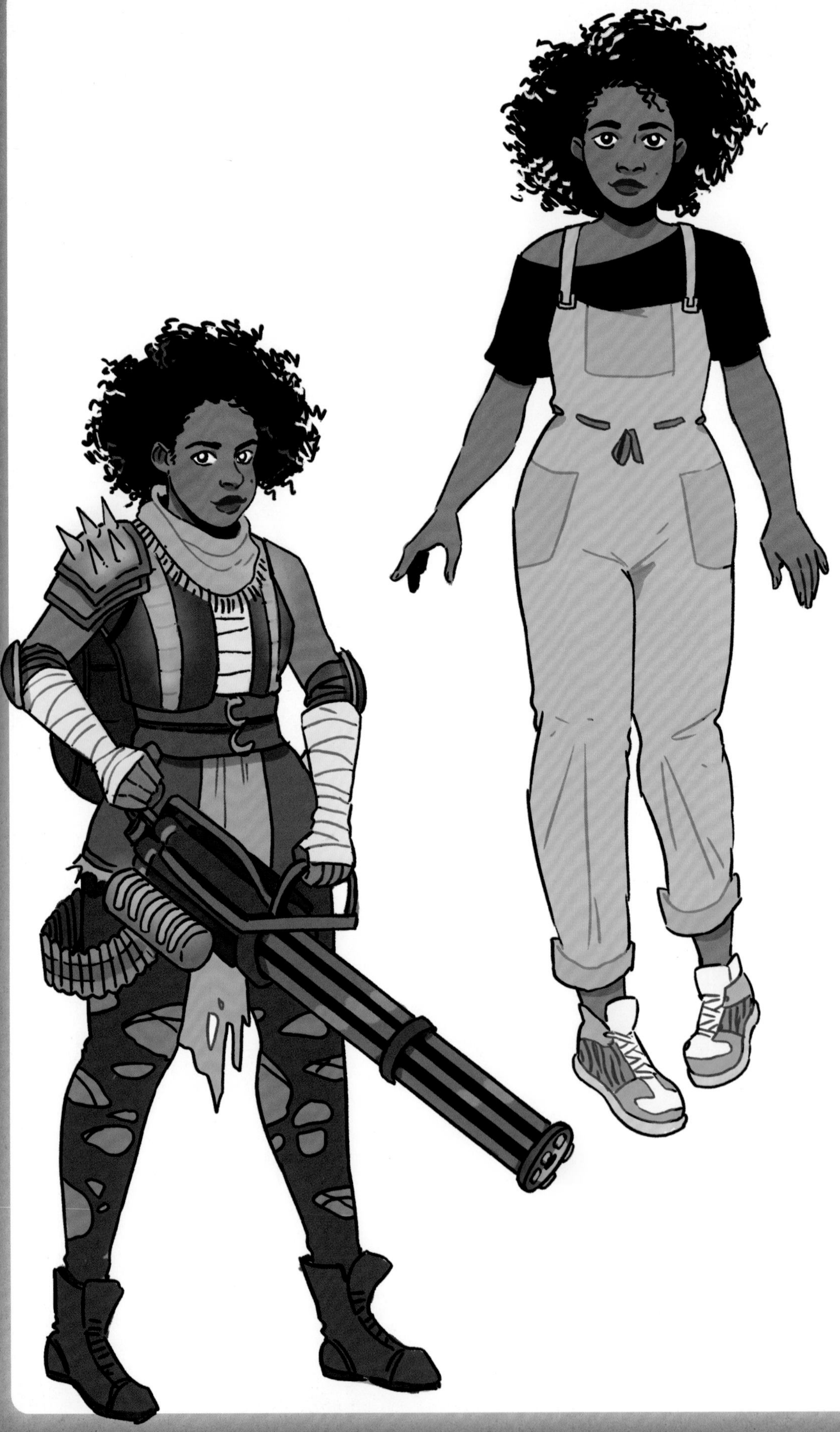

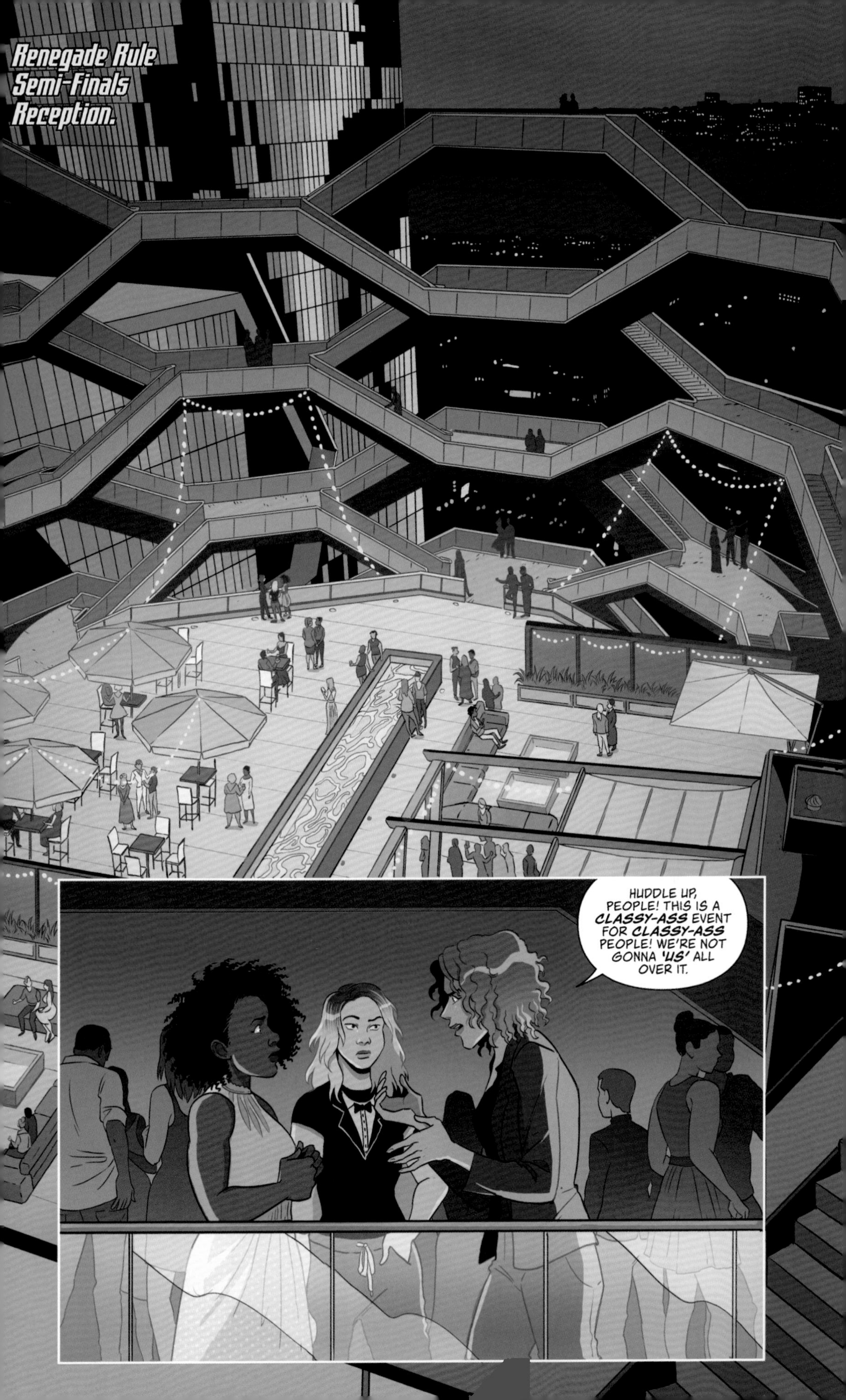
Renegade Rule Semi-Finals Reception.
HUDDLE UP, PEOPLE! THIS IS A CLASSY-ASS EVENT FOR CLASSY-ASS PEOPLE! WE'RE NOT GONNA 'US' ALL OVER IT.

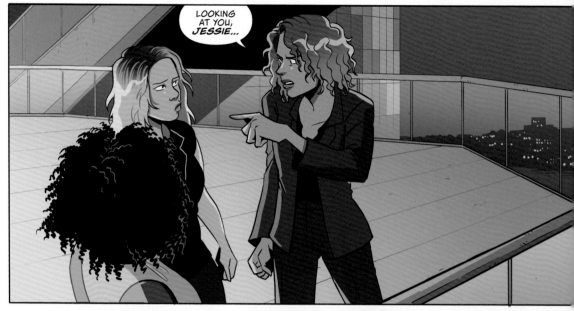

LOOKING AT YOU, **JESSIE**...

JESSIE...

FINE!

HAPPY NOW?

...AND?

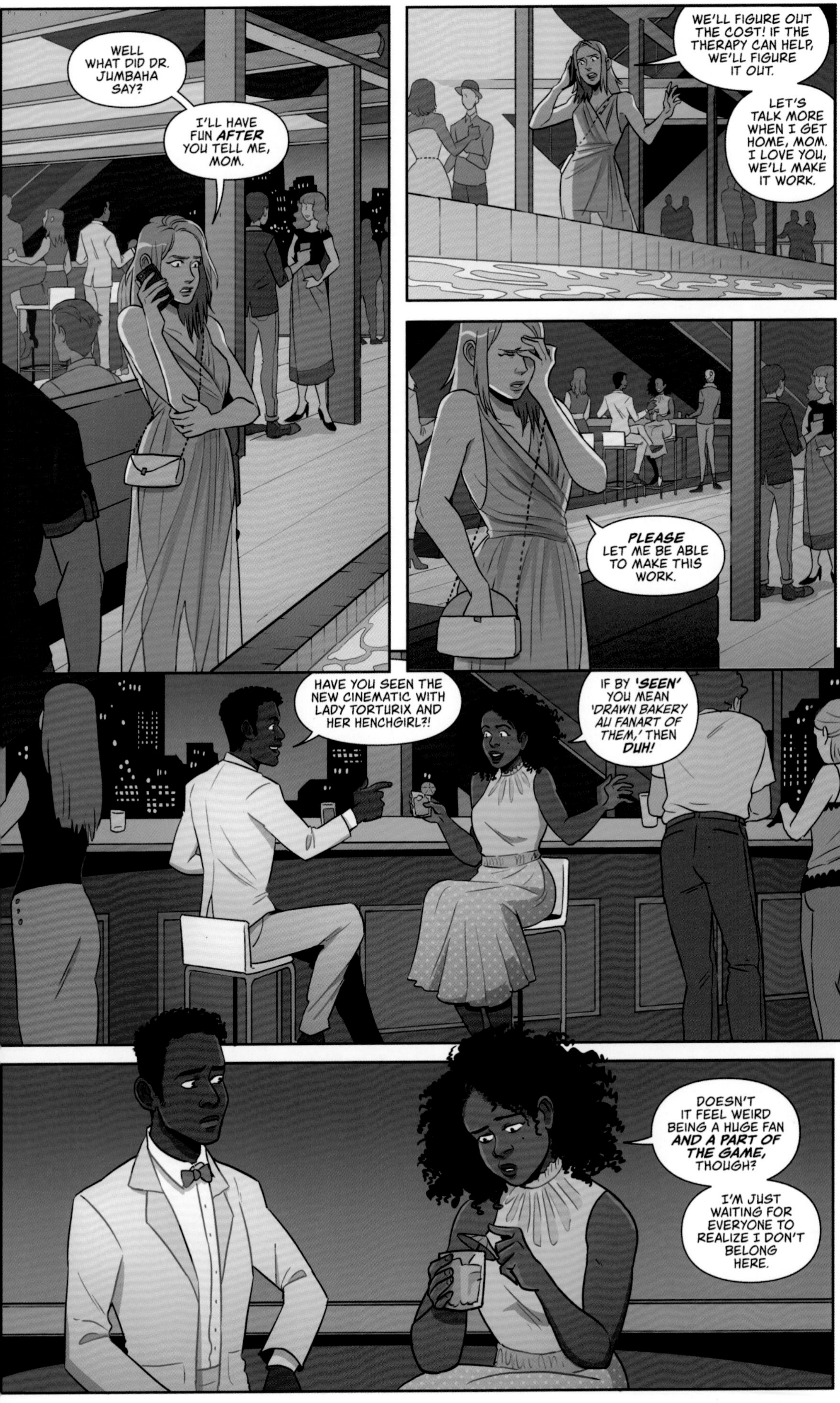
WELL WHAT DID DR. JUMBAHA SAY?
I'LL HAVE FUN AFTER YOU TELL ME, MOM.
WE'LL FIGURE OUT THE COST! IF THE THERAPY CAN HELP, WE'LL FIGURE IT OUT.
LET'S TALK MORE WHEN I GET HOME, MOM. I LOVE YOU, WE'LL MAKE IT WORK.
PLEASE LET ME BE ABLE TO MAKE THIS WORK.
HAVE YOU SEEN THE NEW CINEMATIC WITH LADY TORTURIX AND HER HENCHGIRL?!
IF BY 'SEEN' YOU MEAN 'DRAWN BAKERY AU FANART OF THEM,' THEN DUH!
DOESN'T IT FEEL WEIRD BEING A HUGE FAN AND A PART OF THE GAME, THOUGH?
I'M JUST WAITING FOR EVERYONE TO REALIZE I DON'T BELONG HERE.

WHAT AM I DOING AT A FANCY PARTY LIKE THIS, TONY? THIS SHOULD BE FOR, LIKE, PEOPLE THAT *MATTER.*

I'M NOT A PRO *ANYTHING.*

HEY, THAT'S THE IMPOSTOR SYNDROME TALKING. YOU'RE JUST AS PRO AS THE REST OF US.

YOU'RE GOING TO THE SEMI-FINALS BECAUSE YOU'VE *EARNED* YOUR WAY HERE.

HAVE I? I'M THE LOWEST RANKED PLAYER ON MY TEAM.

DOES NAKAMURA EVEN *HAVE* A RANKING?

SHE'S LABELED NUMBER "*CROISSANT.*"

WE DON'T KNOW HOW THAT WORKS, EITHER.

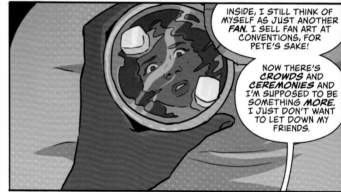

INSIDE, I STILL THINK OF MYSELF AS JUST ANOTHER *FAN.* I SELL FAN ART AT CONVENTIONS, FOR PETE'S SAKE!

NOW THERE'S *CROWDS* AND *CEREMONIES* AND I'M SUPPOSED TO BE SOMETHING *MORE.* I JUST DON'T WANT TO LET DOWN MY FRIENDS.

WELL, PERSONALLY SPEAKING, I KINDA HOPE YOU *DO* LET DOWN YOUR FRIENDS. 'CAUSE THEN *MY* TEAM WINS.

WHAT Y'ALL UP TO? YOU SCOPIN' OUT THE COMPETITION, TONY?

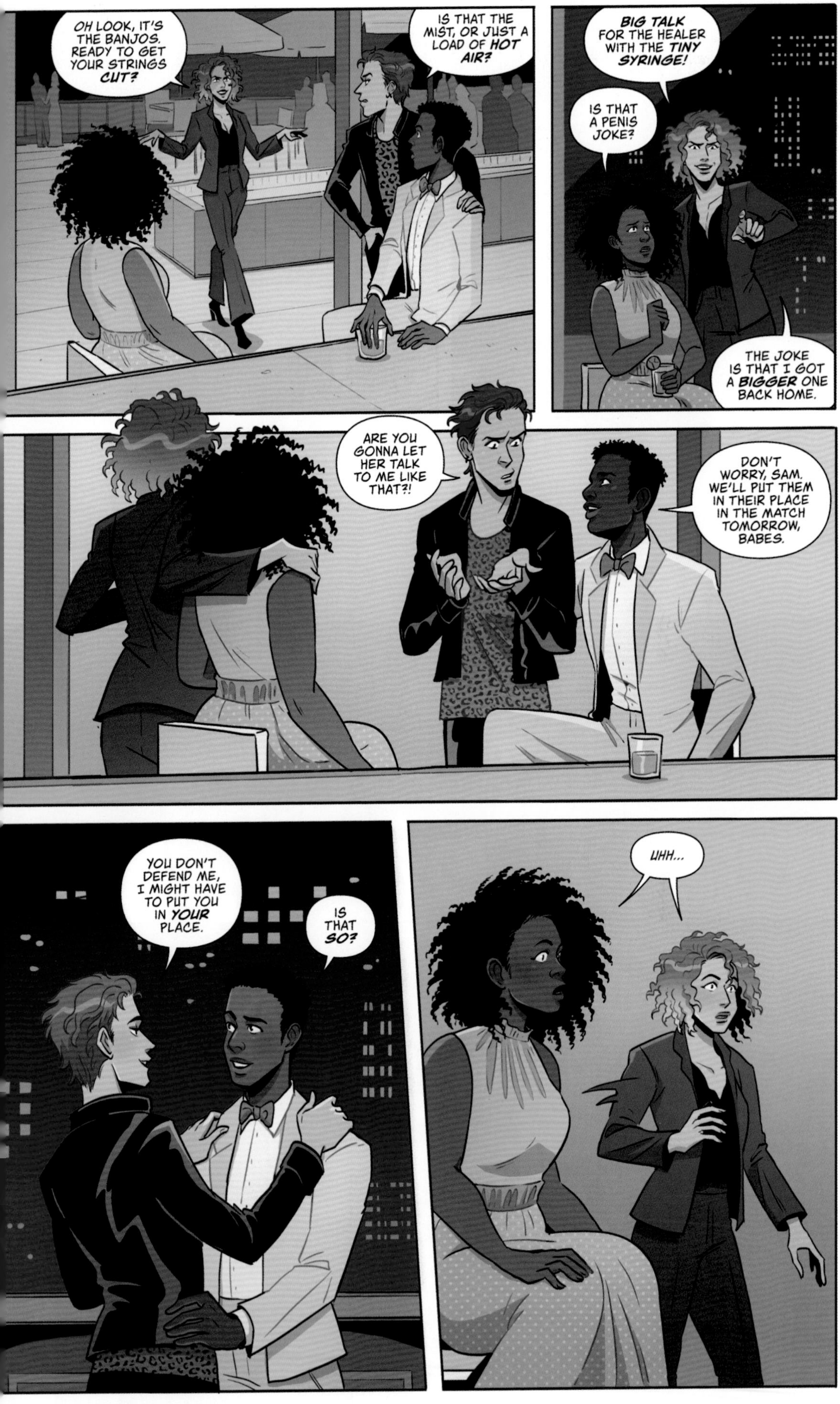

OH LOOK, IT'S THE BANJOS. READY TO GET YOUR STRINGS CUT?
IS THAT THE MIST, OR JUST A LOAD OF HOT AIR?
BIG TALK FOR THE HEALER WITH THE TINY SYRINGE!
IS THAT A PENIS JOKE?
THE JOKE IS THAT I GOT A BIGGER ONE BACK HOME.
ARE YOU GONNA LET HER TALK TO ME LIKE THAT?!
DON'T WORRY, SAM. WE'LL PUT THEM IN THEIR PLACE IN THE MATCH TOMORROW, BABES.
YOU DON'T DEFEND ME, I MIGHT HAVE TO PUT YOU IN YOUR PLACE.
IS THAT SO?
UHH...

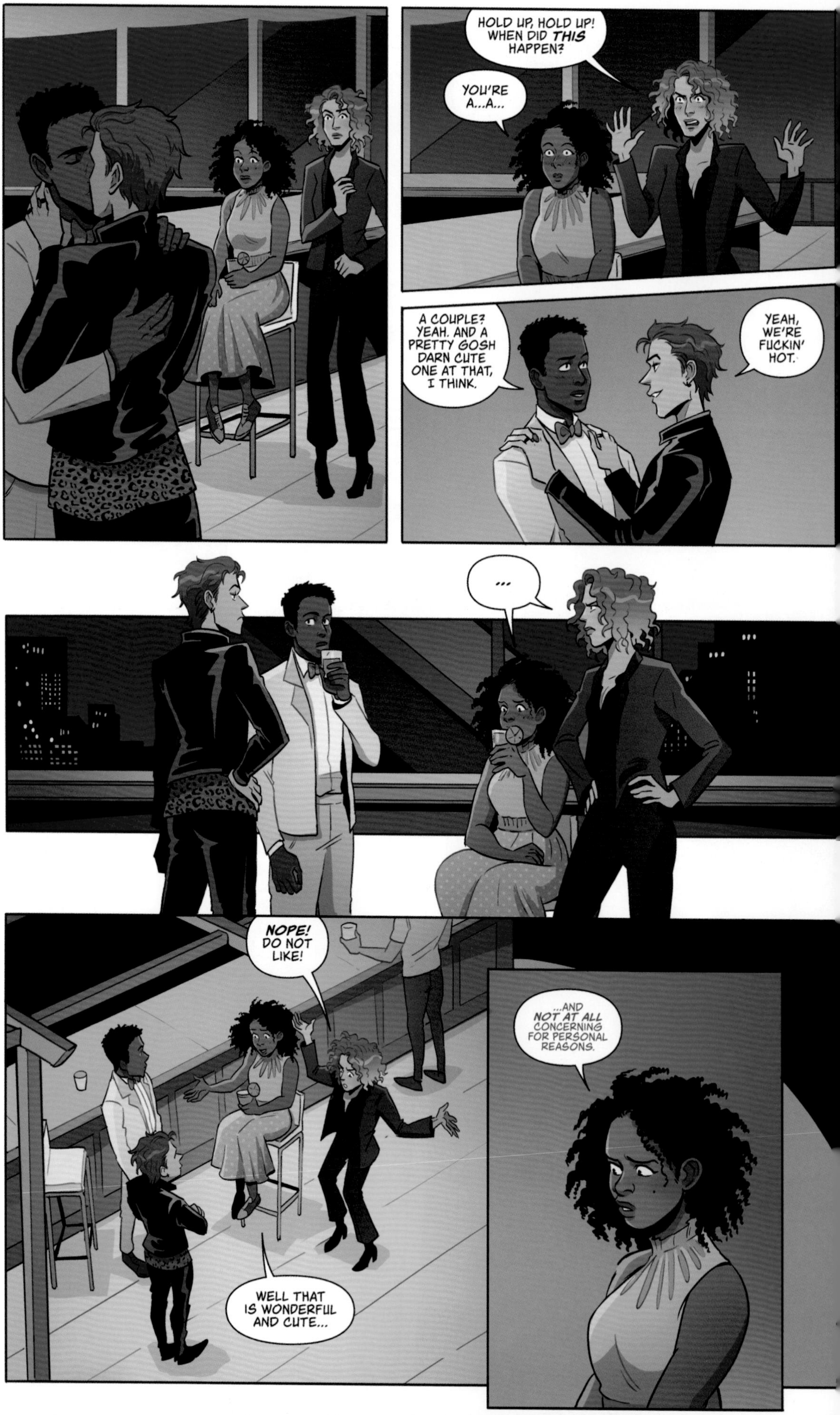
HOLD UP, HOLD UP! WHEN DID THIS HAPPEN?
YOU'RE A...A...
A COUPLE? YEAH. AND A PRETTY GOSH DARN CUTE ONE AT THAT, I THINK.
YEAH, WE'RE FUCKIN' HOT.
...
NOPE! DO NOT LIKE!
WELL THAT IS WONDERFUL AND CUTE...
...AND NOT AT ALL CONCERNING FOR PERSONAL REASONS.

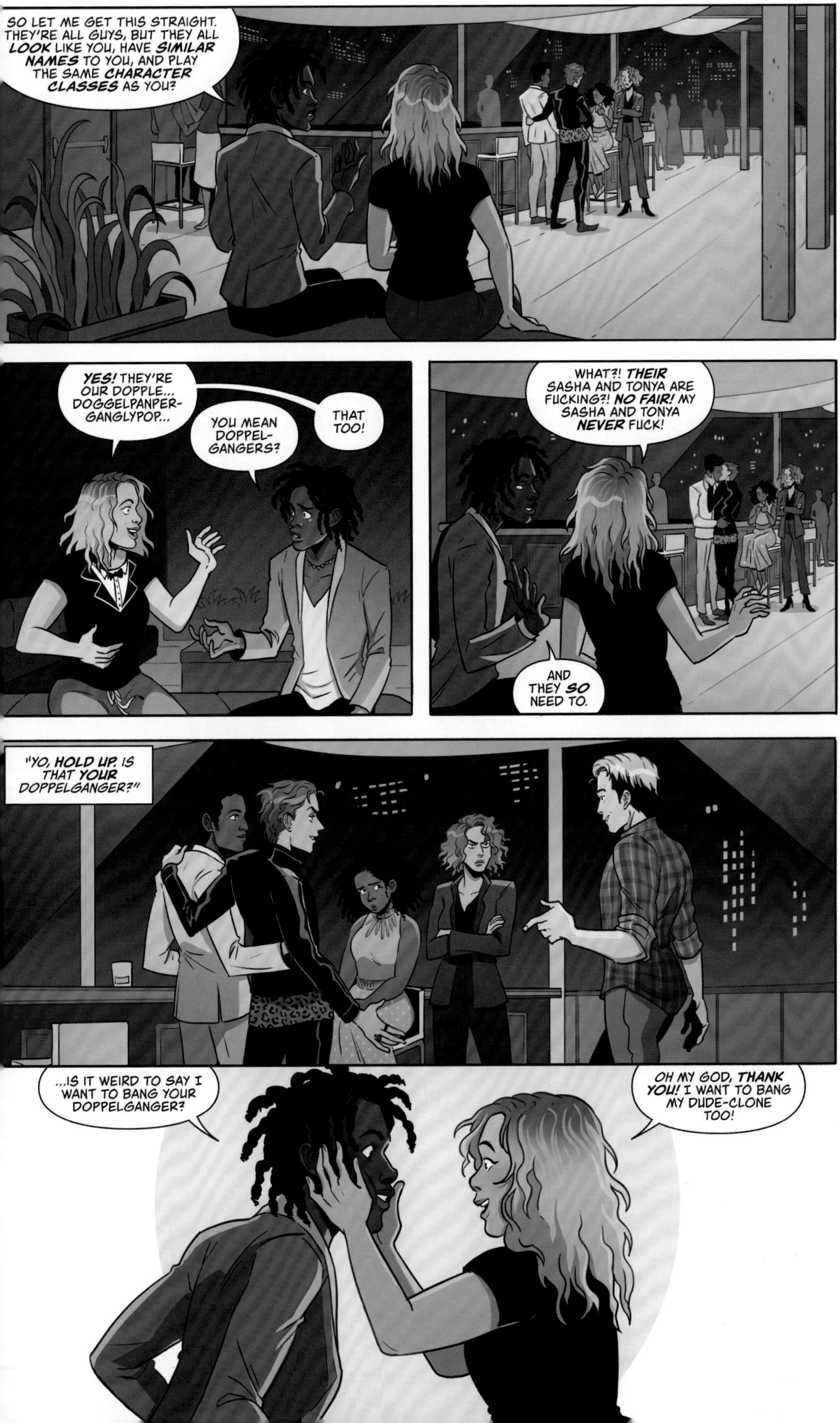
SO LET ME GET THIS STRAIGHT. THEY'RE ALL GUYS, BUT THEY ALL LOOK LIKE YOU, HAVE SIMILAR NAMES TO YOU, AND PLAY THE SAME CHARACTER CLASSES AS YOU?
YES! THEY'RE OUR DOPPLE... DOGGELPANPER-GANGLYPOP...
YOU MEAN DOPPEL-GANGERS?
THAT TOO!
WHAT?! THEIR SASHA AND TONYA ARE FUCKING?! NO FAIR! MY SASHA AND TONYA NEVER FUCK!
AND THEY SO NEED TO.
"YO, HOLD UP. IS THAT YOUR DOPPELGANGER?"
...IS IT WEIRD TO SAY I WANT TO BANG YOUR DOPPELGANGER?
OH MY GOD, THANK YOU! I WANT TO BANG MY DUDE-CLONE TOO!

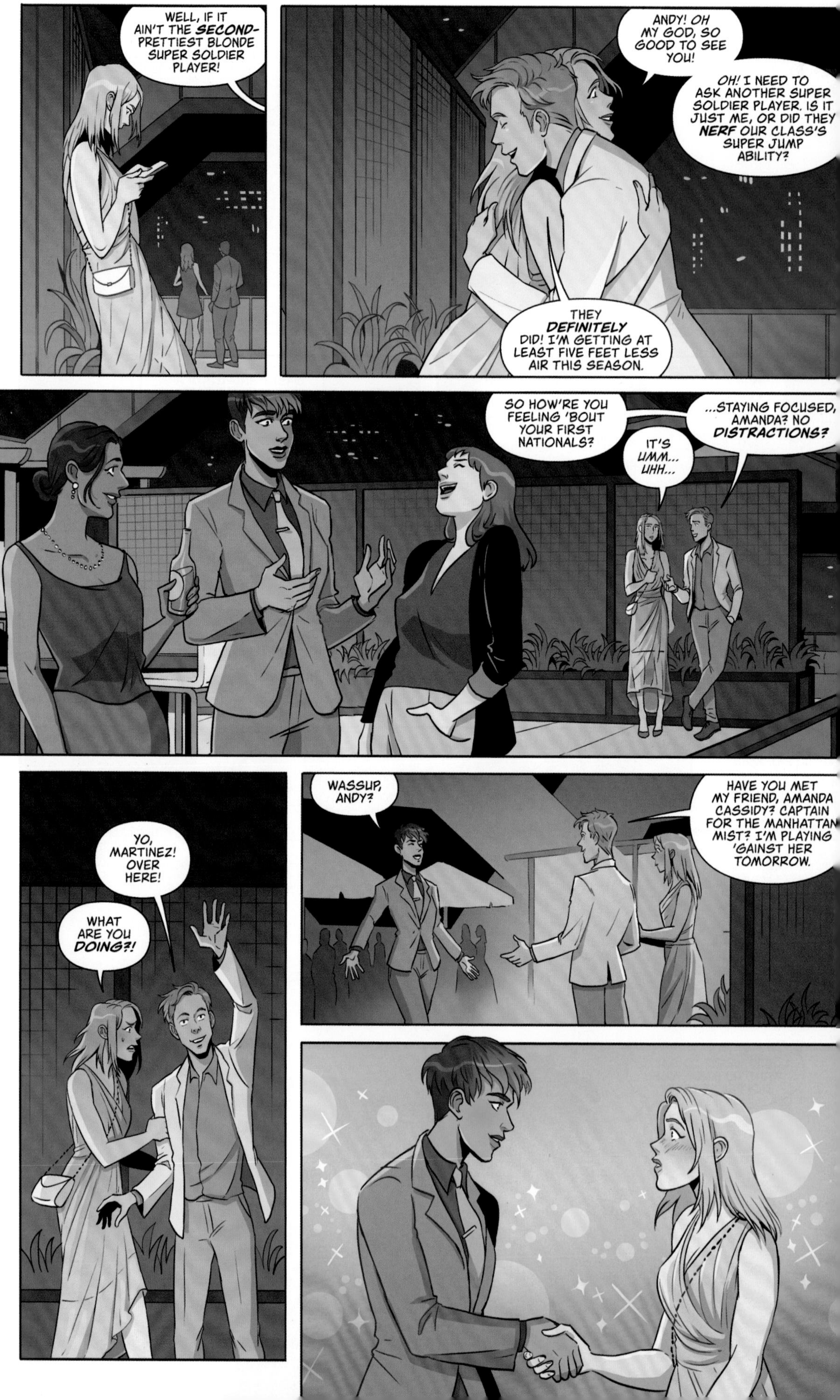
WELL, IF IT AIN'T THE SECOND-PRETTIEST BLONDE SUPER SOLDIER PLAYER!
ANDY! OH MY GOD, SO GOOD TO SEE YOU!
OH! I NEED TO ASK ANOTHER SUPER SOLDIER PLAYER. IS IT JUST ME, OR DID THEY NERF OUR CLASS'S SUPER JUMP ABILITY?
THEY DEFINITELY DID! I'M GETTING AT LEAST FIVE FEET LESS AIR THIS SEASON.
SO HOW'RE YOU FEELING 'BOUT YOUR FIRST NATIONALS?
IT'S UMM... UHH...
...STAYING FOCUSED, AMANDA? NO DISTRACTIONS?
YO, MARTINEZ! OVER HERE!
WHAT ARE YOU DOING?!
WASSUP, ANDY?
HAVE YOU MET MY FRIEND, AMANDA CASSIDY? CAPTAIN FOR THE MANHATTAN MIST? I'M PLAYING 'GAINST HER TOMORROW.

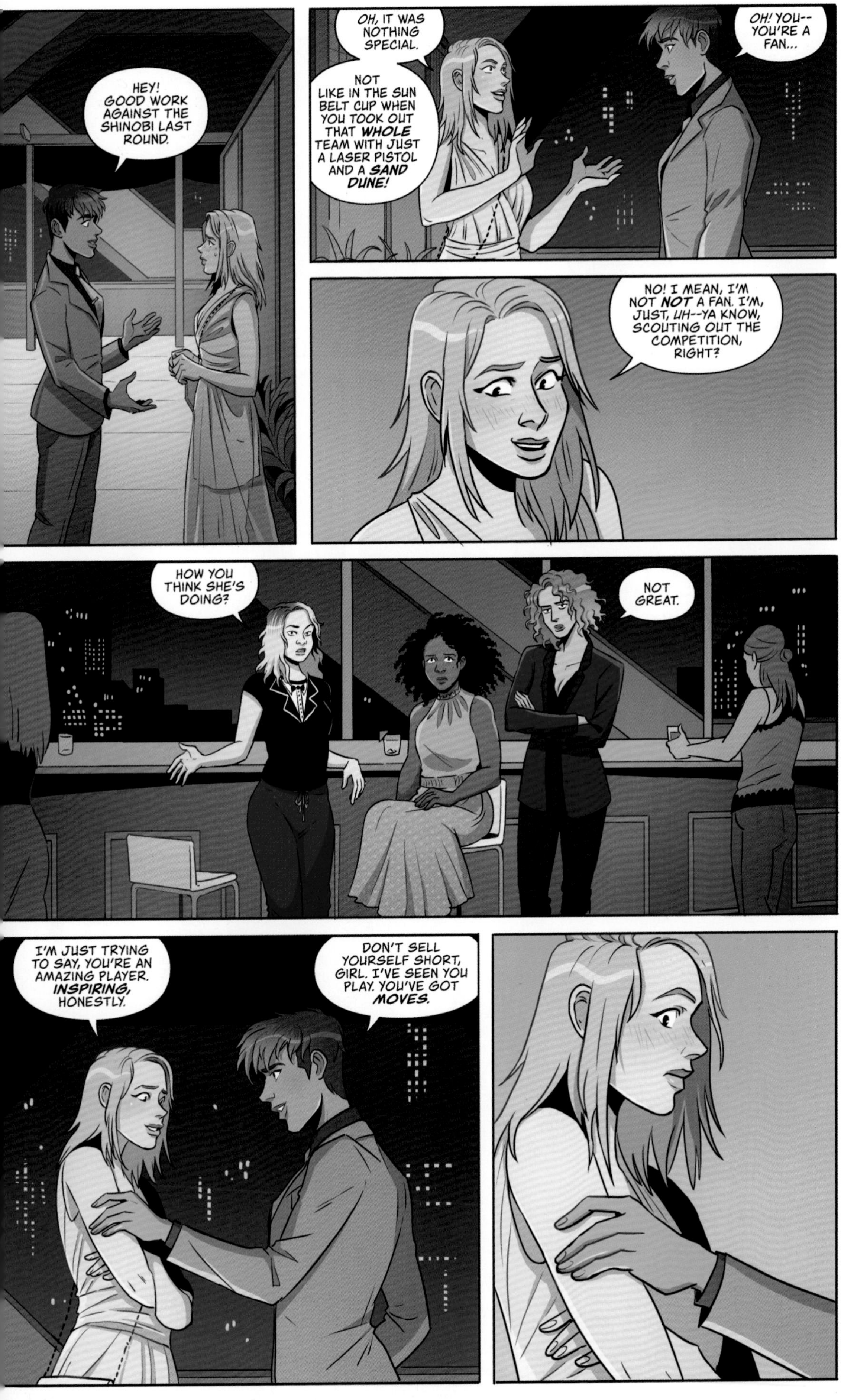
HEY! GOOD WORK AGAINST THE SHINOBI LAST ROUND.
OH, IT WAS NOTHING SPECIAL.
NOT LIKE IN THE SUN BELT CUP WHEN YOU TOOK OUT THAT WHOLE TEAM WITH JUST A LASER PISTOL AND A SAND DUNE!
OH! YOU-- YOU'RE A FAN...
NO! I MEAN, I'M NOT NOT A FAN. I'M, JUST, UH--YA KNOW, SCOUTING OUT THE COMPETITION, RIGHT?
HOW YOU THINK SHE'S DOING?
NOT GREAT.
I'M JUST TRYING TO SAY, YOU'RE AN AMAZING PLAYER. INSPIRING, HONESTLY.
DON'T SELL YOURSELF SHORT, GIRL. I'VE SEEN YOU PLAY. YOU'VE GOT MOVES.

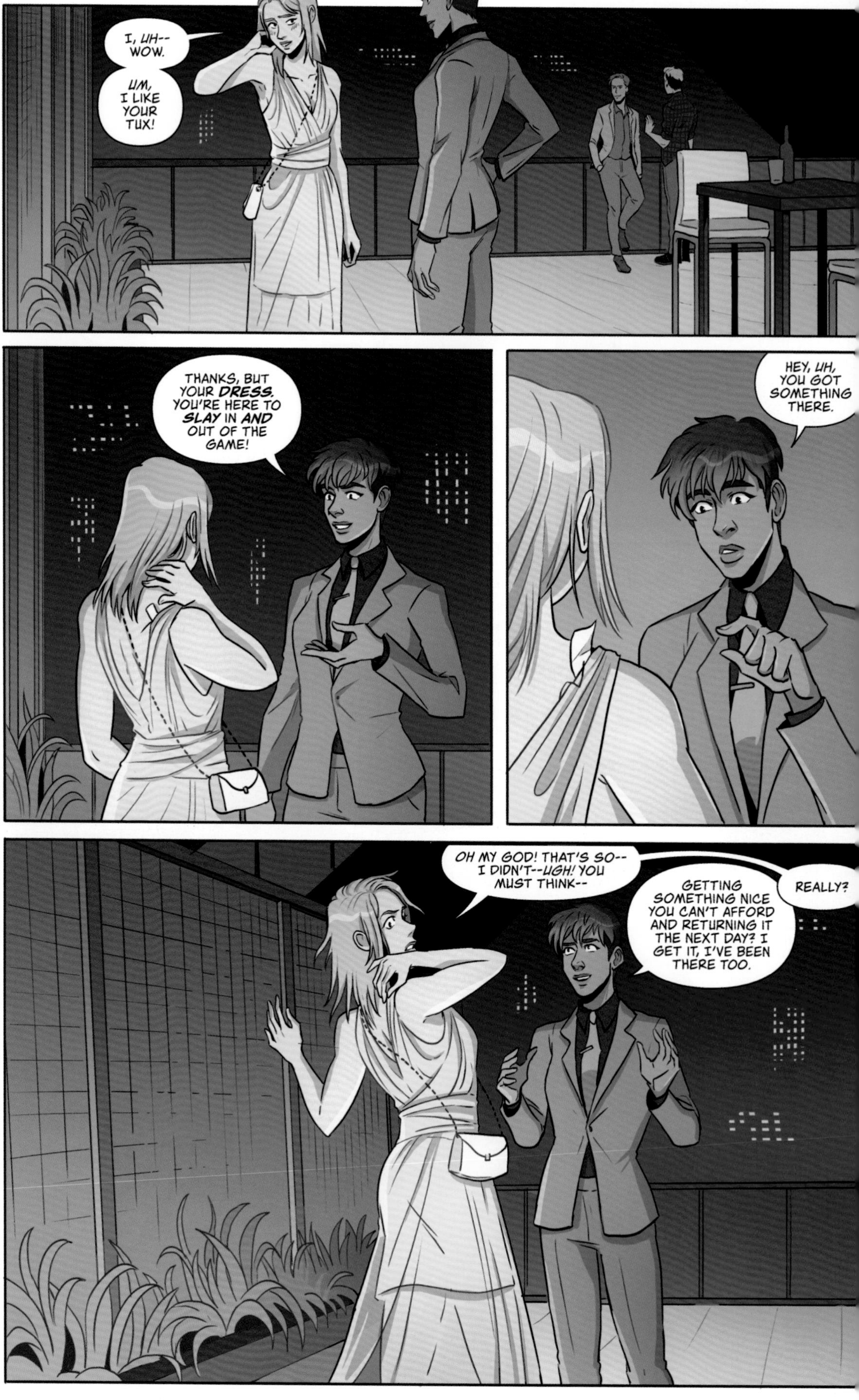

I, UH-- WOW.
UM, I LIKE YOUR TUX!
THANKS, BUT YOUR DRESS. YOU'RE HERE TO SLAY IN AND OUT OF THE GAME!
HEY, UH, YOU GOT SOMETHING THERE.
OH MY GOD! THAT'S SO-- I DIDN'T--UGH! YOU MUST THINK--
GETTING SOMETHING NICE YOU CAN'T AFFORD AND RETURNING IT THE NEXT DAY? I GET IT, I'VE BEEN THERE TOO.
REALLY?

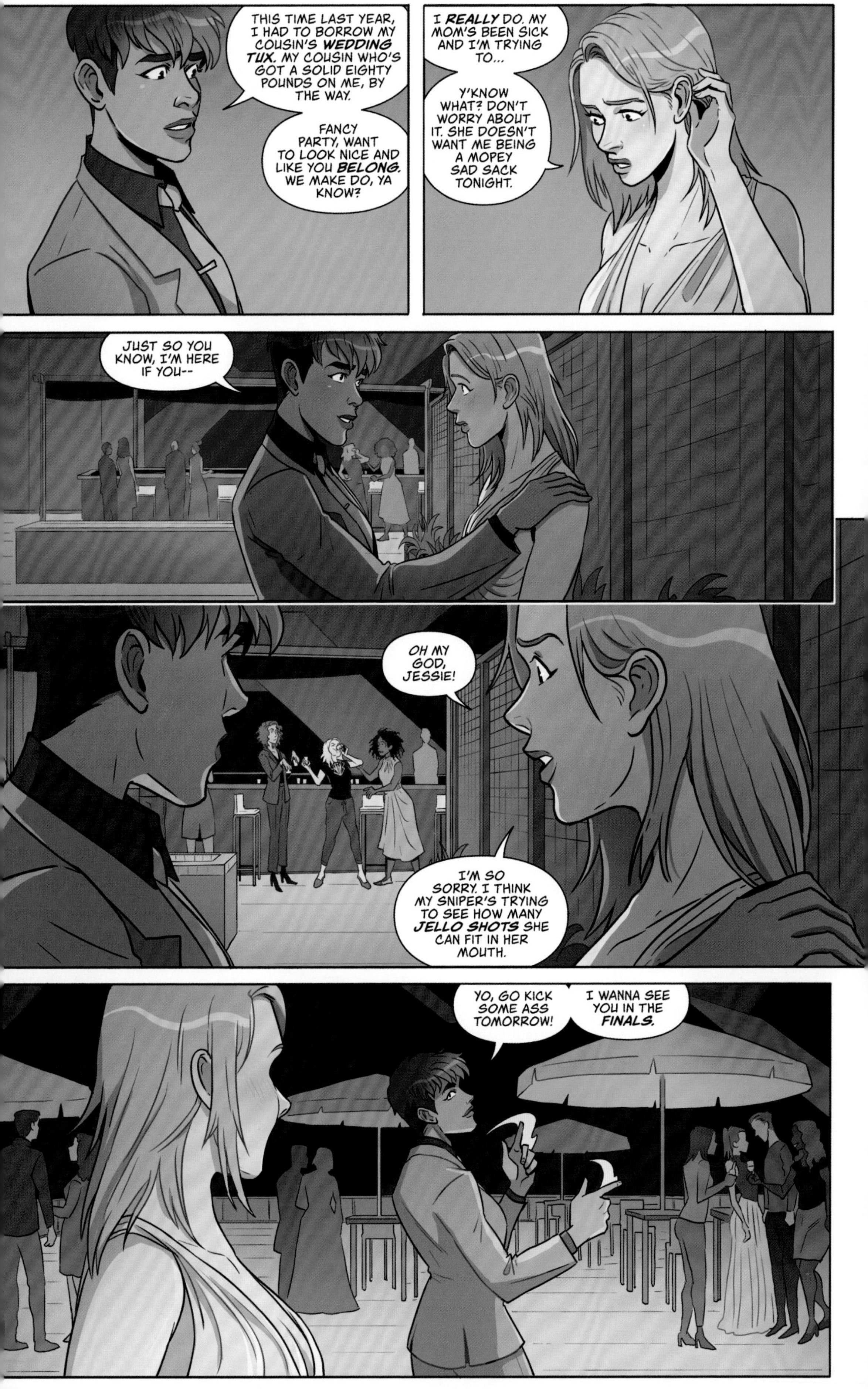
THIS TIME LAST YEAR, I HAD TO BORROW MY COUSIN'S WEDDING TUX. MY COUSIN WHO'S GOT A SOLID EIGHTY POUNDS ON ME, BY THE WAY.
FANCY PARTY, WANT TO LOOK NICE AND LIKE YOU BELONG. WE MAKE DO, YA KNOW?
I REALLY DO. MY MOM'S BEEN SICK AND I'M TRYING TO...
Y'KNOW WHAT? DON'T WORRY ABOUT IT. SHE DOESN'T WANT ME BEING A MOPEY SAD SACK TONIGHT.
JUST SO YOU KNOW, I'M HERE IF YOU--
OH MY GOD, JESSIE!
I'M SO SORRY. I THINK MY SNIPER'S TRYING TO SEE HOW MANY JELLO SHOTS SHE CAN FIT IN HER MOUTH.
YO, GO KICK SOME ASS TOMORROW!
I WANNA SEE YOU IN THE FINALS.

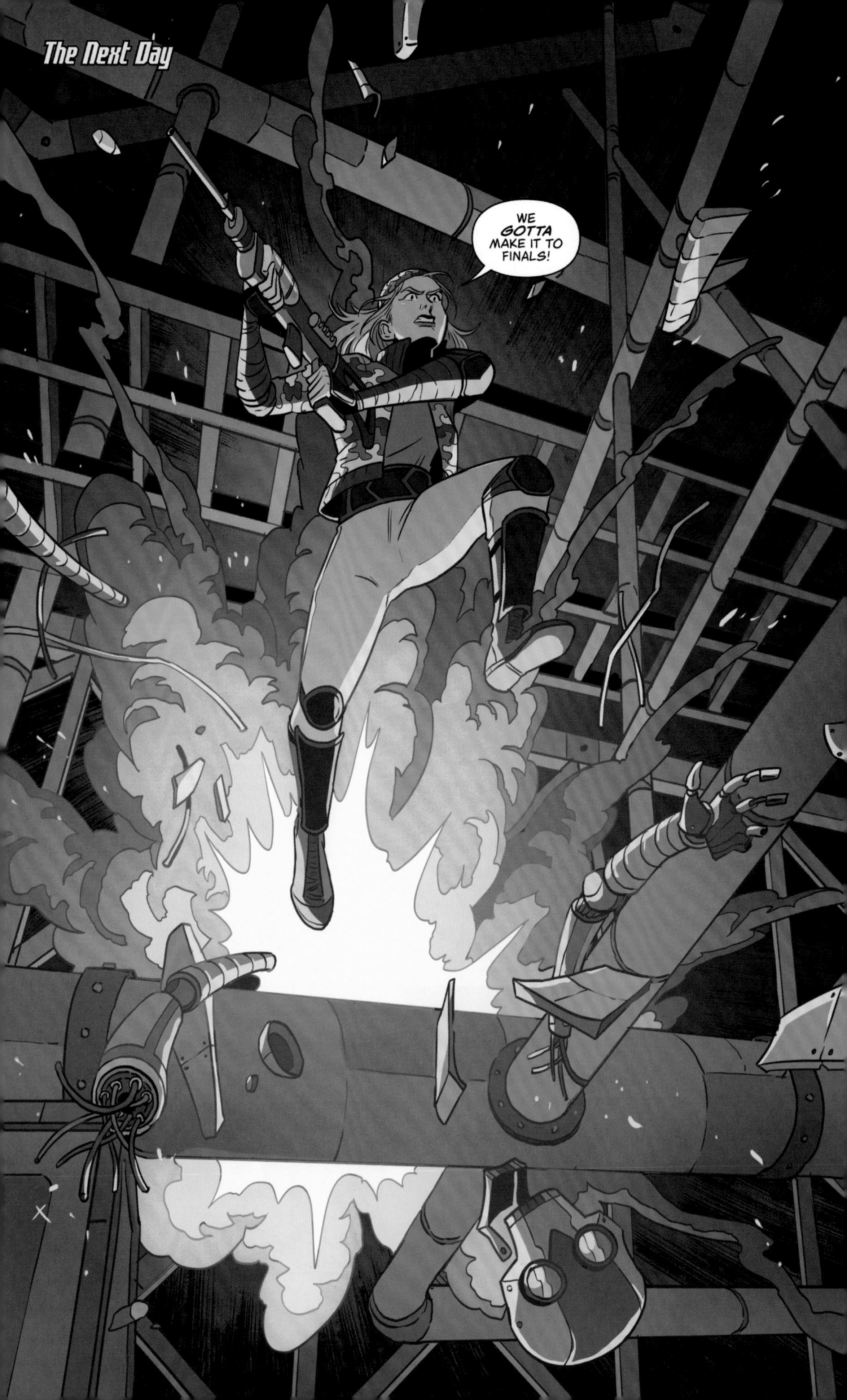
The Next Day
WE GOTTA MAKE IT TO FINALS!

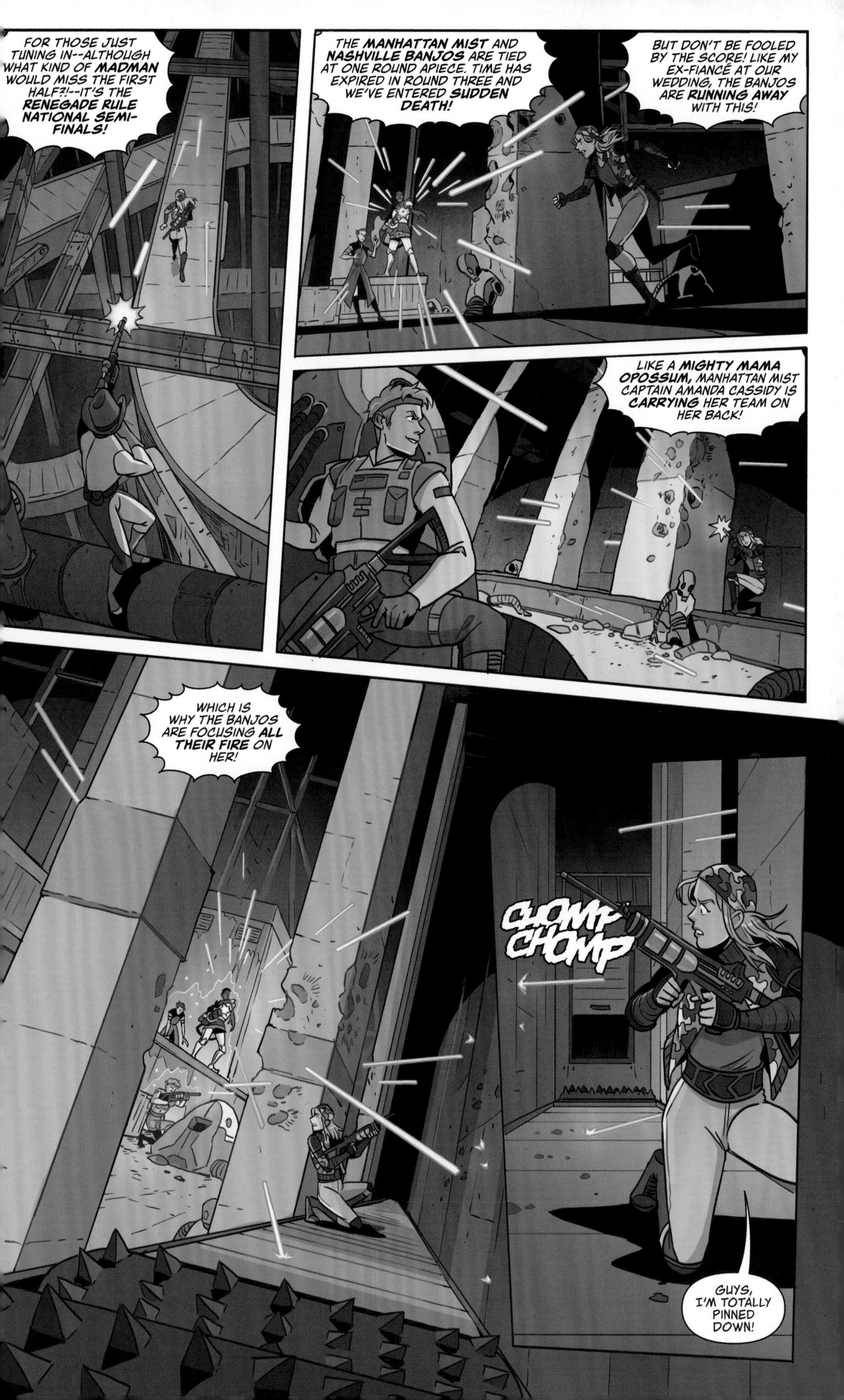
FOR THOSE JUST TUNING IN--ALTHOUGH WHAT KIND OF MADMAN WOULD MISS THE FIRST HALF?!--IT'S THE RENEGADE RULE NATIONAL SEMI-FINALS!
THE MANHATTAN MIST AND NASHVILLE BANJOS ARE TIED AT ONE ROUND APIECE. TIME HAS EXPIRED IN ROUND THREE AND WE'VE ENTERED SUDDEN DEATH!
BUT DON'T BE FOOLED BY THE SCORE! LIKE MY EX-FIANCÉ AT OUR WEDDING, THE BANJOS ARE RUNNING AWAY WITH THIS!
LIKE A MIGHTY MAMA OPOSSUM, MANHATTAN MIST CAPTAIN AMANDA CASSIDY IS CARRYING HER TEAM ON HER BACK!
WHICH IS WHY THE BANJOS ARE FOCUSING ALL THEIR FIRE ON HER!
CHOMP CHOMP
GUYS, I'M TOTALLY PINNED DOWN!

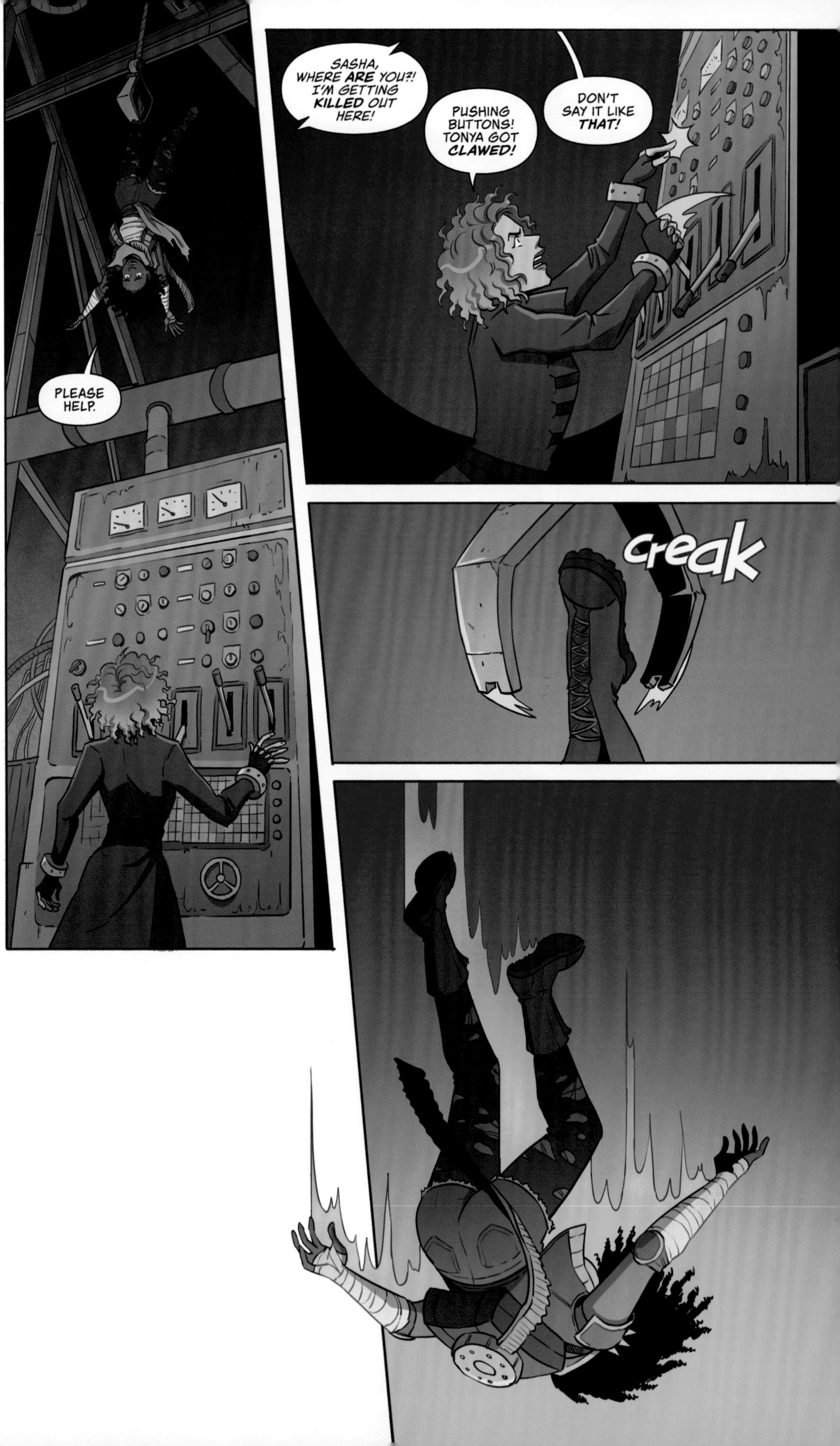
PLEASE HELP.
SASHA, WHERE ARE YOU?! I'M GETTING KILLED OUT HERE!
PUSHING BUTTONS! TONYA GOT CLAWED!
DON'T SAY IT LIKE THAT!
creak

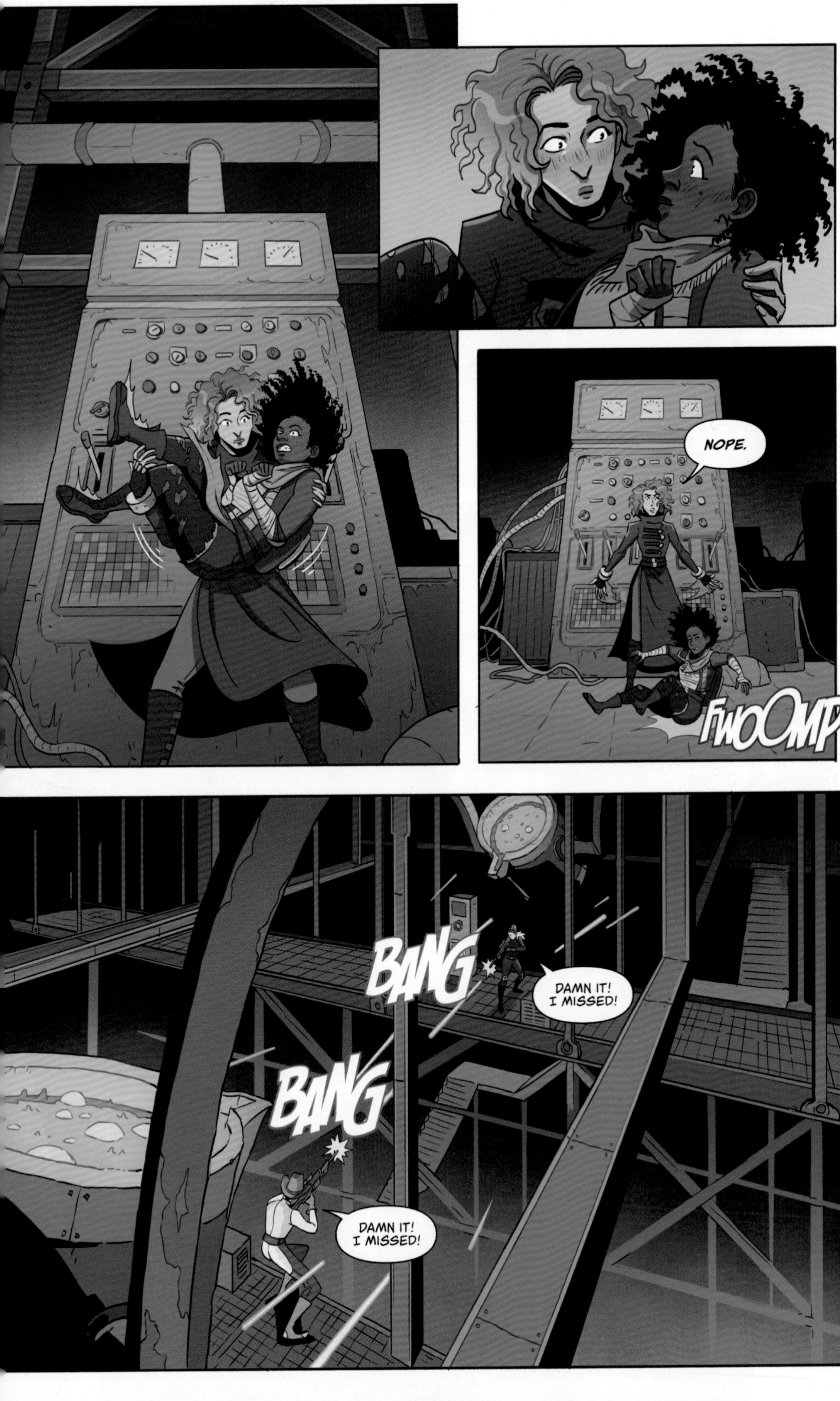
NOPE.
FWOOMP
BANG
DAMN IT! I MISSED!
BANG
DAMN IT! I MISSED!

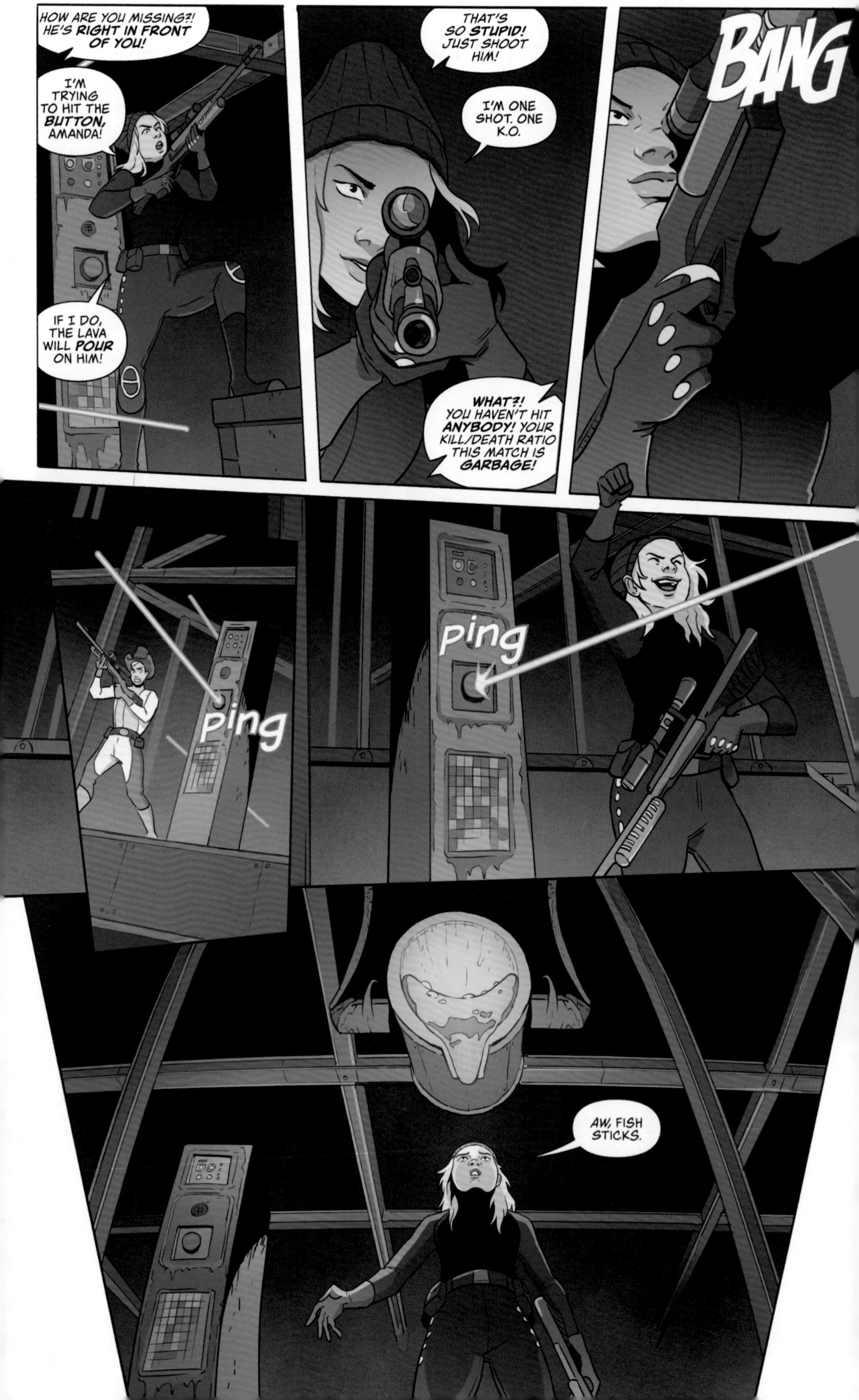
HOW ARE YOU MISSING?! HE'S **RIGHT IN FRONT OF YOU!**
I'M TRYING TO HIT THE **BUTTON,** AMANDA!
IF I DO, THE LAVA WILL **POUR** ON HIM!
THAT'S SO **STUPID!** JUST SHOOT HIM!
I'M ONE SHOT. ONE K.O.
WHAT?! YOU HAVEN'T HIT **ANYBODY!** YOUR KILL/DEATH RATIO THIS MATCH IS **GARBAGE!**
BANG
ping
ping
AW, FISH STICKS.

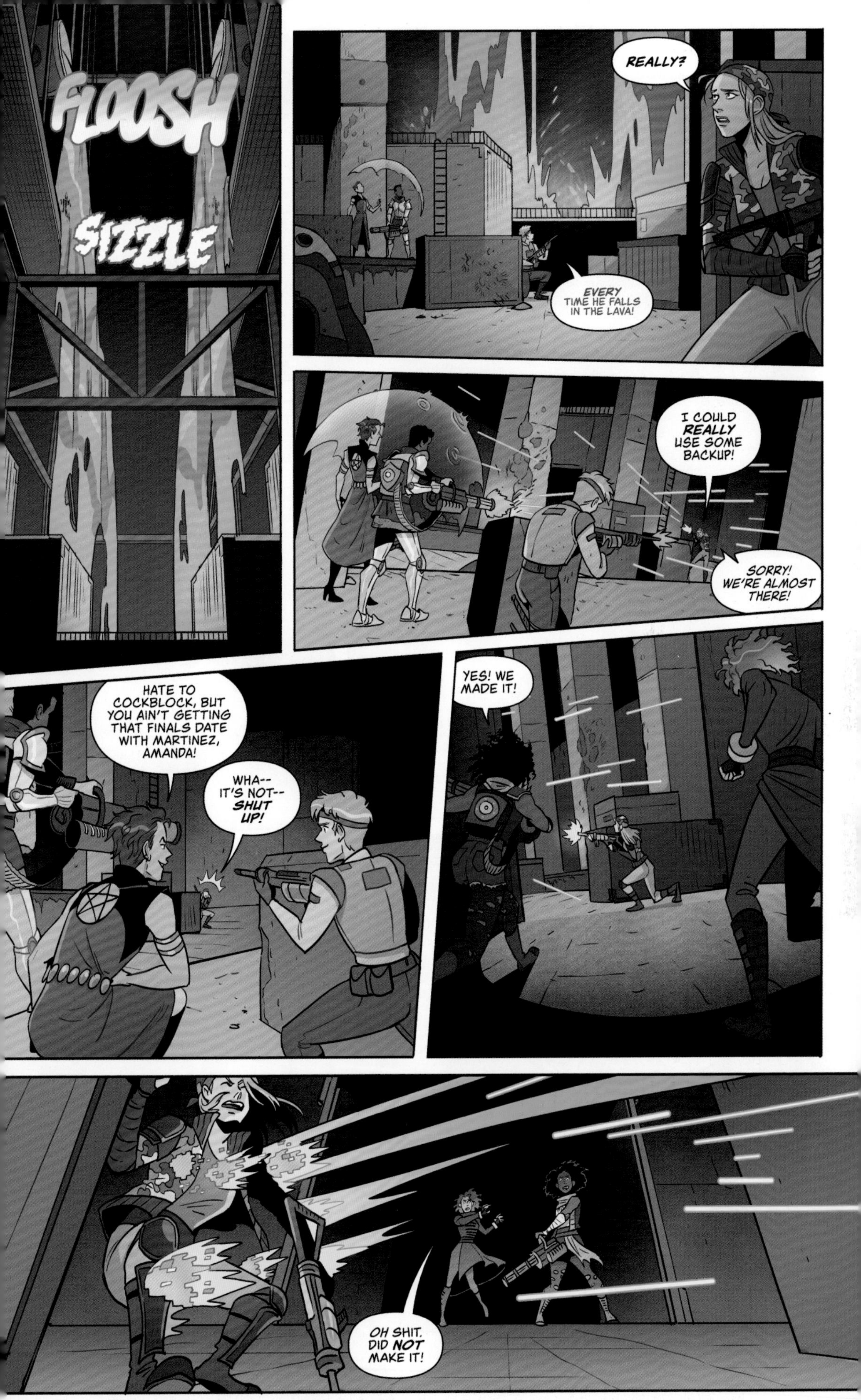
FLOOSH
SIZZLE
REALLY?
EVERY TIME HE FALLS IN THE LAVA!
I COULD REALLY USE SOME BACKUP!
SORRY! WE'RE ALMOST THERE!
HATE TO COCKBLOCK, BUT YOU AIN'T GETTING THAT FINALS DATE WITH MARTINEZ, AMANDA!
WHA-- IT'S NOT-- SHUT UP!
YES! WE MADE IT!
OH SHIT. DID NOT MAKE IT!

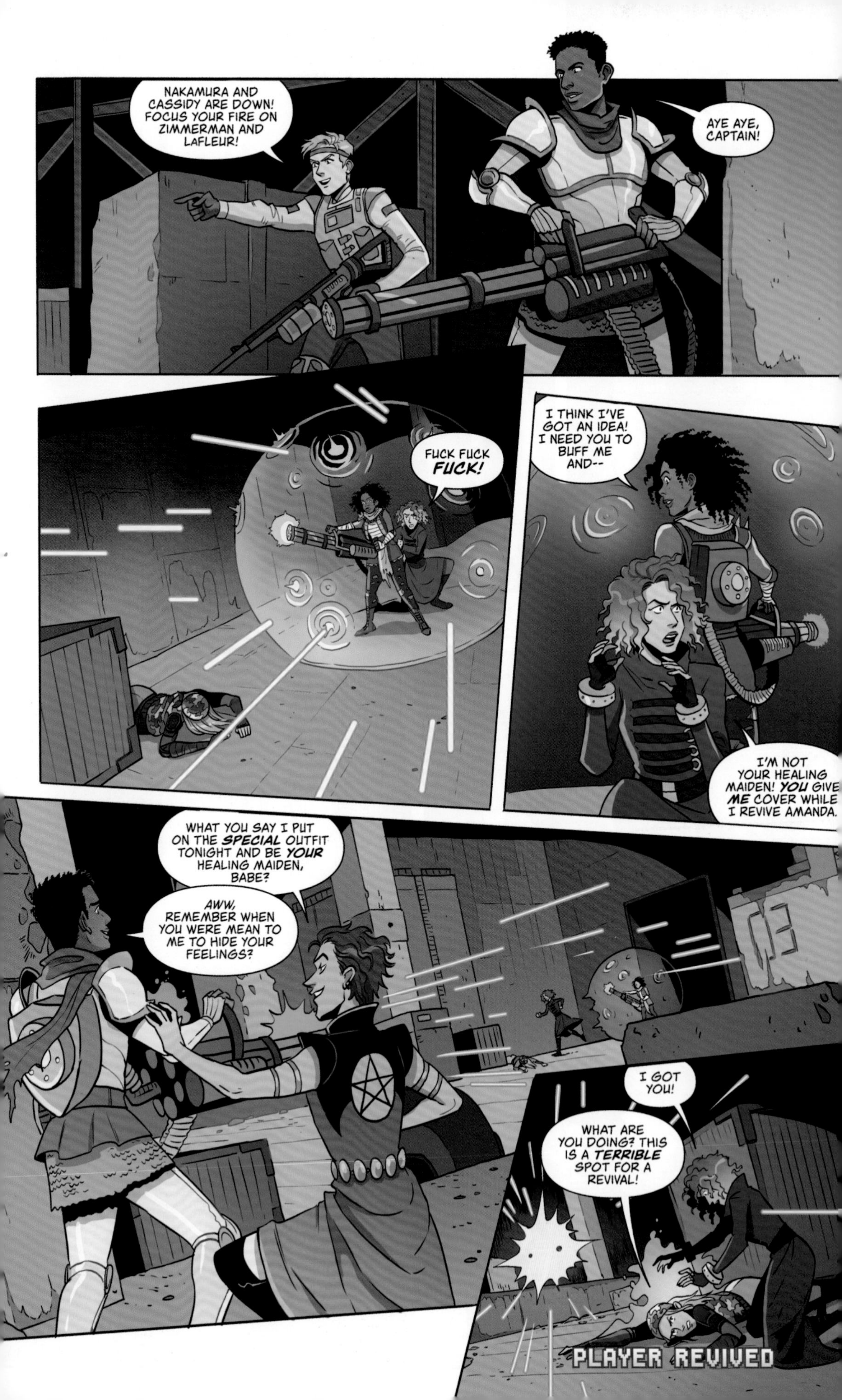
NAKAMURA AND CASSIDY ARE DOWN! FOCUS YOUR FIRE ON ZIMMERMAN AND LAFLEUR!
AYE AYE, CAPTAIN!
FUCK FUCK *FUCK!*
I THINK I'VE GOT AN IDEA! I NEED YOU TO BUFF ME AND--
I'M NOT YOUR HEALING MAIDEN! *YOU* GIVE *ME* COVER WHILE I REVIVE AMANDA.
WHAT YOU SAY I PUT ON THE *SPECIAL* OUTFIT TONIGHT AND BE *YOUR* HEALING MAIDEN, BABE?
AWW, REMEMBER WHEN YOU WERE MEAN TO ME TO HIDE YOUR FEELINGS?
I GOT YOU!
WHAT ARE YOU DOING? THIS IS A *TERRIBLE* SPOT FOR A REVIVAL!
PLAYER REVIVED

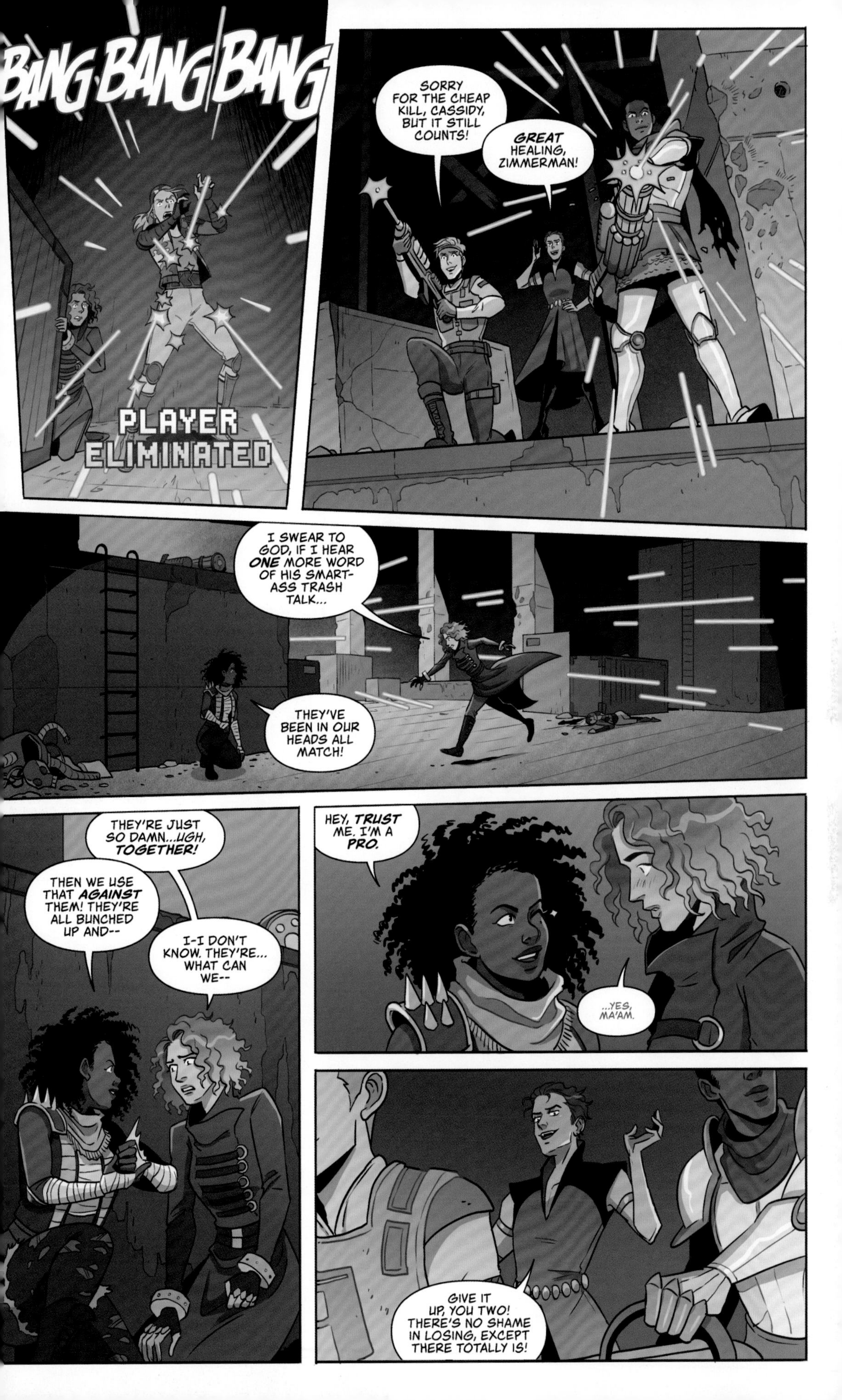

BANG BANG BANG
PLAYER ELIMINATED
SORRY FOR THE CHEAP KILL, CASSIDY, BUT IT STILL COUNTS!
GREAT HEALING, ZIMMERMAN!
I SWEAR TO GOD, IF I HEAR ONE MORE WORD OF HIS SMART-ASS TRASH TALK...
THEY'VE BEEN IN OUR HEADS ALL MATCH!
THEY'RE JUST SO DAMN...UGH, TOGETHER!
THEN WE USE THAT AGAINST THEM! THEY'RE ALL BUNCHED UP AND--
I-I DON'T KNOW. THEY'RE... WHAT CAN WE--
HEY, TRUST ME. I'M A PRO.
...YES, MA'AM.
GIVE IT UP, YOU TWO! THERE'S NO SHAME IN LOSING, EXCEPT THERE TOTALLY IS!

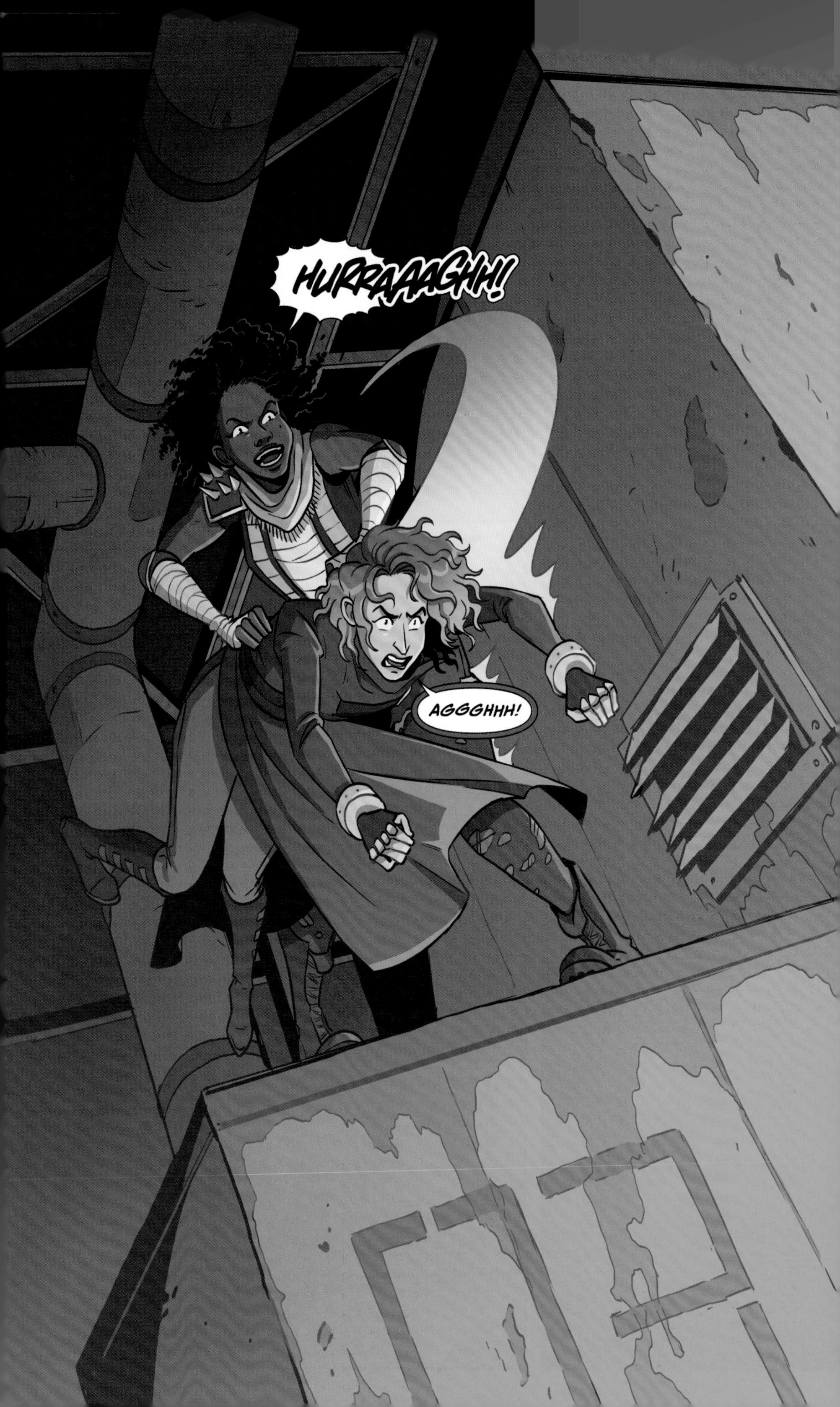
HURRAAAAGHH!
AGGGHHH!

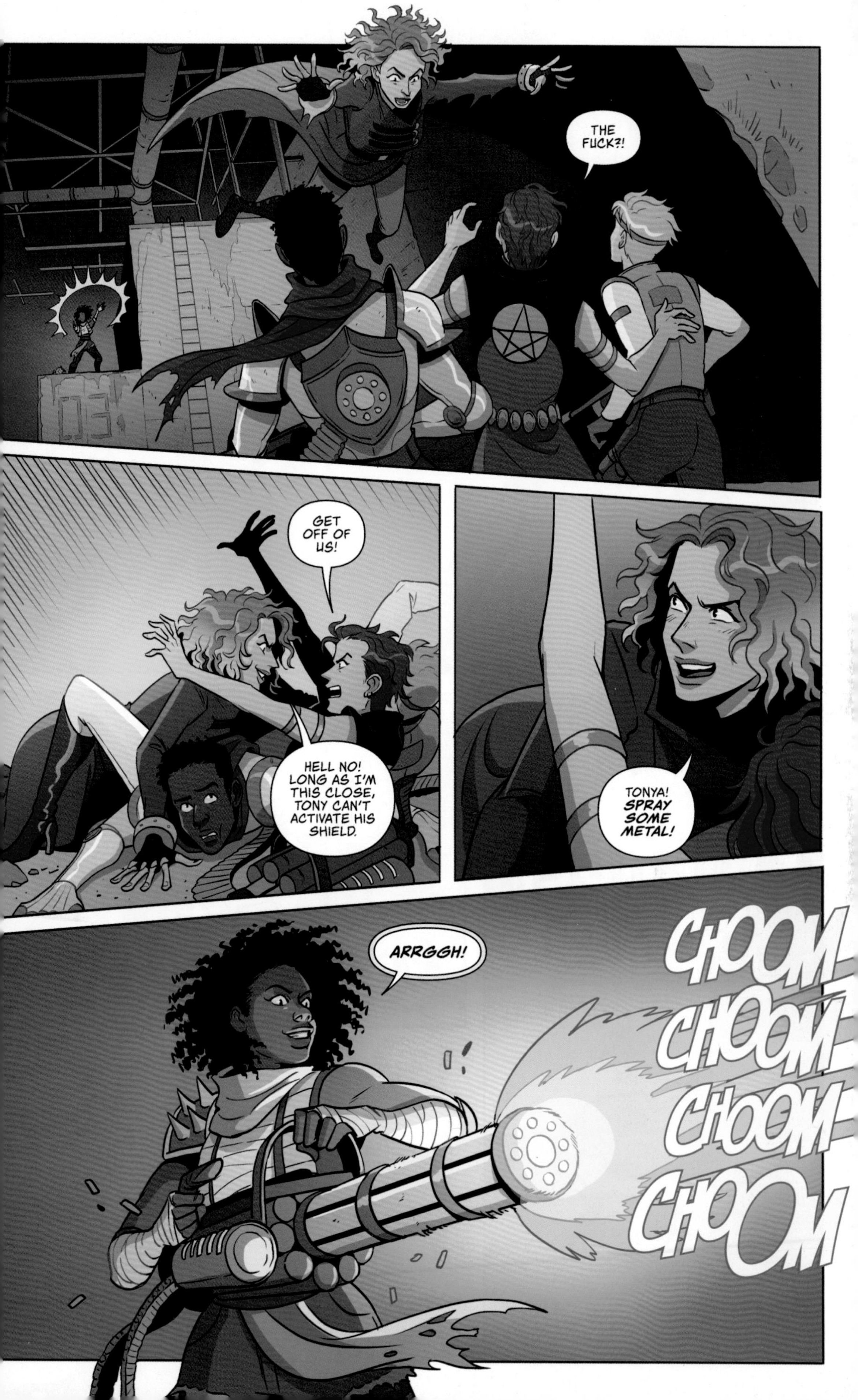
THE FUCK?!
GET OFF OF US!
HELL NO! LONG AS I'M THIS CLOSE, TONY CAN'T ACTIVATE HIS SHIELD.
TONYA! SPRAY SOME METAL!
ARRGGH!
CHOOM
CHOOM
CHOOM
CHOOM

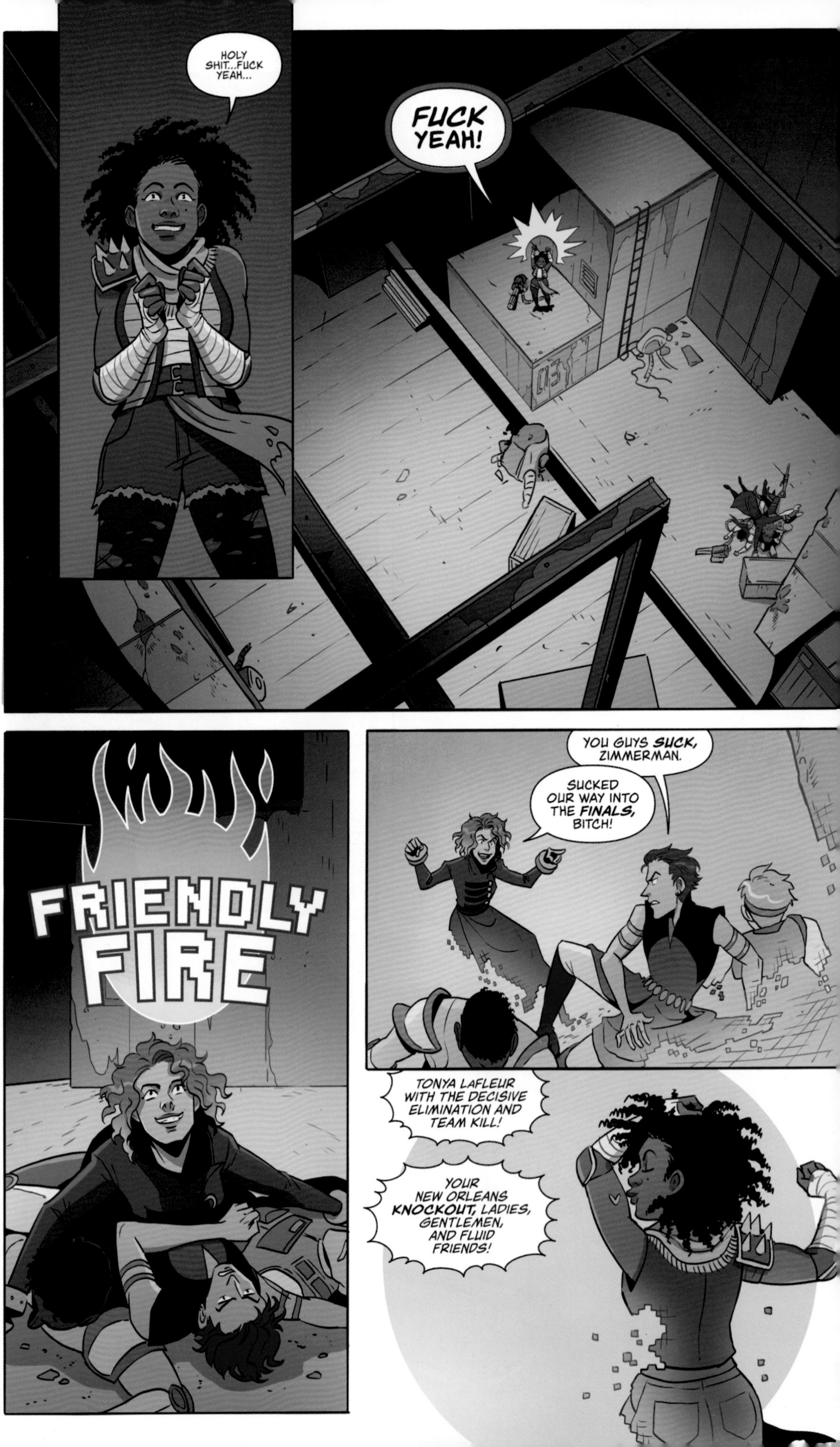
HOLY SHIT...FUCK YEAH...
FUCK YEAH!
FRIENDLY FIRE
YOU GUYS SUCK, ZIMMERMAN.
SUCKED OUR WAY INTO THE FINALS, BITCH!
TONYA LAFLEUR WITH THE DECISIVE ELIMINATION AND TEAM KILL!
YOUR NEW ORLEANS KNOCKOUT, LADIES, GENTLEMEN, AND FLUID FRIENDS!

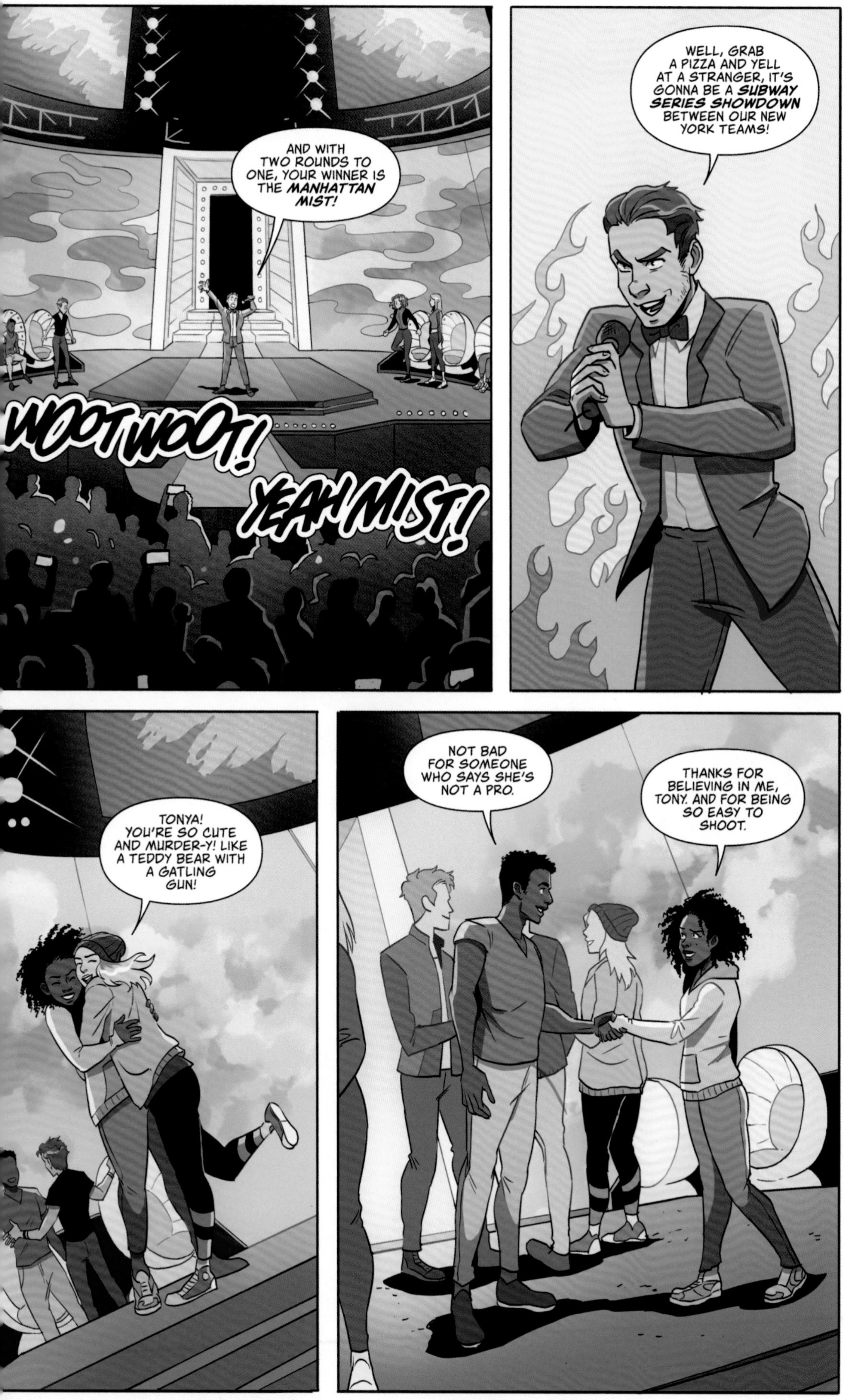
AND WITH TWO ROUNDS TO ONE, YOUR WINNER IS THE *MANHATTAN MIST!*
WOOT WOOT!
YEAH MIST!
WELL, GRAB A PIZZA AND YELL AT A STRANGER, IT'S GONNA BE A ***SUBWAY SERIES SHOWDOWN*** BETWEEN OUR NEW YORK TEAMS!
TONYA! YOU'RE SO CUTE AND MURDER-Y! LIKE A TEDDY BEAR WITH A GATLING GUN!
NOT BAD FOR SOMEONE WHO SAYS SHE'S NOT A PRO.
THANKS FOR BELIEVING IN ME, TONY. AND FOR BEING SO EASY TO SHOOT.

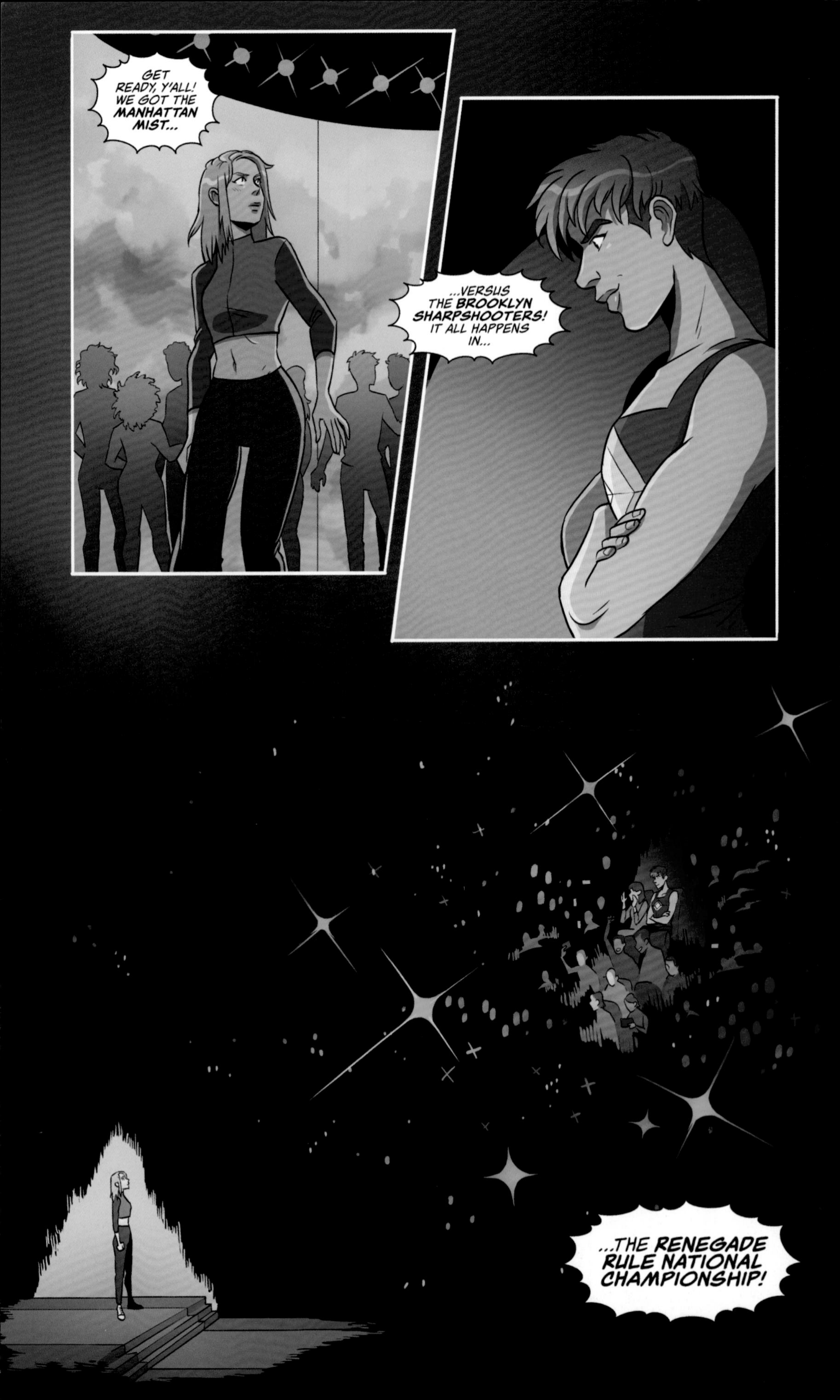
GET READY, Y'ALL! WE GOT THE MANHATTAN MIST...
...VERSUS THE BROOKLYN SHARPSHOOTERS! IT ALL HAPPENS IN...
...THE RENEGADE RULE NATIONAL CHAMPIONSHIP!

CHAPTER FOUR

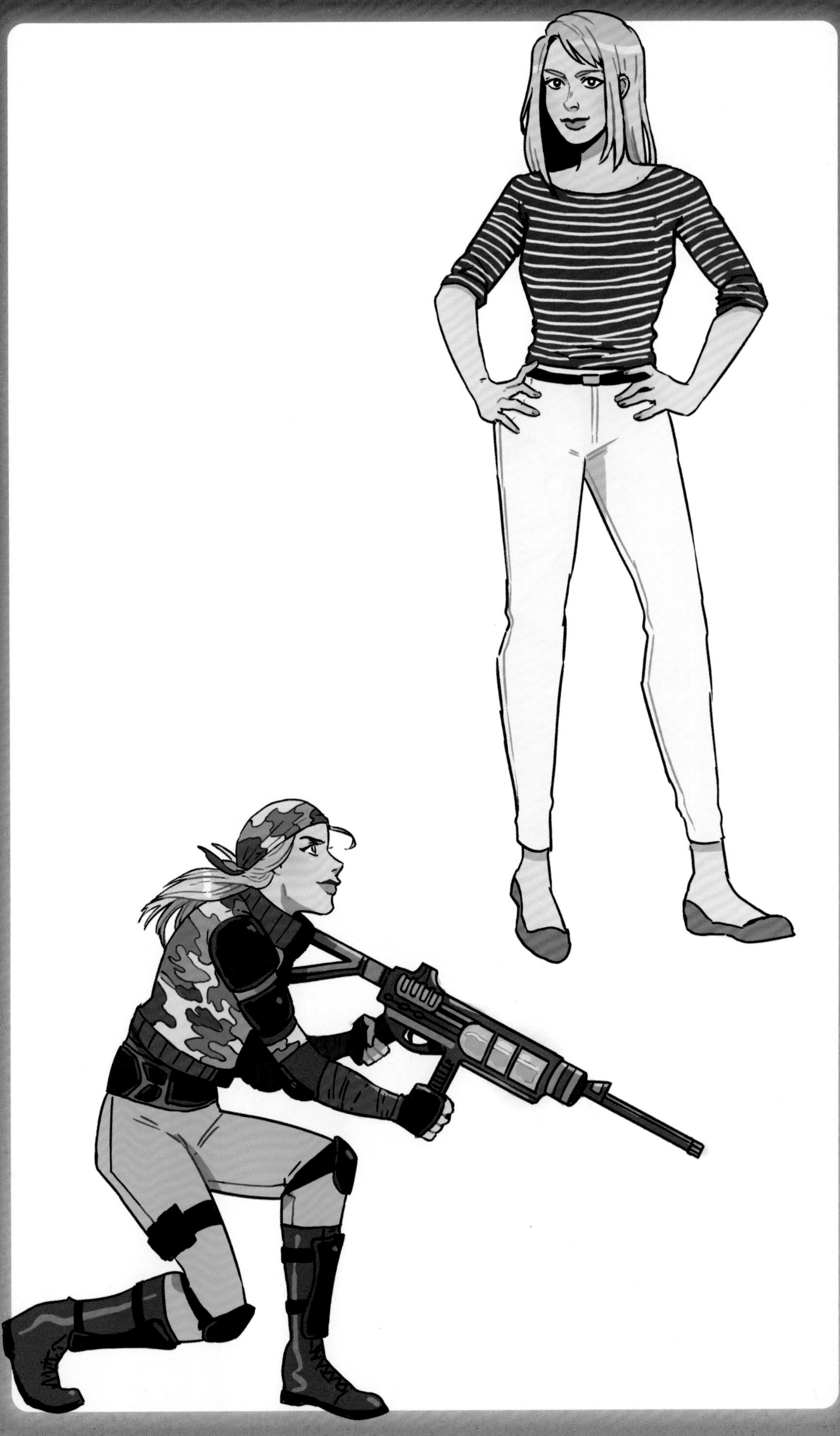

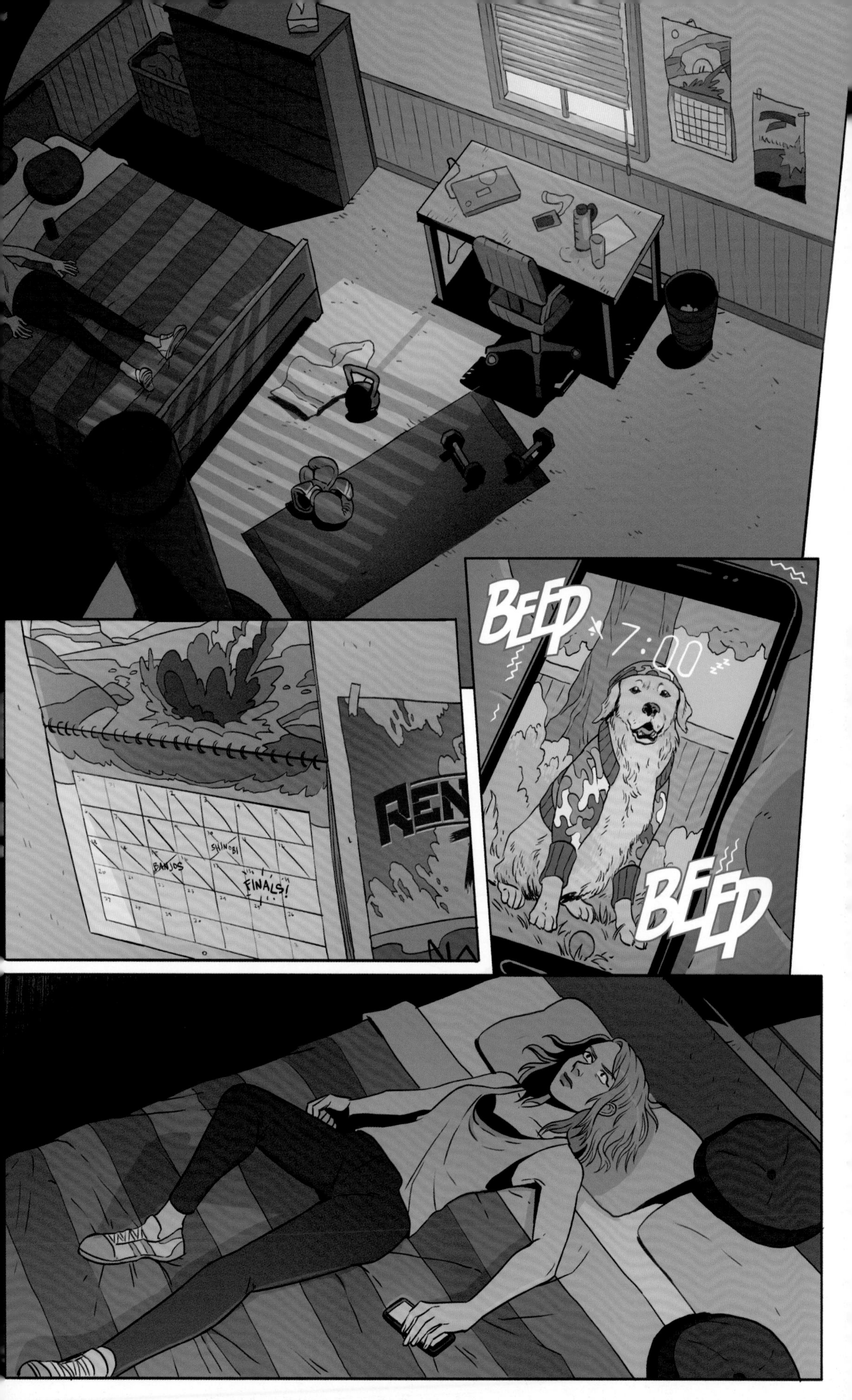

BANJOS
SHINOBI
FINALS!
BEEP
7:00
BEEP

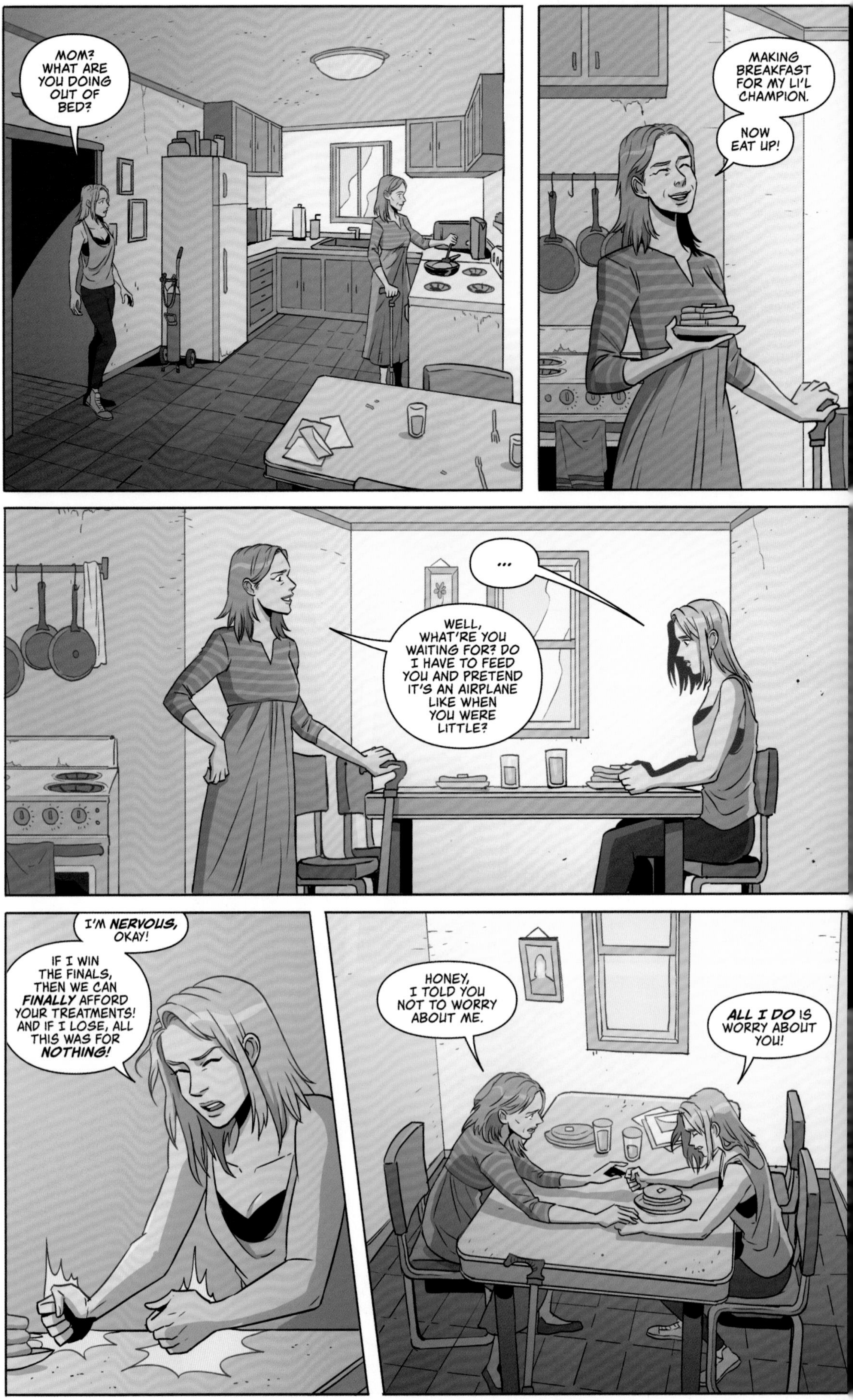
MOM? WHAT ARE YOU DOING OUT OF BED?
MAKING BREAKFAST FOR MY LI'L CHAMPION.
NOW EAT UP!
...
WELL, WHAT'RE YOU WAITING FOR? DO I HAVE TO FEED YOU AND PRETEND IT'S AN AIRPLANE LIKE WHEN YOU WERE LITTLE?
I'M **NERVOUS**, OKAY!
IF I WIN THE FINALS, THEN WE CAN **FINALLY** AFFORD YOUR TREATMENTS! AND IF I LOSE, ALL THIS WAS FOR **NOTHING!**
HONEY, I TOLD YOU NOT TO WORRY ABOUT ME.
ALL I DO IS WORRY ABOUT YOU!

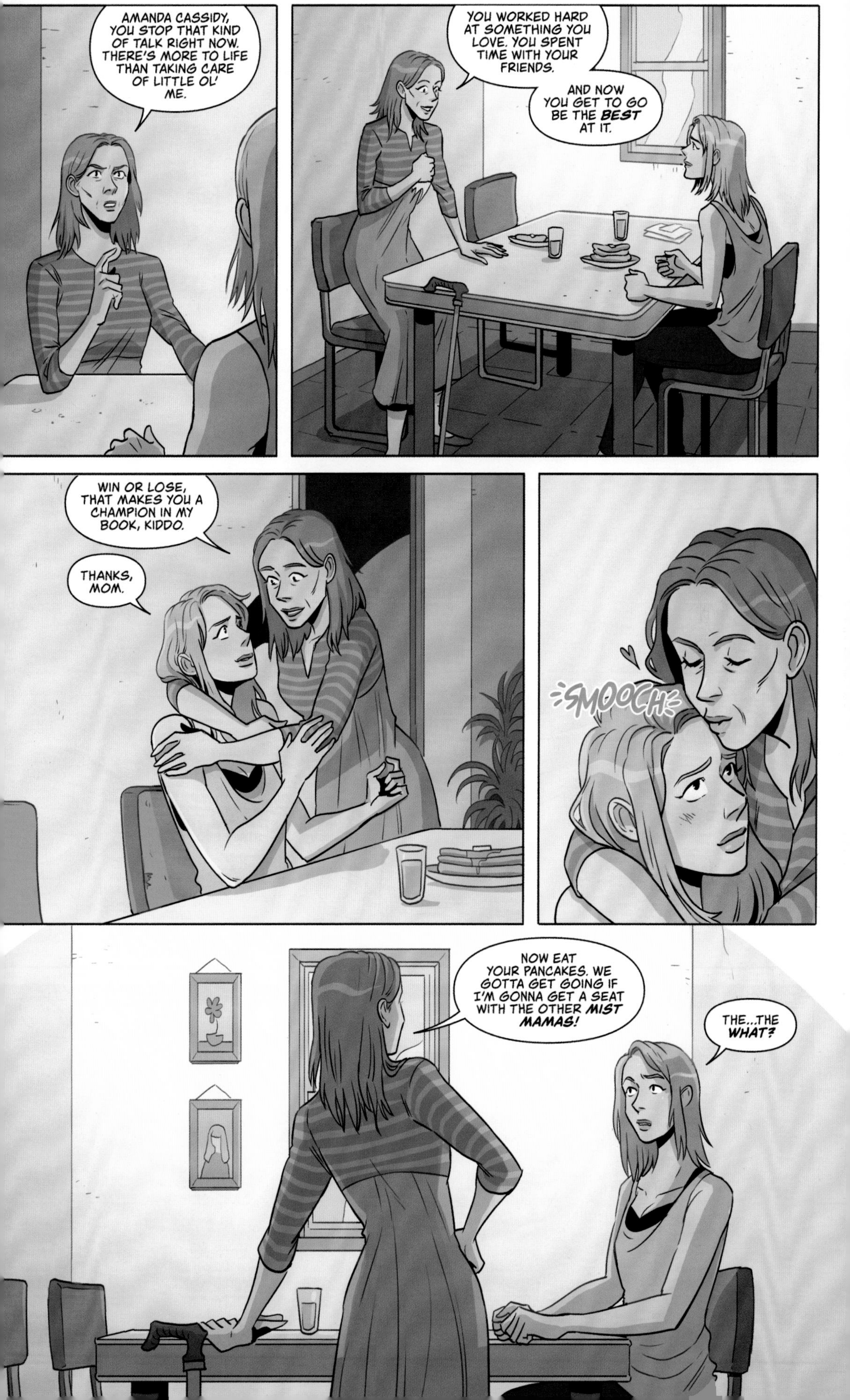
AMANDA CASSIDY, YOU STOP THAT KIND OF TALK RIGHT NOW. THERE'S MORE TO LIFE THAN TAKING CARE OF LITTLE OL' ME.
YOU WORKED HARD AT SOMETHING YOU LOVE. YOU SPENT TIME WITH YOUR FRIENDS.
AND NOW YOU GET TO GO BE THE BEST AT IT.
WIN OR LOSE, THAT MAKES YOU A CHAMPION IN MY BOOK, KIDDO.
THANKS, MOM.
SMOOCH
NOW EAT YOUR PANCAKES. WE GOTTA GET GOING IF I'M GONNA GET A SEAT WITH THE OTHER MIST MAMAS!
THE...THE WHAT?

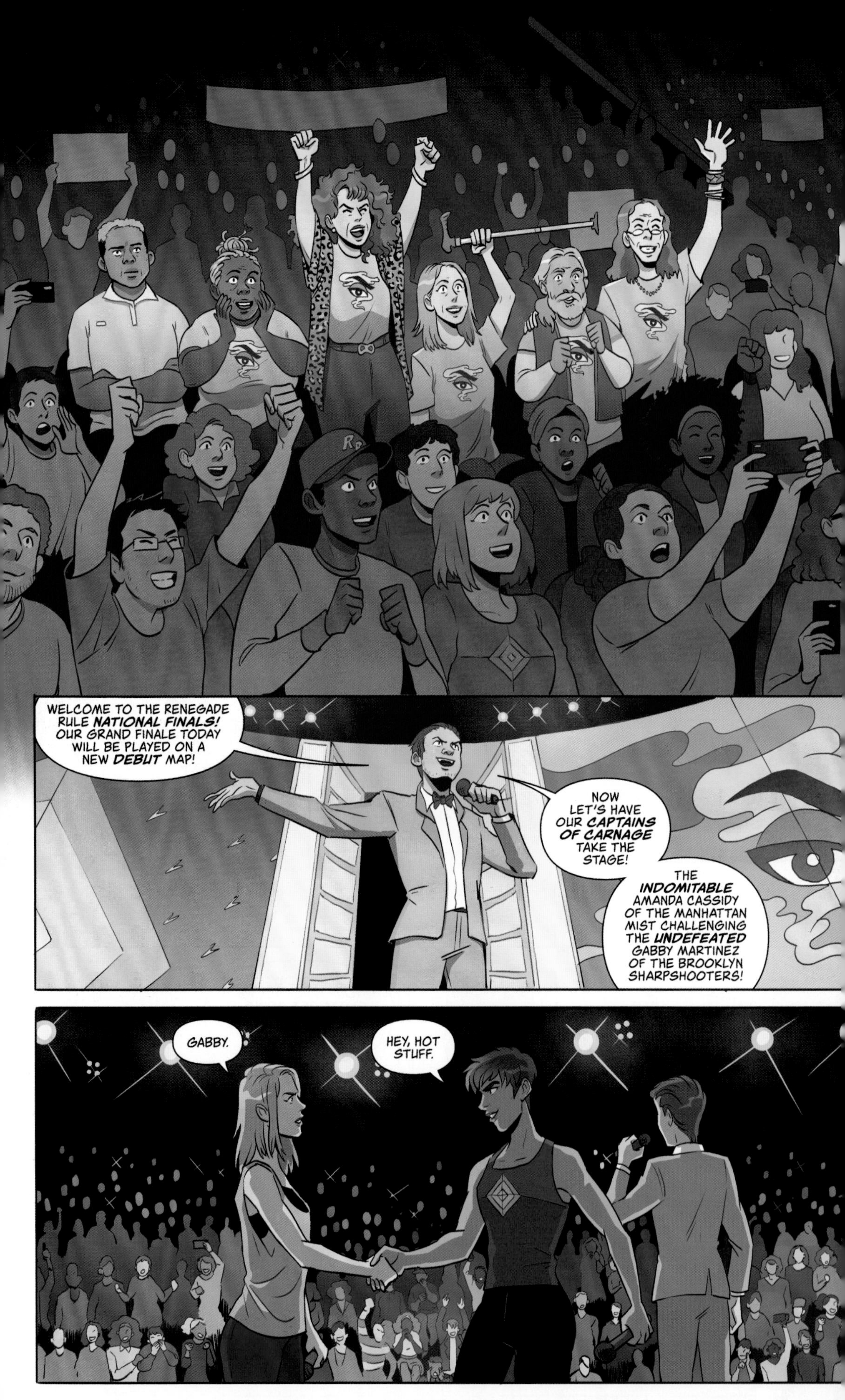
WELCOME TO THE RENEGADE RULE NATIONAL FINALS! OUR GRAND FINALE TODAY WILL BE PLAYED ON A NEW DEBUT MAP!
NOW LET'S HAVE OUR CAPTAINS OF CARNAGE TAKE THE STAGE!
THE INDOMITABLE AMANDA CASSIDY OF THE MANHATTAN MIST CHALLENGING THE UNDEFEATED GABBY MARTINEZ OF THE BROOKLYN SHARPSHOOTERS!
GABBY.
HEY, HOT STUFF.

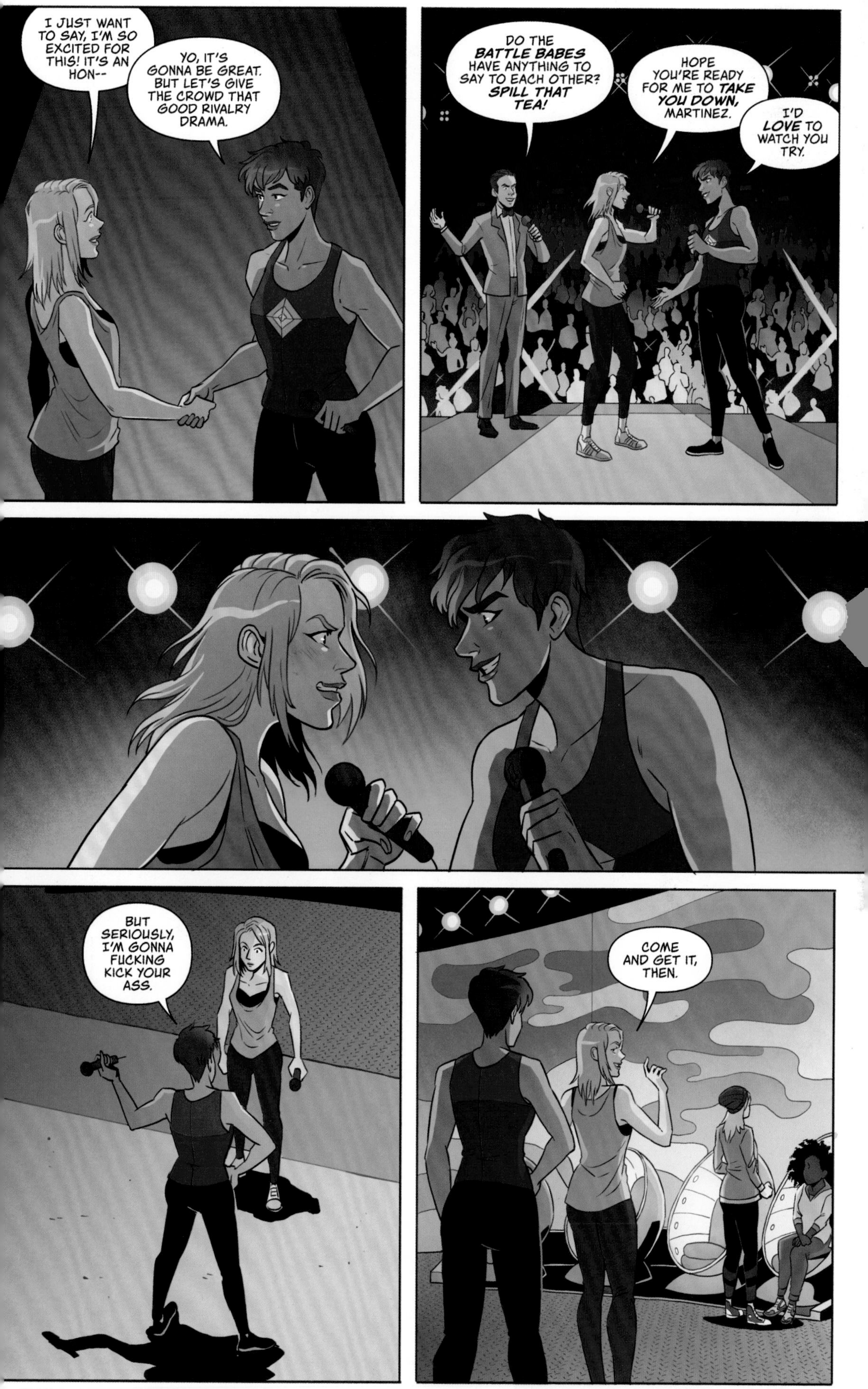
I JUST WANT TO SAY, I'M SO EXCITED FOR THIS! IT'S AN HON--
YO, IT'S GONNA BE GREAT. BUT LET'S GIVE THE CROWD THAT GOOD RIVALRY DRAMA.
DO THE BATTLE BABES HAVE ANYTHING TO SAY TO EACH OTHER? SPILL THAT TEA!
HOPE YOU'RE READY FOR ME TO TAKE YOU DOWN, MARTINEZ.
I'D LOVE TO WATCH YOU TRY.
BUT SERIOUSLY, I'M GONNA FUCKING KICK YOUR ASS.
COME AND GET IT, THEN.

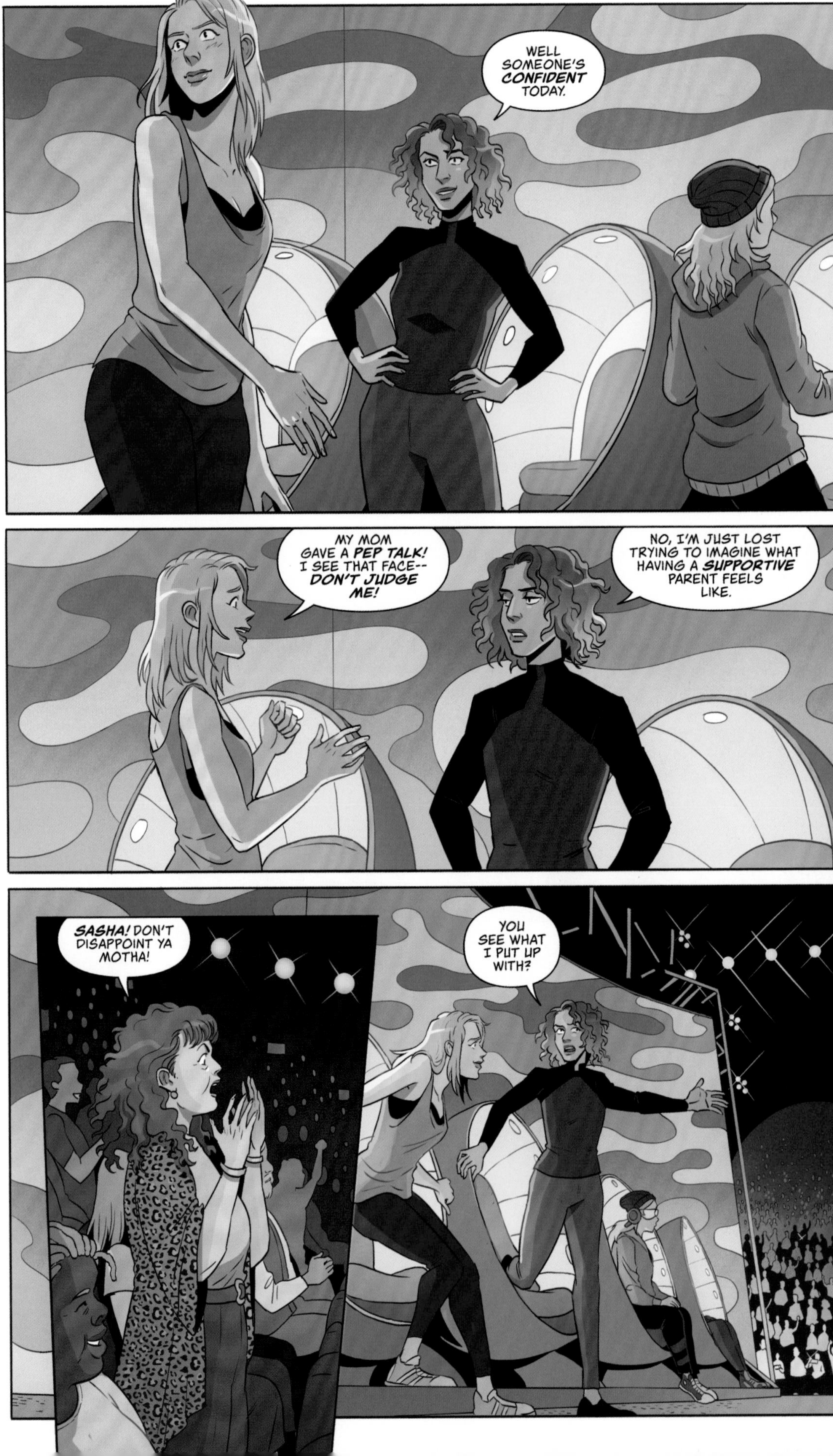
WELL SOMEONE'S **CONFIDENT** TODAY.
MY MOM GAVE A **PEP TALK!** I SEE THAT FACE-- **DON'T JUDGE ME!**
NO, I'M JUST LOST TRYING TO IMAGINE WHAT HAVING A **SUPPORTIVE** PARENT FEELS LIKE.
SASHA! DON'T DISAPPOINT YA MOTHA!
YOU SEE WHAT I PUT UP WITH?

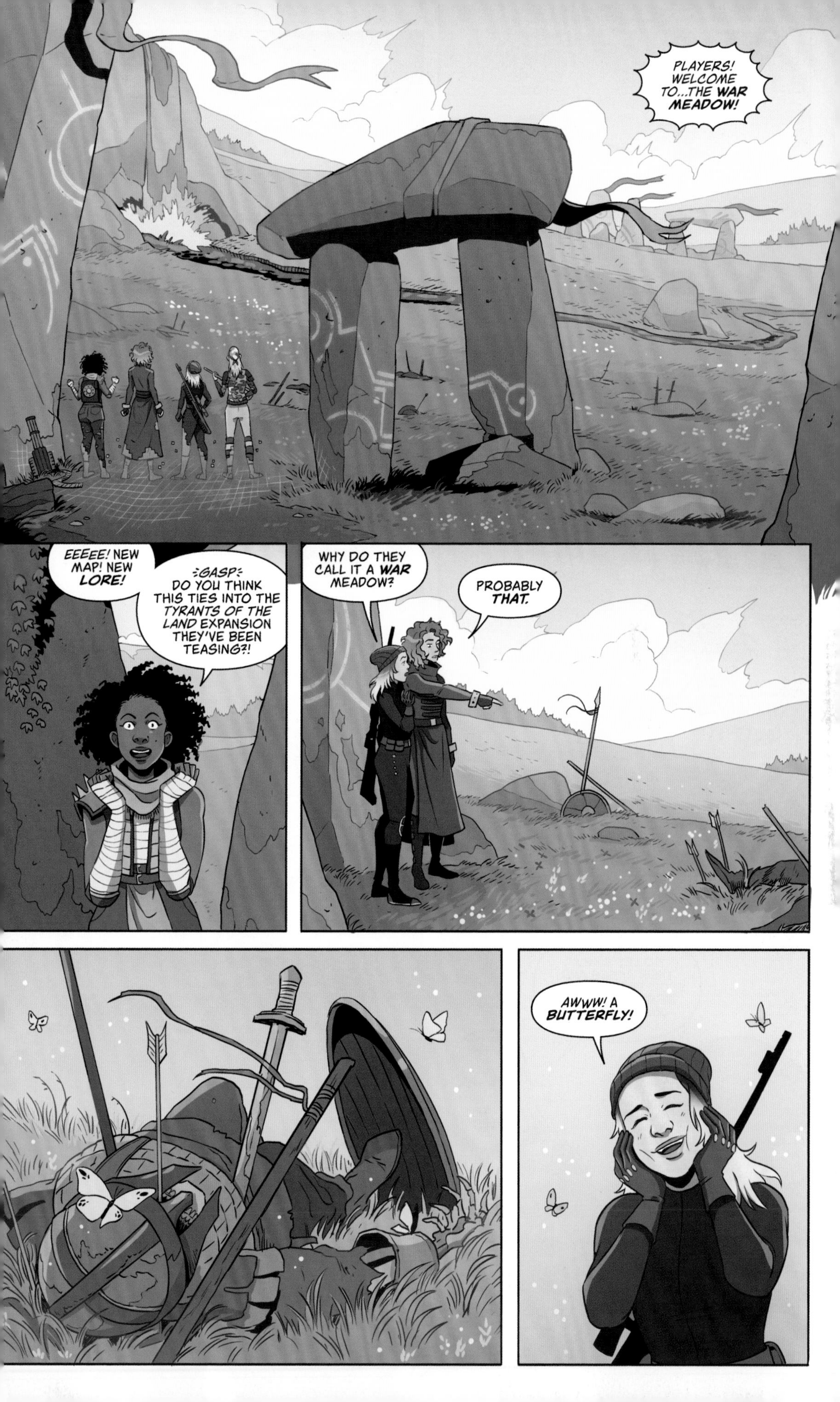

PLAYERS! WELCOME TO...THE *WAR MEADOW!*
EEEEE! NEW MAP! NEW **LORE!**
GASP
DO YOU THINK THIS TIES INTO THE *TYRANTS OF THE LAND* EXPANSION THEY'VE BEEN TEASING?!
WHY DO THEY CALL IT A ***WAR*** MEADOW?
PROBABLY ***THAT.***
AWWW! A ***BUTTERFLY!***

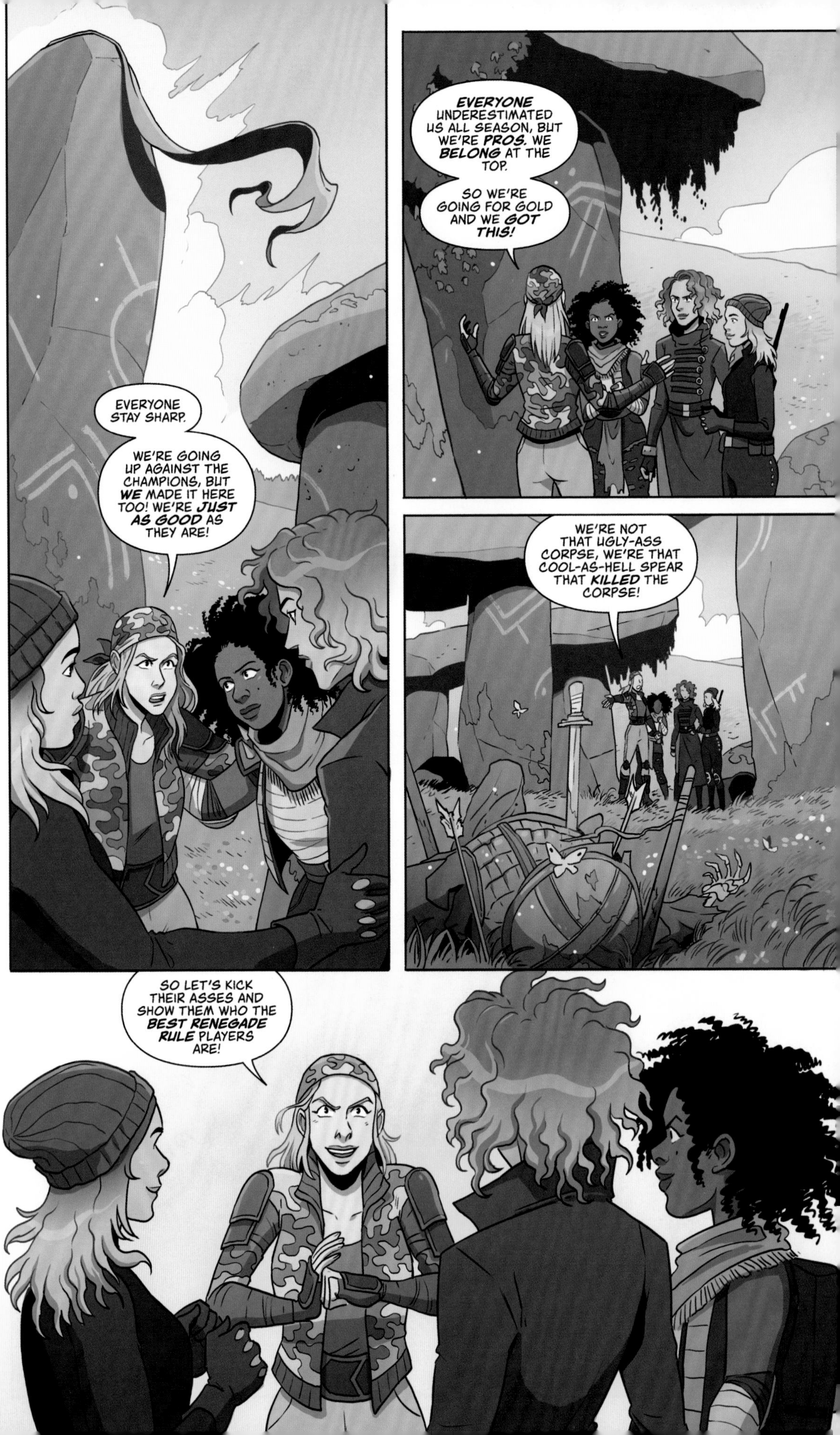
EVERYONE STAY SHARP.
WE'RE GOING UP AGAINST THE CHAMPIONS, BUT WE MADE IT HERE TOO! WE'RE JUST AS GOOD AS THEY ARE!
EVERYONE UNDERESTIMATED US ALL SEASON, BUT WE'RE PROS. WE BELONG AT THE TOP.
SO WE'RE GOING FOR GOLD AND WE GOT THIS!
WE'RE NOT THAT UGLY-ASS CORPSE, WE'RE THAT COOL-AS-HELL SPEAR THAT KILLED THE CORPSE!
SO LET'S KICK THEIR ASSES AND SHOW THEM WHO THE BEST RENEGADE RULE PLAYERS ARE!

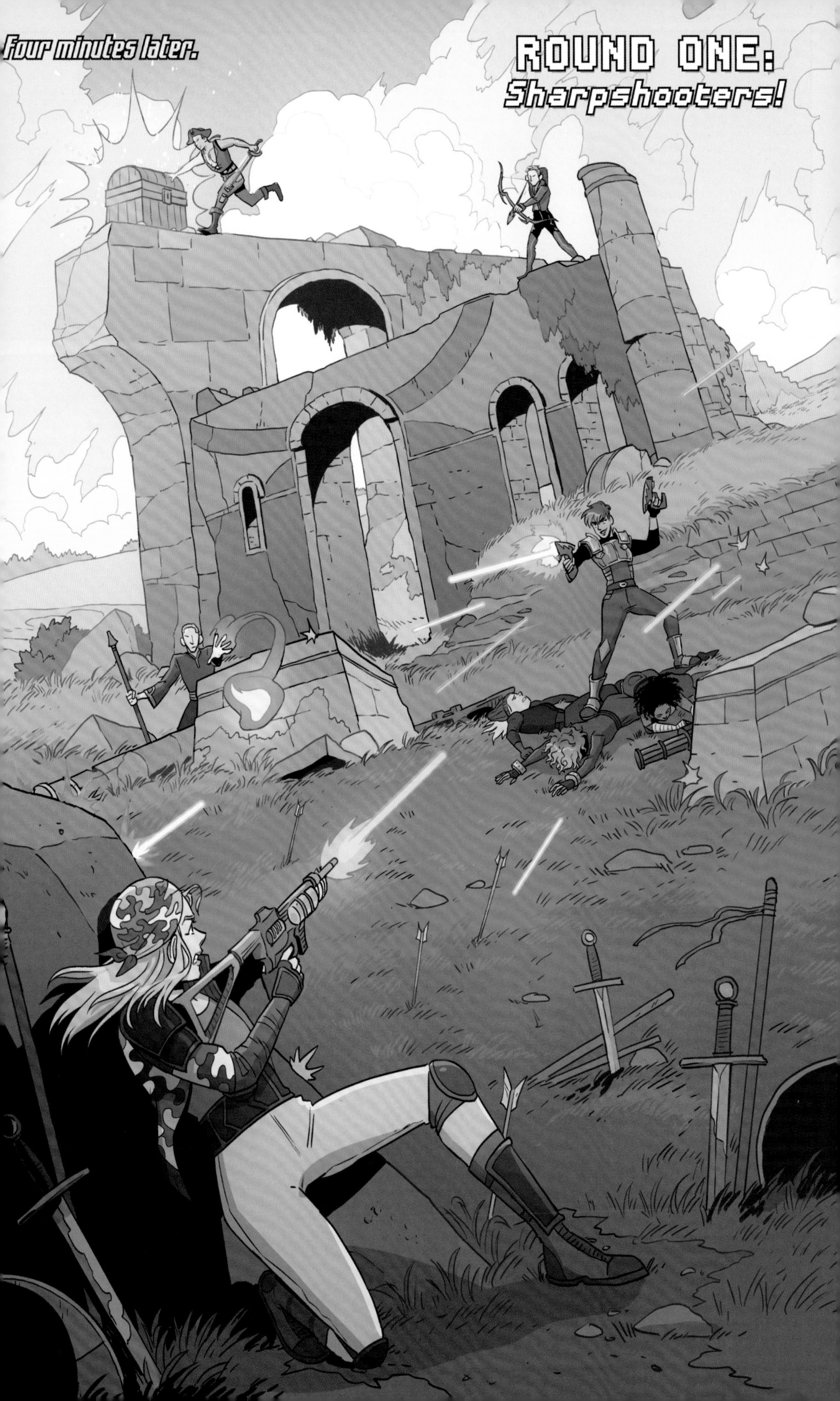
Four minutes later.
ROUND ONE:
Sharpshooters!

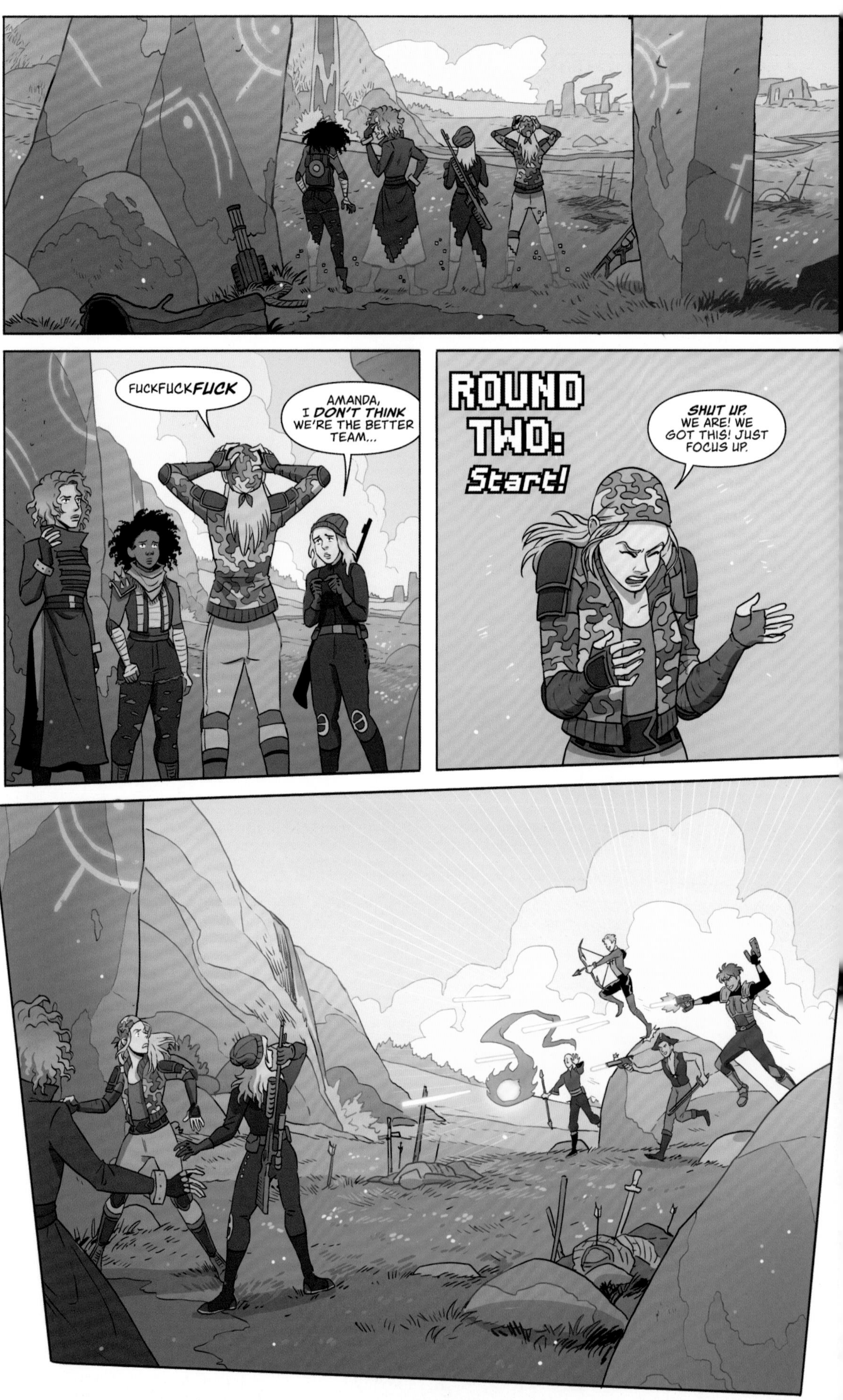

FUCKFUCKFUCK
AMANDA, I DON'T THINK WE'RE THE BETTER TEAM...
ROUND TWO: Start!
SHUT UP. WE ARE! WE GOT THIS! JUST FOCUS UP.

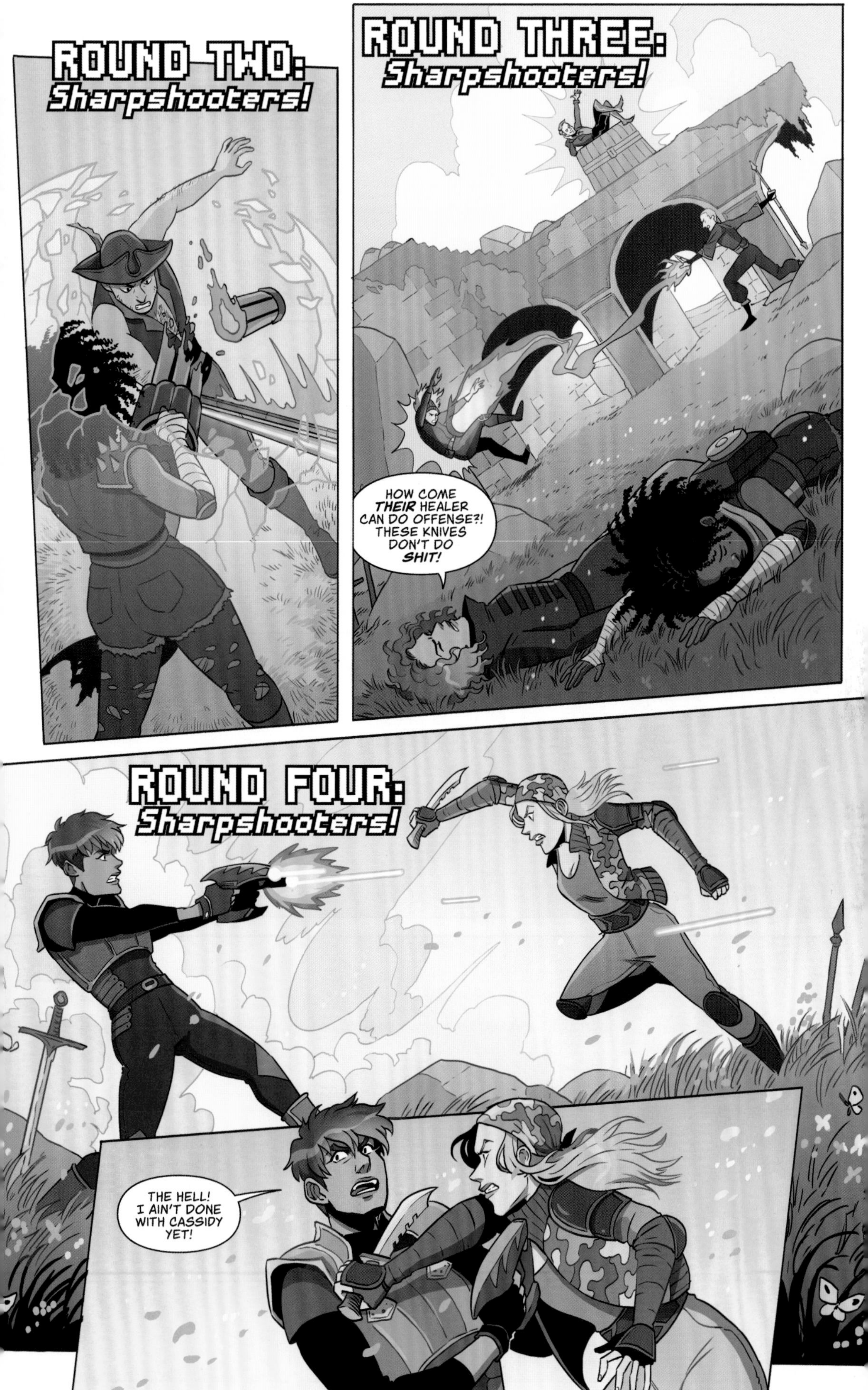
ROUND TWO:
Sharpshooters!
ROUND THREE:
Sharpshooters!
HOW COME THEIR HEALER CAN DO OFFENSE?! THESE KNIVES DON'T DO SHIT!
ROUND FOUR:
Sharpshooters!
THE HELL! I AIN'T DONE WITH CASSIDY YET!

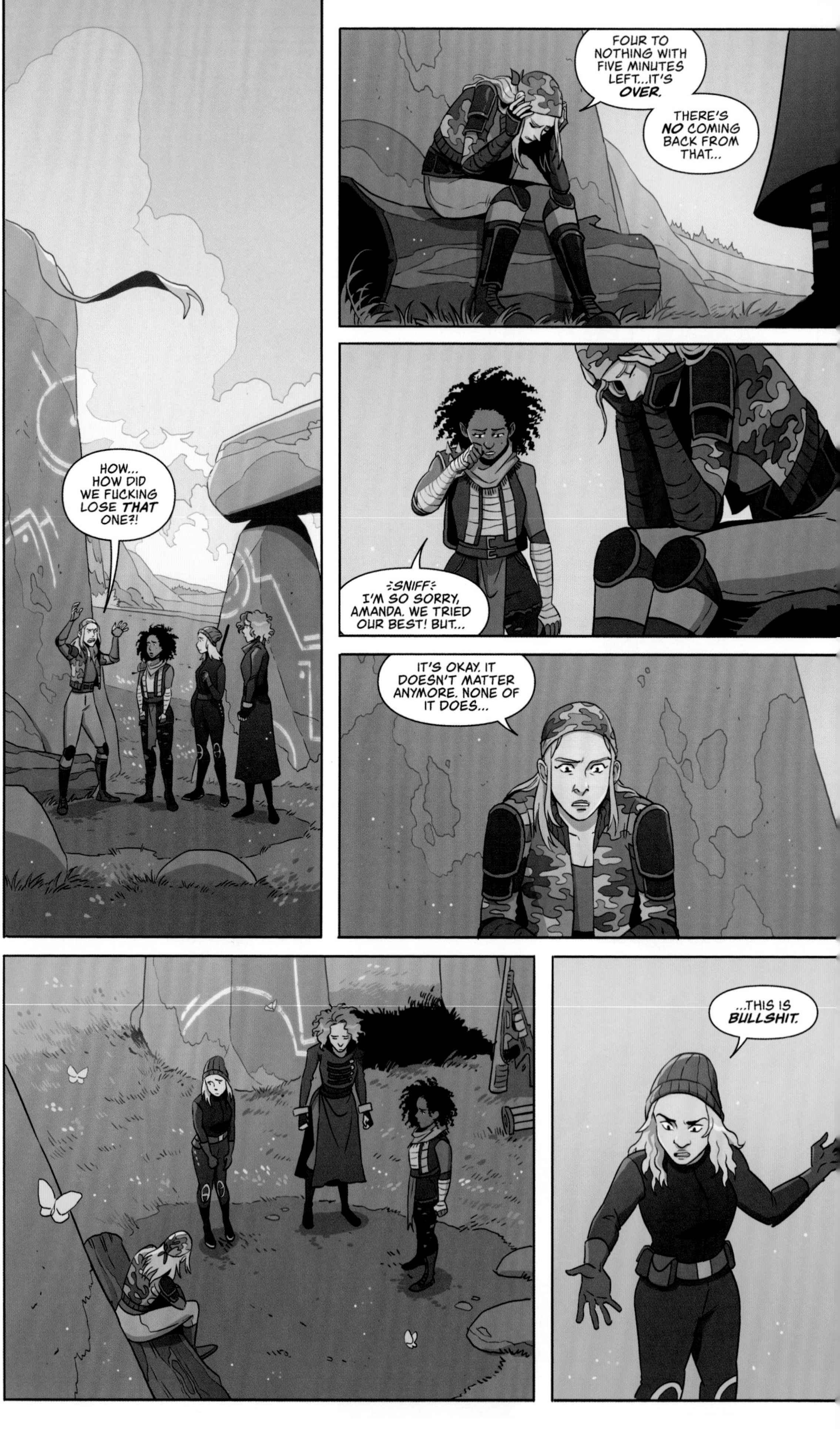
HOW... HOW DID WE FUCKING LOSE THAT ONE?!
FOUR TO NOTHING WITH FIVE MINUTES LEFT...IT'S OVER.
THERE'S NO COMING BACK FROM THAT...
SNIFF
I'M SO SORRY, AMANDA. WE TRIED OUR BEST! BUT...
IT'S OKAY. IT DOESN'T MATTER ANYMORE. NONE OF IT DOES...
...THIS IS BULLSHIT.

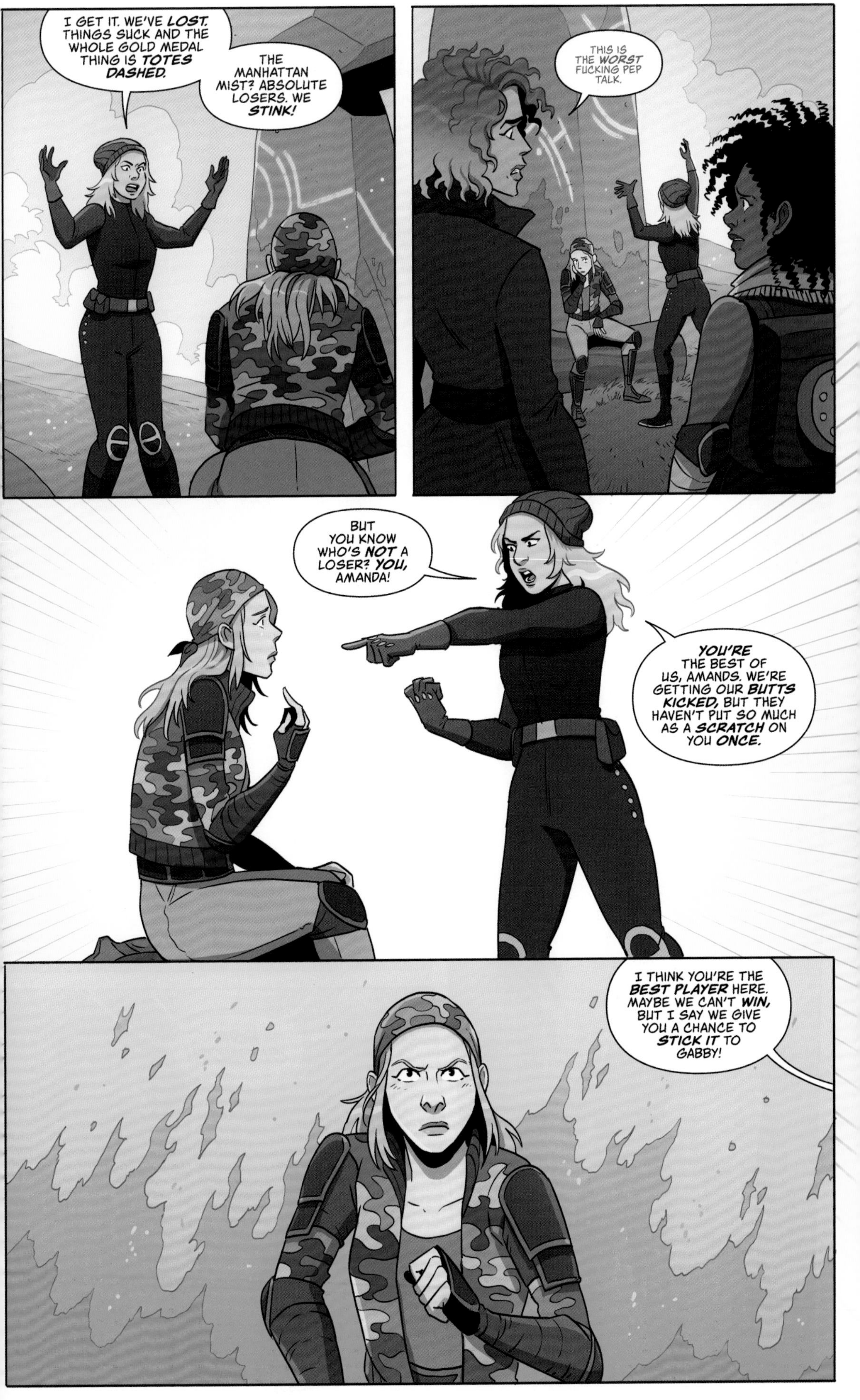

I GET IT. WE'VE LOST. THINGS SUCK AND THE WHOLE GOLD MEDAL THING IS TOTES DASHED.
THE MANHATTAN MIST? ABSOLUTE LOSERS. WE STINK!
THIS IS THE WORST FUCKING PEP TALK.
BUT YOU KNOW WHO'S NOT A LOSER? YOU, AMANDA!
YOU'RE THE BEST OF US, AMANDS. WE'RE GETTING OUR BUTTS KICKED, BUT THEY HAVEN'T PUT SO MUCH AS A SCRATCH ON YOU ONCE.
I THINK YOU'RE THE BEST PLAYER HERE. MAYBE WE CAN'T WIN, BUT I SAY WE GIVE YOU A CHANCE TO STICK IT TO GABBY!

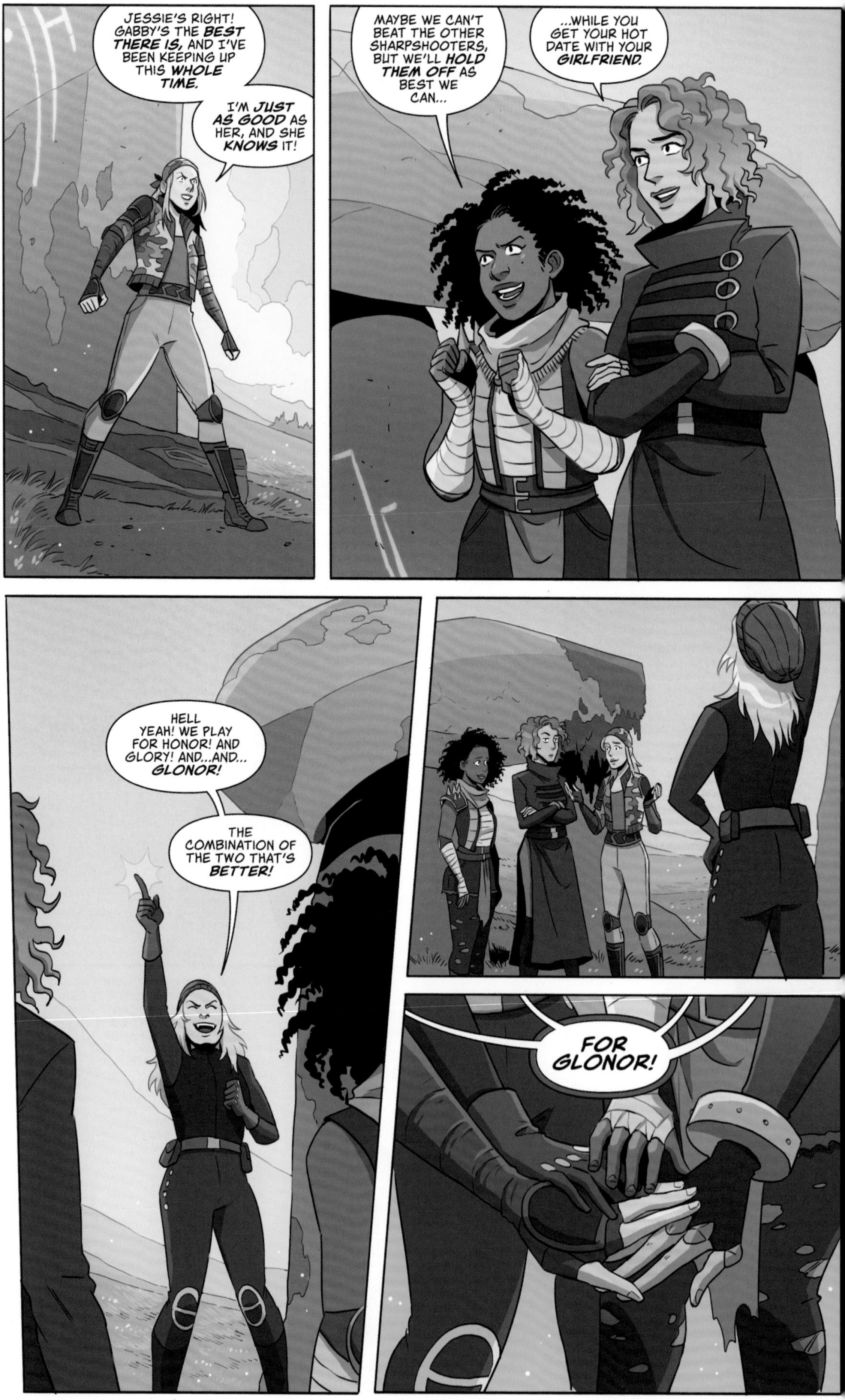
JESSIE'S RIGHT! GABBY'S THE **BEST THERE IS,** AND I'VE BEEN KEEPING UP THIS **WHOLE TIME.**
I'M **JUST AS GOOD** AS HER, AND SHE **KNOWS** IT!
MAYBE WE CAN'T BEAT THE OTHER SHARPSHOOTERS, BUT WE'LL **HOLD THEM OFF** AS BEST WE CAN...
...WHILE YOU GET YOUR HOT DATE WITH YOUR **GIRLFRIEND.**
HELL YEAH! WE PLAY FOR HONOR! AND GLORY! AND...AND... **GLONOR!**
THE COMBINATION OF THE TWO THAT'S **BETTER!**
FOR GLONOR!

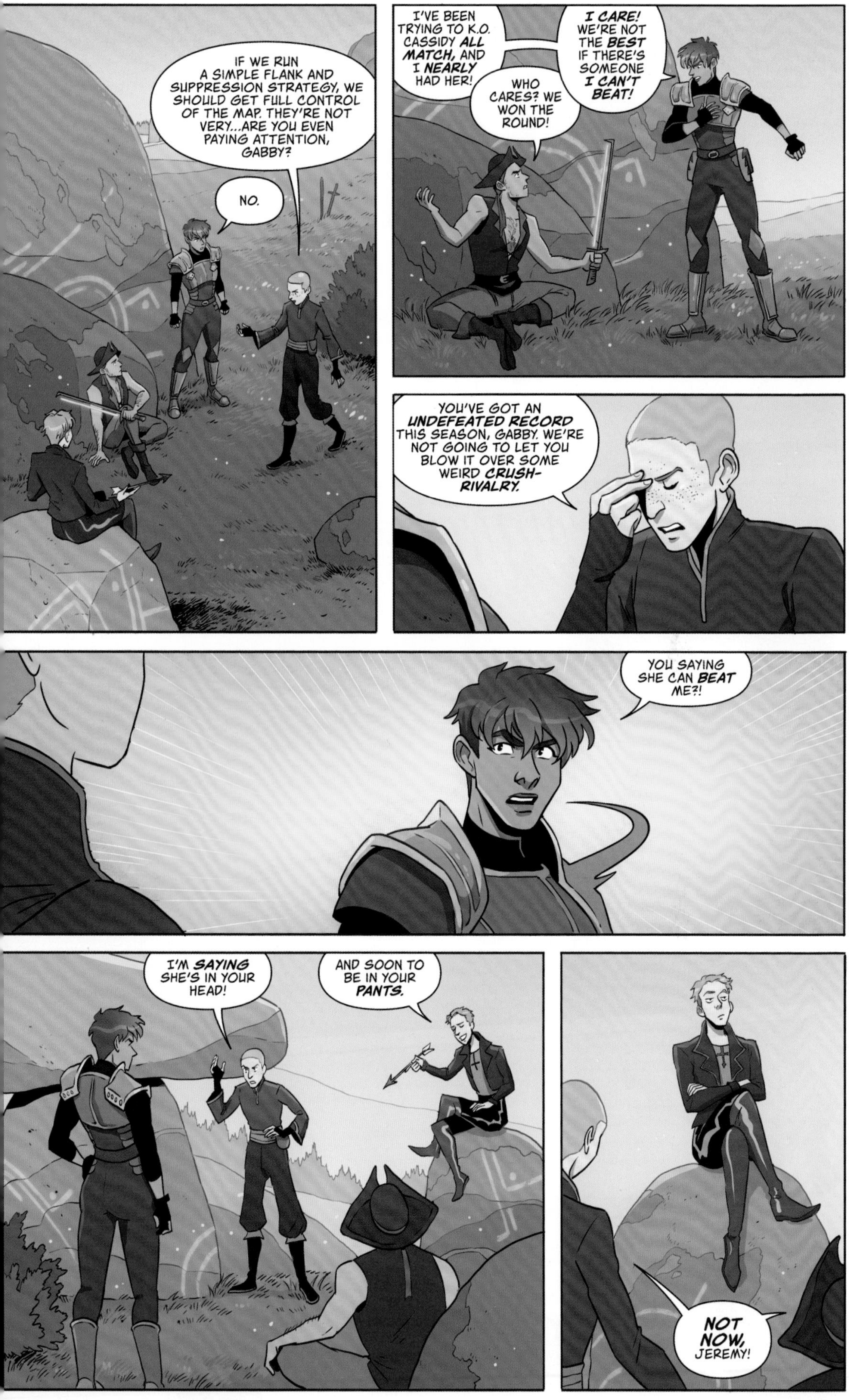
IF WE RUN A SIMPLE FLANK AND SUPPRESSION STRATEGY, WE SHOULD GET FULL CONTROL OF THE MAP. THEY'RE NOT VERY...ARE YOU EVEN PAYING ATTENTION, GABBY?
NO.
I'VE BEEN TRYING TO K.O. CASSIDY ALL MATCH, AND I NEARLY HAD HER!
WHO CARES? WE WON THE ROUND!
I CARE! WE'RE NOT THE BEST IF THERE'S SOMEONE I CAN'T BEAT!
YOU'VE GOT AN UNDEFEATED RECORD THIS SEASON, GABBY. WE'RE NOT GOING TO LET YOU BLOW IT OVER SOME WEIRD CRUSH-RIVALRY.
YOU SAYING SHE CAN BEAT ME?!
I'M SAYING SHE'S IN YOUR HEAD!
AND SOON TO BE IN YOUR PANTS.
NOT NOW, JEREMY!

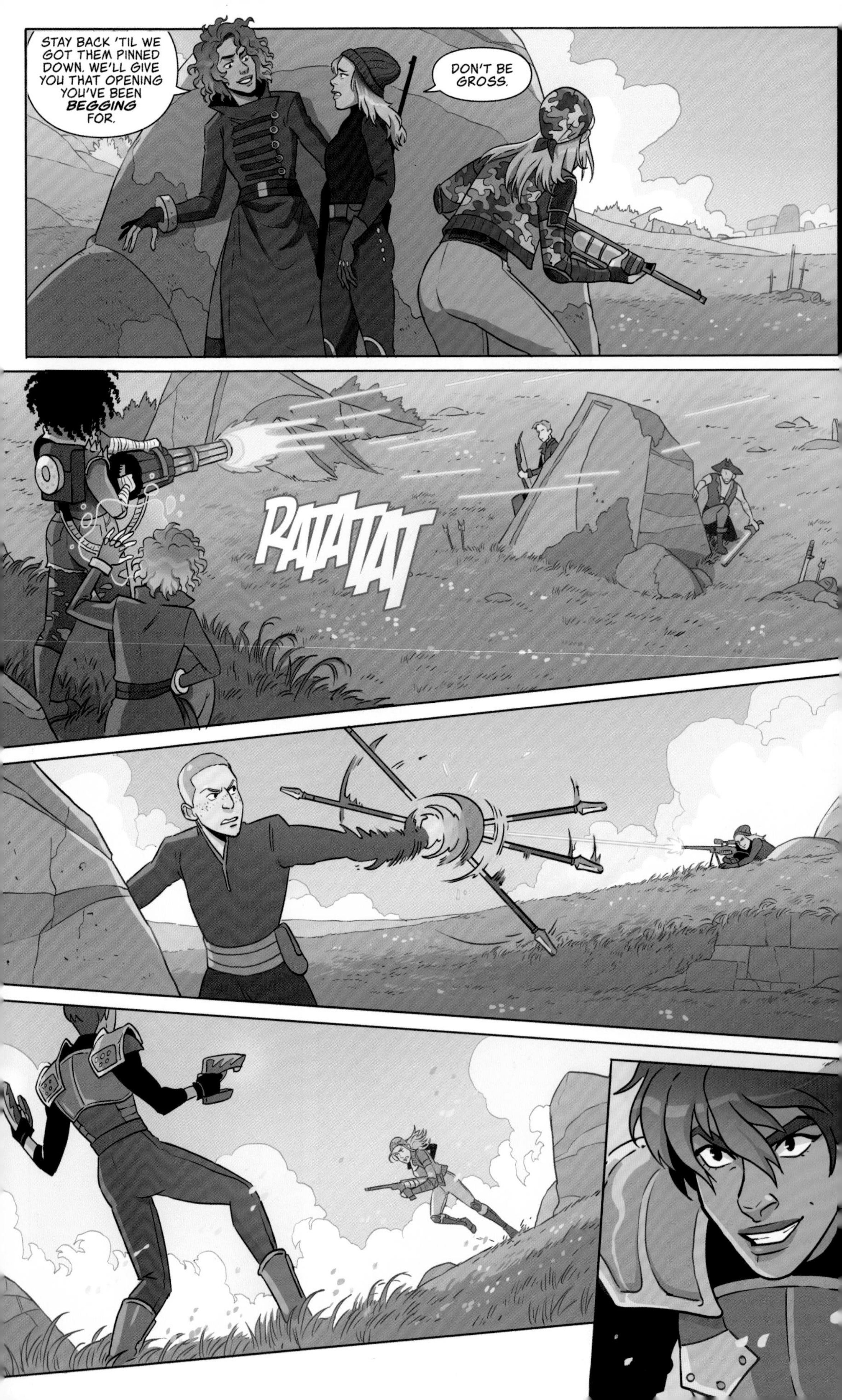
STAY BACK 'TIL WE GOT THEM PINNED DOWN. WE'LL GIVE YOU THAT OPENING YOU'VE BEEN *BEGGING* FOR.
DON'T BE GROSS.
RATATAT

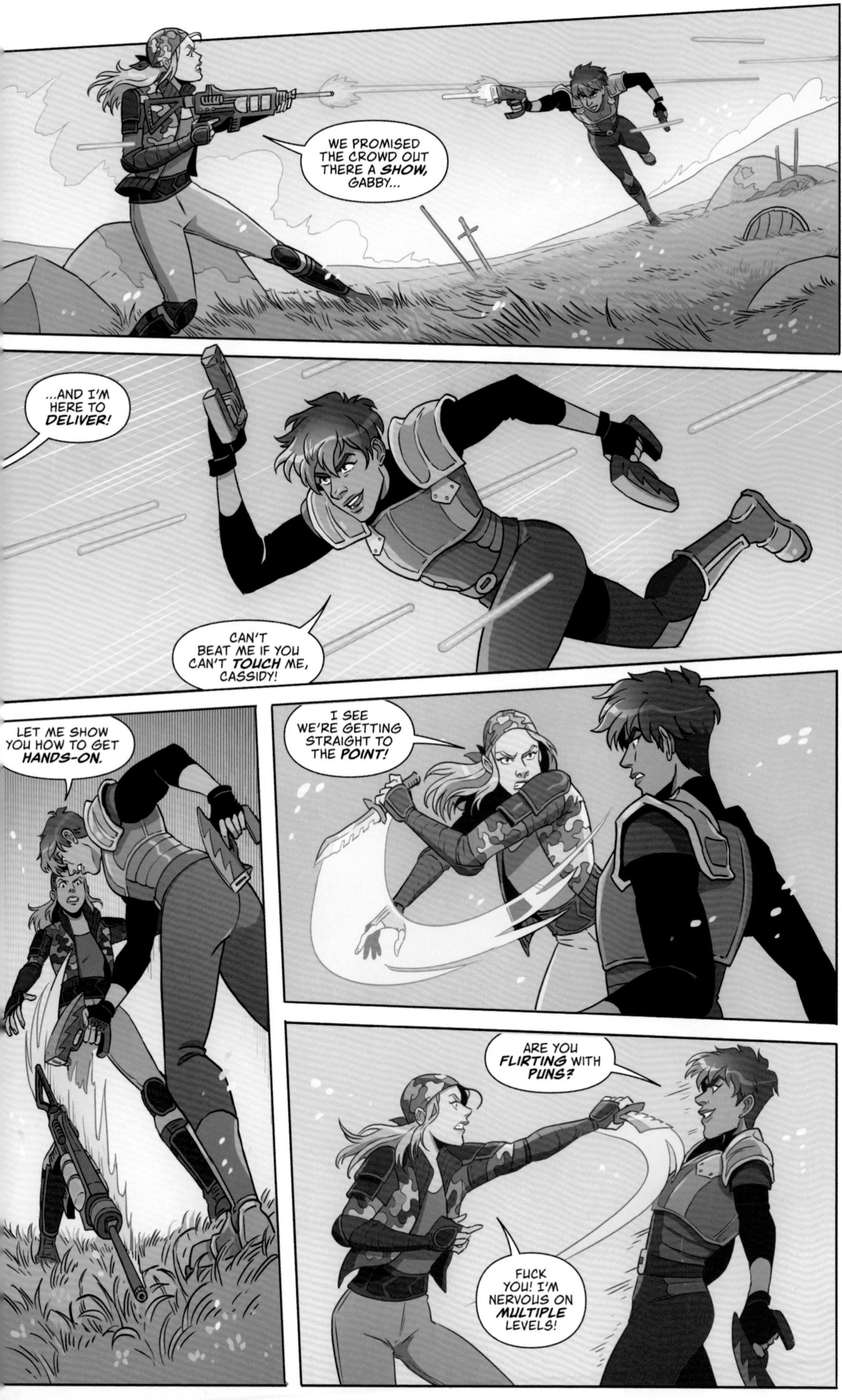
WE PROMISED THE CROWD OUT THERE A SHOW, GABBY...
...AND I'M HERE TO DELIVER!
CAN'T BEAT ME IF YOU CAN'T TOUCH ME, CASSIDY!
LET ME SHOW YOU HOW TO GET HANDS-ON.
I SEE WE'RE GETTING STRAIGHT TO THE POINT!
ARE YOU FLIRTING WITH PUNS?
FUCK YOU! I'M NERVOUS ON MULTIPLE LEVELS!

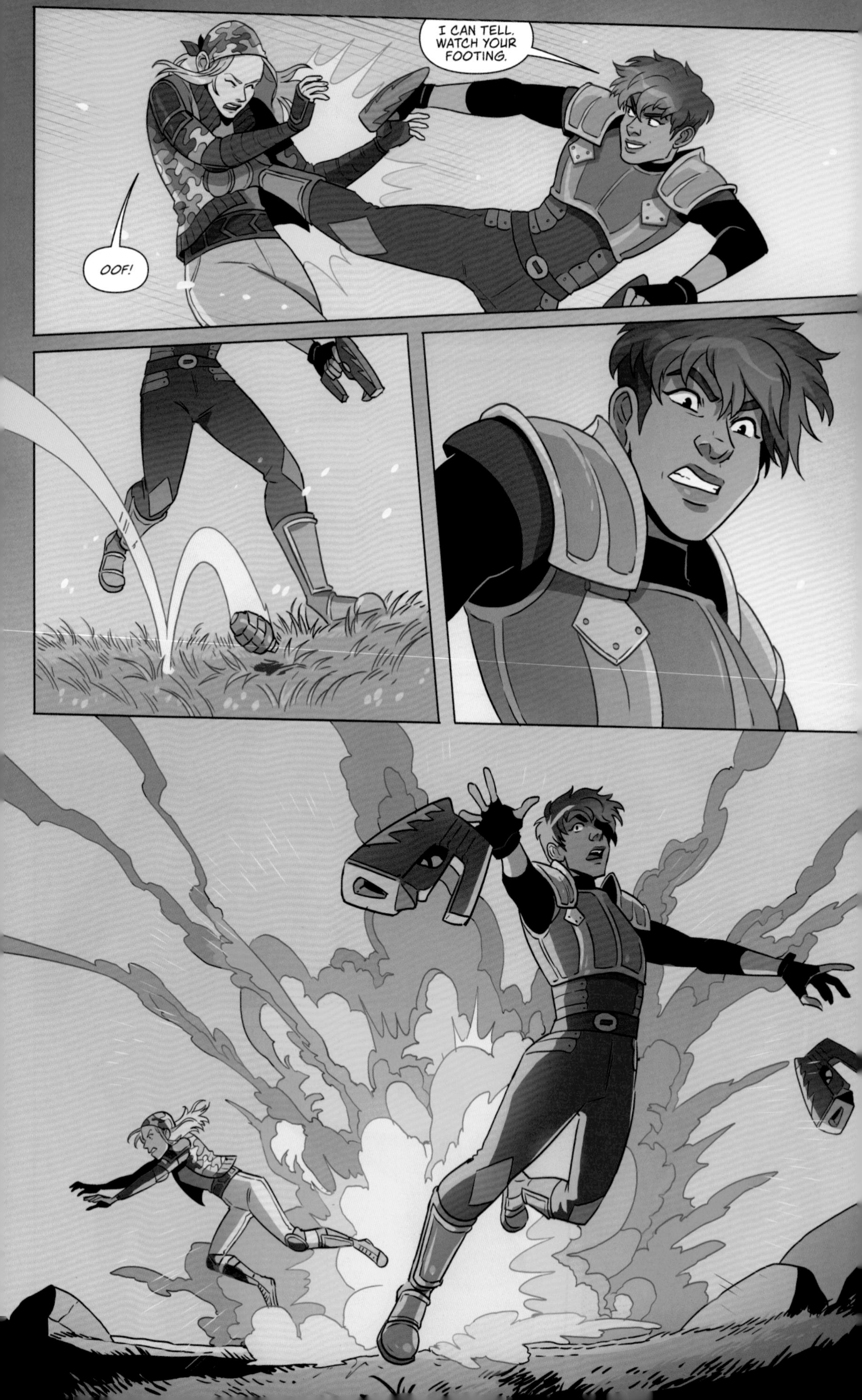
I CAN TELL. WATCH YOUR FOOTING.
OOF!

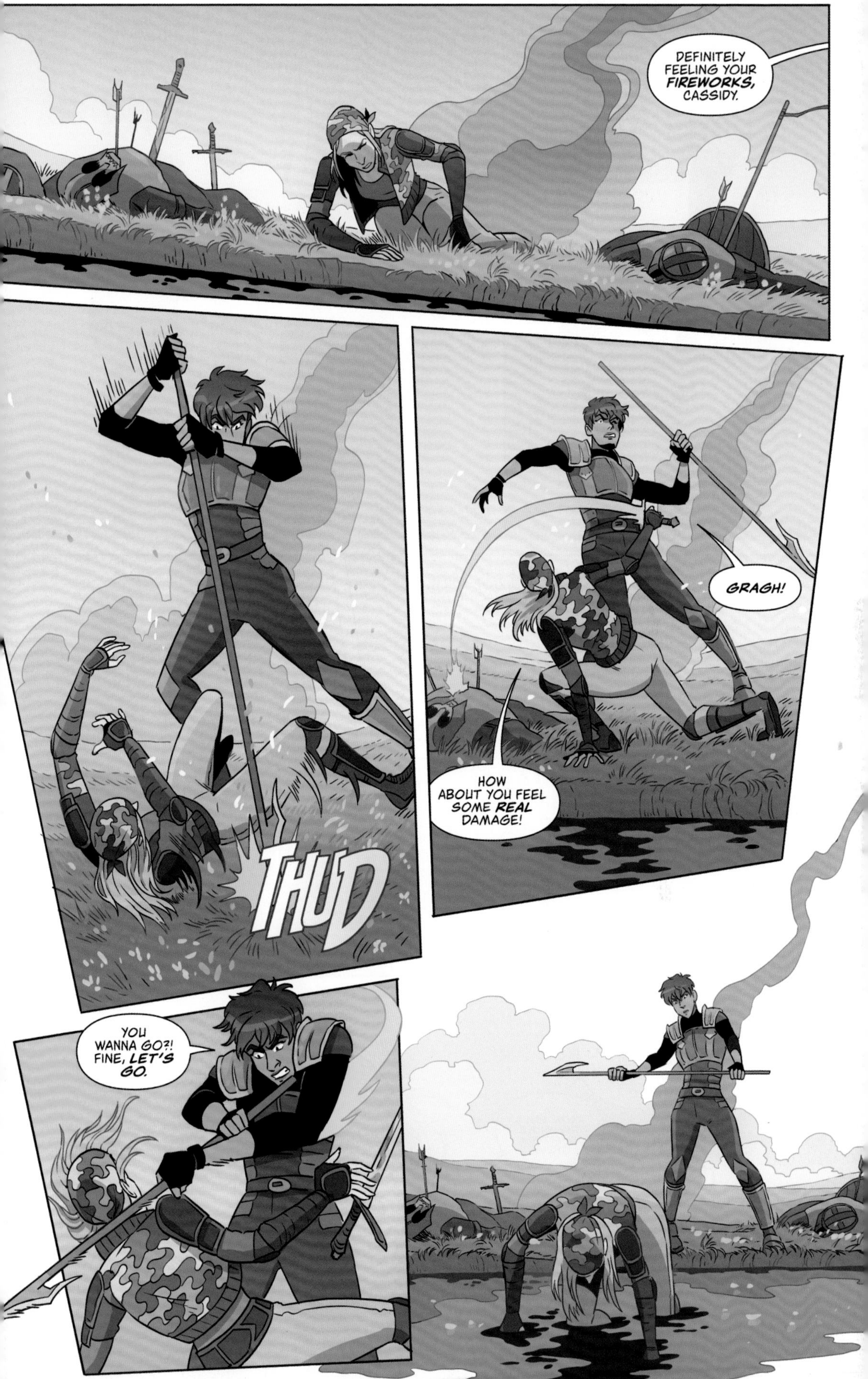
DEFINITELY FEELING YOUR **FIREWORKS,** CASSIDY.
THUD
HOW ABOUT YOU FEEL SOME ***REAL*** DAMAGE!
GRAGH!
YOU WANNA GO?! FINE, ***LET'S GO.***

I GOTTA HAND IT TO YA, CASSIDY, YOU'RE ONE HELL OF A PLAYER.

AND I KNOW THIS IS WEIRD TIMING, WHAT WITH THE WHOLE "I KICKED YOUR ASS" THING, BUT...YOU'RE *CUTE* AS HELL.

I *KNOW* I SHOULD WAIT 'TIL THE MATCH IS OVER, BUT LIKE... YOU WANT TO *GO OUT* AFTER THIS?

...

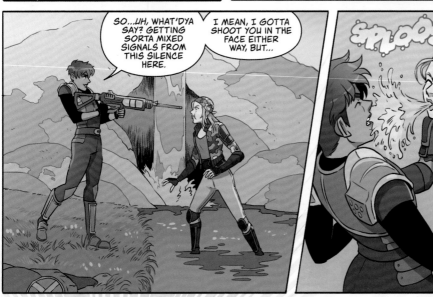

SO...UH, WHAT'DYA SAY? GETTING SORTA MIXED SIGNALS FROM THIS SILENCE HERE.

I MEAN, I GOTTA SHOOT YOU IN THE FACE EITHER WAY, BUT...

SPLOOSH!

YOU'VE GOT NO IDEA HOW LONG I'VE *DREAMED* ABOUT THIS MOMENT!

YA KNOW, MINUS THE WHOLE *SPITTING* THING.

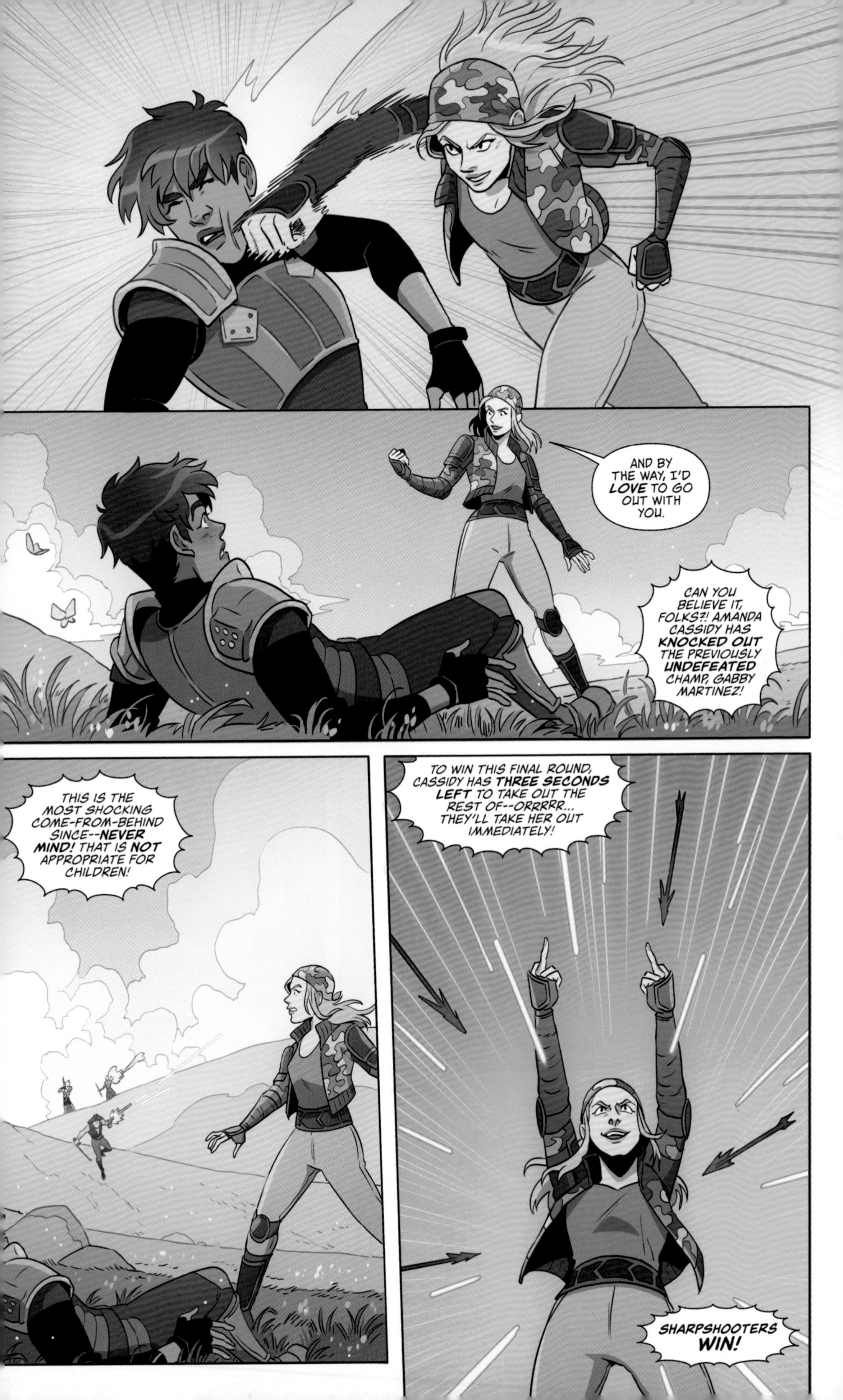
AND BY THE WAY, I'D LOVE TO GO OUT WITH YOU.
CAN YOU BELIEVE IT, FOLKS?! AMANDA CASSIDY HAS KNOCKED OUT THE PREVIOUSLY UNDEFEATED CHAMP, GABBY MARTINEZ!
THIS IS THE MOST SHOCKING COME-FROM-BEHIND SINCE--NEVER MIND! THAT IS NOT APPROPRIATE FOR CHILDREN!
TO WIN THIS FINAL ROUND, CASSIDY HAS THREE SECONDS LEFT TO TAKE OUT THE REST OF--ORRRRR... THEY'LL TAKE HER OUT IMMEDIATELY!
SHARPSHOOTERS WIN!

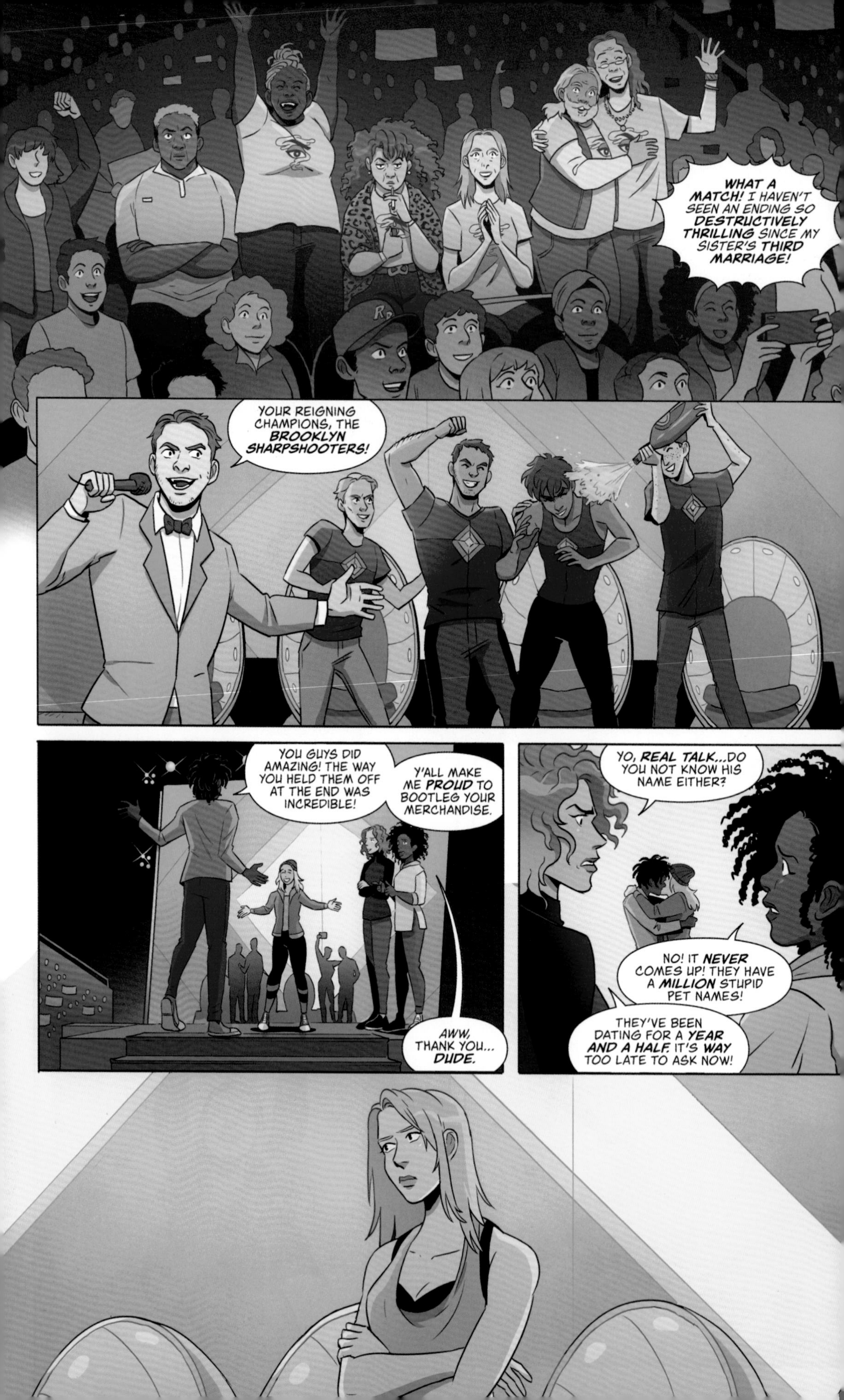
WHAT A MATCH! I HAVEN'T SEEN AN ENDING SO DESTRUCTIVELY THRILLING SINCE MY SISTER'S THIRD MARRIAGE!
YOUR REIGNING CHAMPIONS, THE BROOKLYN SHARPSHOOTERS!
YOU GUYS DID AMAZING! THE WAY YOU HELD THEM OFF AT THE END WAS INCREDIBLE!
Y'ALL MAKE ME PROUD TO BOOTLEG YOUR MERCHANDISE.
AWW, THANK YOU... DUDE.
YO, REAL TALK...DO YOU NOT KNOW HIS NAME EITHER?
NO! IT NEVER COMES UP! THEY HAVE A MILLION STUPID PET NAMES!
THEY'VE BEEN DATING FOR A YEAR AND A HALF. IT'S WAY TOO LATE TO ASK NOW!

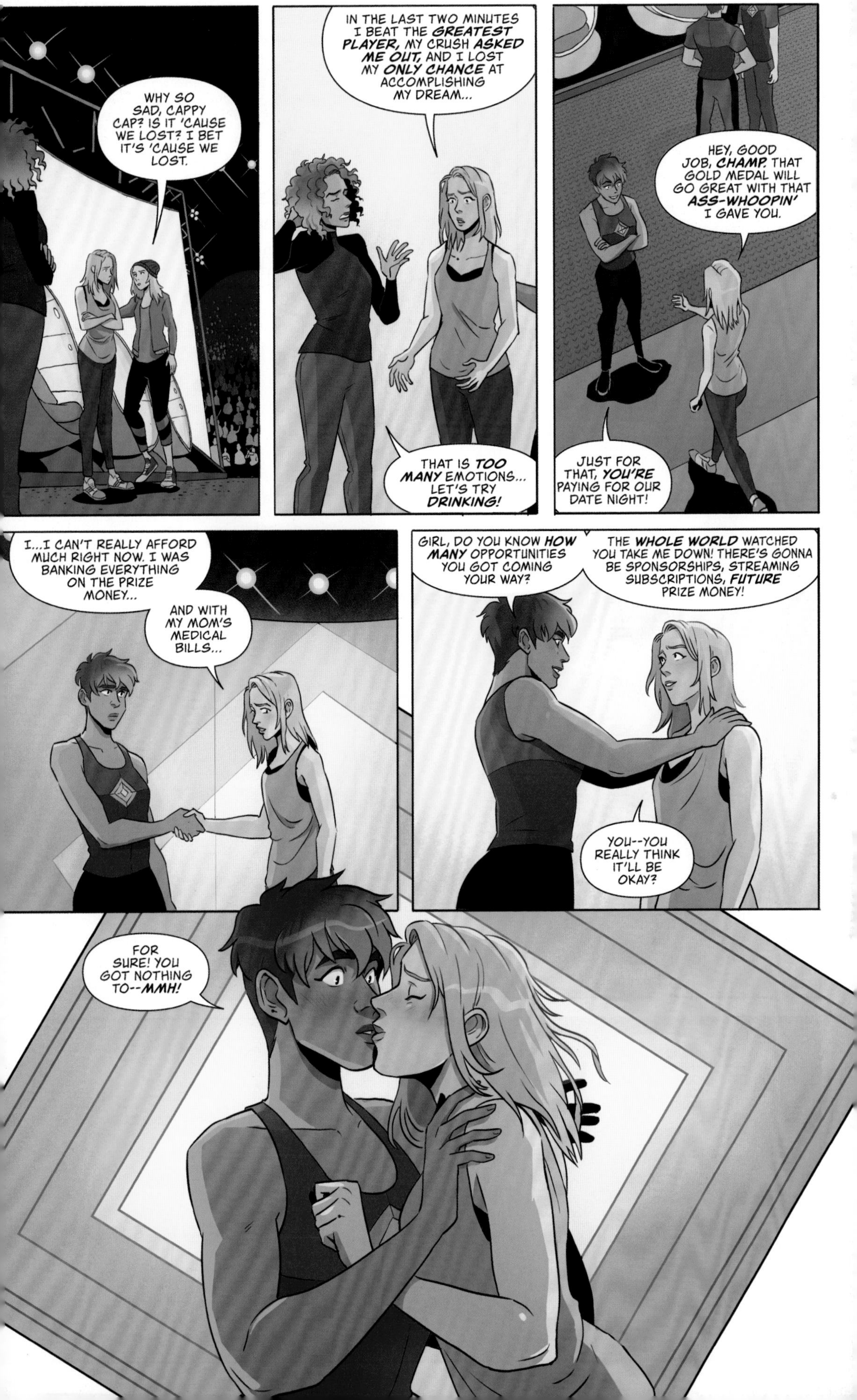

WHY SO SAD, CAPPY CAP? IS IT 'CAUSE WE LOST? I BET IT'S 'CAUSE WE LOST.
IN THE LAST TWO MINUTES I BEAT THE **GREATEST PLAYER**, MY CRUSH **ASKED ME OUT**, AND I LOST MY **ONLY CHANCE** AT ACCOMPLISHING MY DREAM...
THAT IS **TOO MANY** EMOTIONS... LET'S TRY **DRINKING**!
HEY, GOOD JOB, **CHAMP**. THAT GOLD MEDAL WILL GO GREAT WITH THAT **ASS-WHOOPIN'** I GAVE YOU.
JUST FOR THAT, **YOU'RE** PAYING FOR OUR DATE NIGHT!
I...I CAN'T REALLY AFFORD MUCH RIGHT NOW. I WAS BANKING EVERYTHING ON THE PRIZE MONEY...
AND WITH MY MOM'S MEDICAL BILLS...
GIRL, DO YOU KNOW **HOW MANY** OPPORTUNITIES YOU GOT COMING YOUR WAY?
THE **WHOLE WORLD** WATCHED YOU TAKE ME DOWN! THERE'S GONNA BE SPONSORSHIPS, STREAMING SUBSCRIPTIONS, **FUTURE** PRIZE MONEY!
YOU--YOU REALLY THINK IT'LL BE OKAY?
FOR SURE! YOU GOT NOTHING TO--**MMH!**

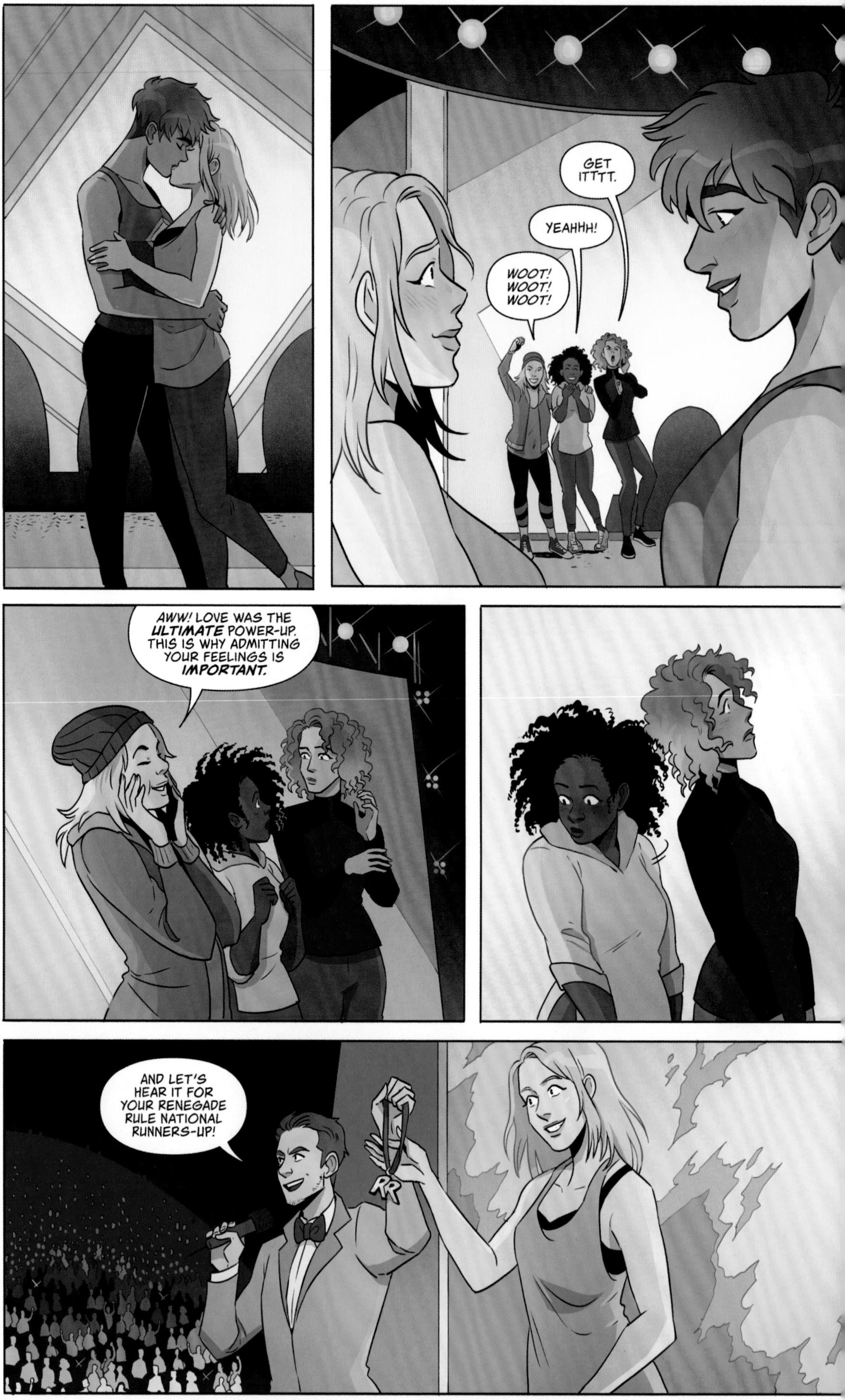

GET ITTTT.
YEAHHH!
WOOT! WOOT! WOOT!
AWW! LOVE WAS THE ULTIMATE POWER-UP. THIS IS WHY ADMITTING YOUR FEELINGS IS IMPORTANT.
AND LET'S HEAR IT FOR YOUR RENEGADE RULE NATIONAL RUNNERS-UP!
RR

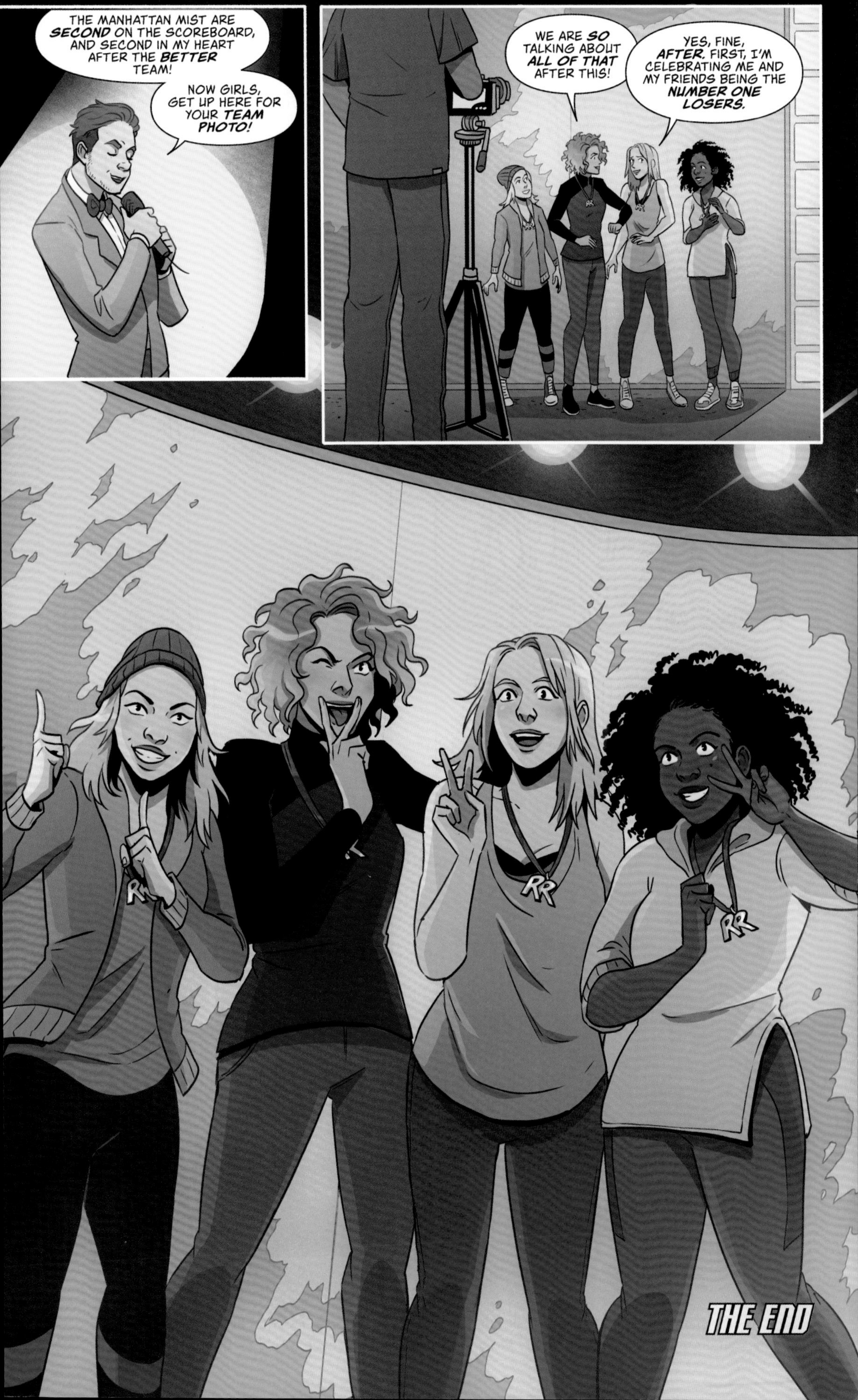

THE MANHATTAN MIST ARE SECOND ON THE SCOREBOARD, AND SECOND IN MY HEART AFTER THE BETTER TEAM!
NOW GIRLS, GET UP HERE FOR YOUR TEAM PHOTO!
WE ARE SO TALKING ABOUT ALL OF THAT AFTER THIS!
YES, FINE, AFTER. FIRST, I'M CELEBRATING ME AND MY FRIENDS BEING THE NUMBER ONE LOSERS.
RR
THE END

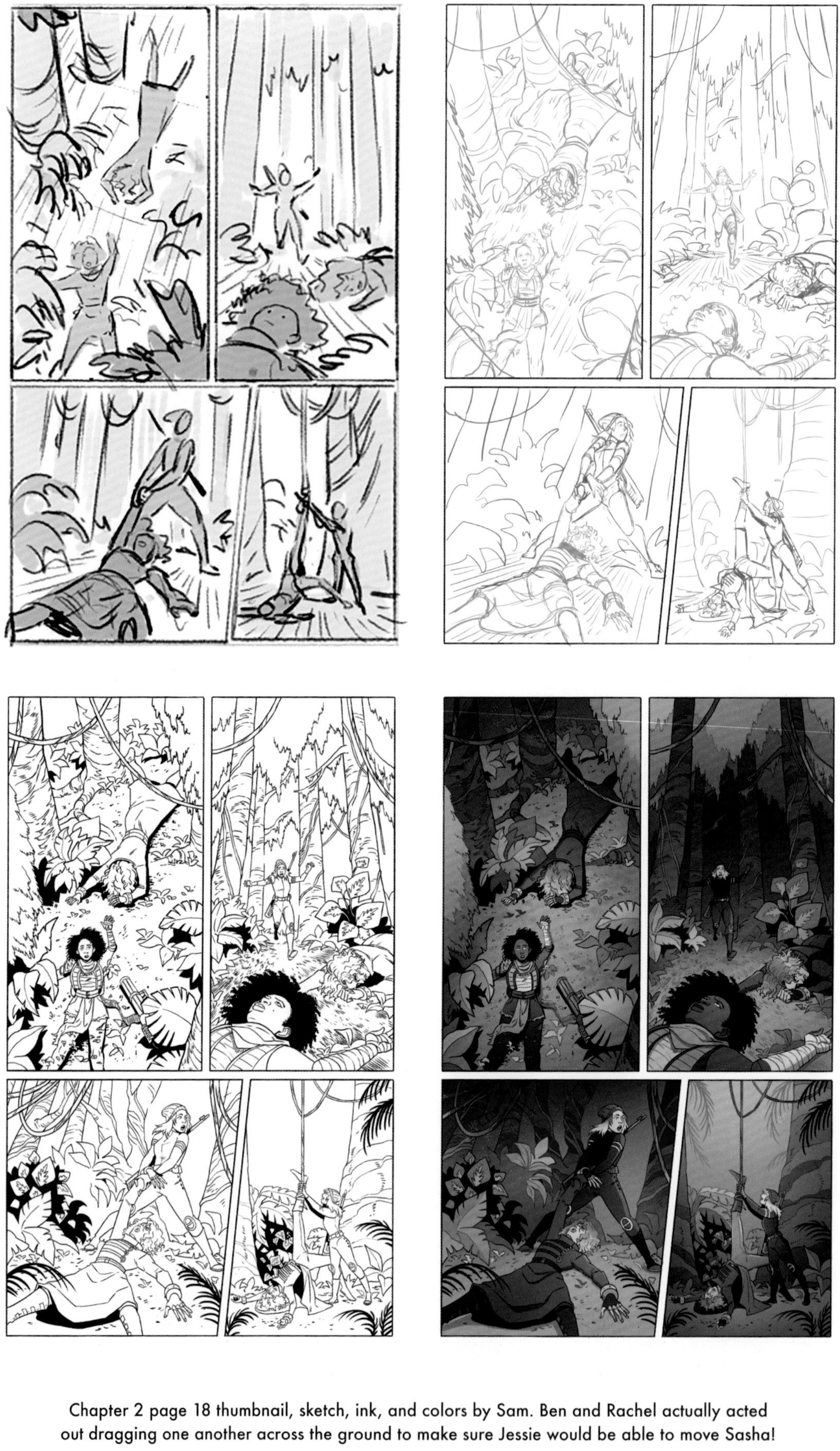

Chapter 2 page 18 thumbnail, sketch, ink, and colors by Sam. Ben and Rachel actually acted out dragging one another across the ground to make sure Jessie would be able to move Sasha!

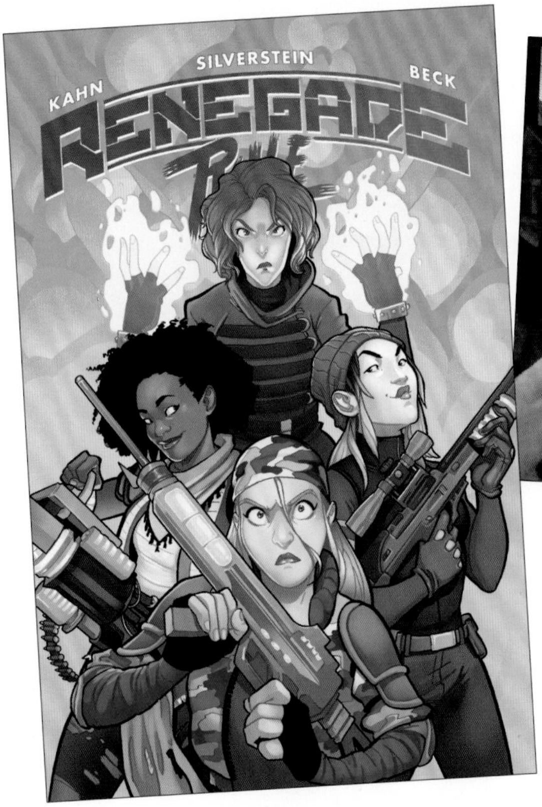
SILVERSTEIN
KAHN
BECK
RENEGADE

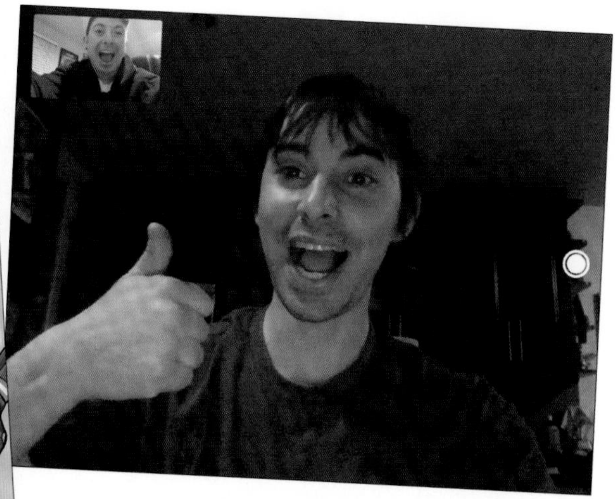

Top left: Variant cover art from *Renegade Rule* #1, the only single issue of the comic ever published, by Ro Stein and Ted Brandt. *Top right:* A screen cap of Rachel and Ben celebrating after they typed "The End." *Bottom:* In-game and real-world character designs for the Sharpshooters team members.

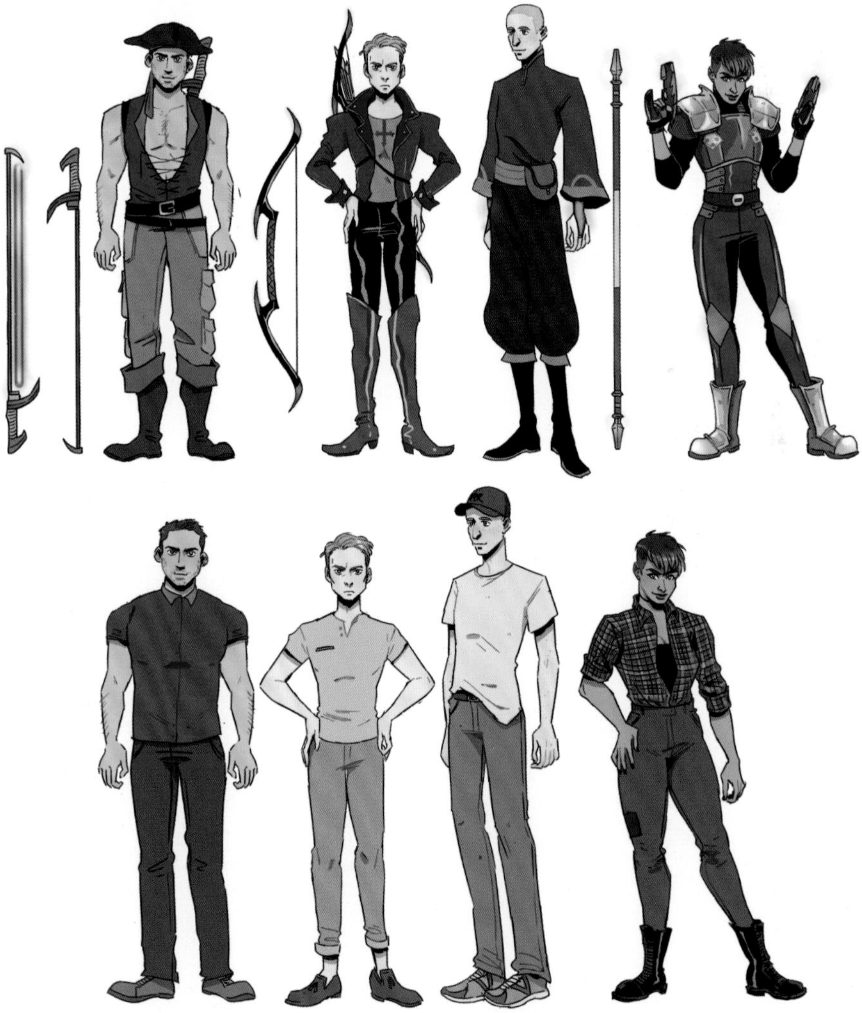

BEN "BEE" KAHN is an Ignatz Award-nominated comics writer. Their previous works include the comics series *Heavenly Blues* (Scout Comics) and *Gryffen: Galaxy's Most Wanted* (SBI Press). They can usually be found shuttered away in their shoebox-sized New York apartment, afraid to leave the city.

RACHEL SILVERSTEIN is a Long Island, NY-based law school graduate. She has published articles in the *Touro Law Review* about comic book law and holds a Master's degree in elephant paleontology. Really!

SAM BECK is an illustrator and cartoonist living in Toronto. She likes to explore themes of identity and relationships through the lens of fantasy and sci-fi. She has done work for Dark Horse, Vault Comics, BOOM! Studios, and Wonderbound.